NOW PERU IS MINE

Narrating Native Histories

Narrating Native Histories aims to foster a rethinking of the ethical, methodological, and conceptual frameworks within which we locate our work on Native histories and cultures. We seek to create a space for effective and ongoing conversations between North and South, Natives and non-Natives, academics and activists, throughout the Americas and the Pacific region.

This series encourages analyses that contribute to an understanding of Native peoples' relationships with nation-states, including histories of expropriation and exclusion as well as projects for autonomy and sovereignty. We encourage collaborative work that recognizes Native intellectuals, cultural interpreters, and alternative knowledge producers, as well as projects that question the relationship between orality and literacy.

Manuel Llamojha Mitma and Jaymie Patricia Heilman

NOW PERU IS MINE

THE LIFE AND TIMES OF A CAMPESINO ACTIVIST

Duke University Press / Durham and London / 2016

Printed in the United States of America on acid-free paper ∞
Designed by Heather Hensley
Typeset in Minion Pro by Copperline

Library of Congress Cataloging-in-Publication Data
Names: Llamojha Mitma, Manuel, [date] author. | Heilman,
Jaymie Patricia, author.
Title: Now Peru is mine : the life and times of a campesino activist /
Manuel Llamojha Mitma and Jaymie Patricia Heilman.
Other titles: Narrating native histories.
Description: Durham : Duke University Press, 2016. | Series: Narrating
native histories | Includes bibliographical references and index.
Identifiers: LCCN 2016020793 (print)
LCCN 2016022036 (ebook)
ISBN 9780822362180 (hardcover : alk. paper)
ISBN 9780822362388 (pbk. : alk. paper)
ISBN 9780822373759 (e-book)
Subjects: LCSH: Llamojha Mitma, Manuel, [date] | Political
activists—Peru—Biography. | Peru—Politics and government—
20th century.
Classification: LCC F3448.4.L53 L53 2016 (print) |
LCC F3448.4.L53 (ebook) | DDC 985.06/3—dc23
LC record available at https://lccn.loc.gov/2016020793

Cover art: Llamojha, location unknown, 1965. Photo courtesy
of Manuel Llamojha Mitma.

DON MANUEL'S DEDICATION:

To my wife.
We struggled so hard together.

And to my children,
who supported me in the fight.

CONTENTS

A NOTE ON PLACE

Peru is divided into twenty-four departments, like American states. Until a major administrative reform in 2006, these departments were governed by nationally appointed prefects. Departments are subdivided into provinces, which were led by subprefects until the 2006 administrative change. Provinces are divided into districts, and districts house numerous communities and towns.

Much of Manuel Llamojha's life history is situated in the Peruvian department of Ayacucho. Its capital city, located in the province of Huamanga, is also named Ayacucho. For purposes of clarity, I refer to the capital as "the city of Ayacucho" throughout the text. Llamojha was born in the community of Concepción. Until 1954, Concepción belonged to the district of Vischongo in Cangallo province. In 1954, Concepción and the communities surrounding it were reorganized as a district, also named Concepción. In 1984, the province of Cangallo was divided in two, when the province of Vilcashuamán was established. The community and district of Concepción now belong to the province of Vilcashuamán.

ACKNOWLEDGMENTS

As part of our co-authorship, Manuel Llamojha Mitma and I agreed that he would compose this book's dedication, and I would write the acknowledgments. My most important thanks, then, go to don Manuel. His incredible talents as a leader, historian, and storyteller form this book's foundation, and I am grateful that he so generously shared his memories with me. I continue to be amazed by his intellectual energy, his accomplishments as an activist, and his astonishing determination. It has been an enormous privilege to work with him.

María Llamojha Puklla took an active part in this book from its earliest moments, showing much enthusiasm, generosity, and kindness. I thank her for arranging interviews, for answering countless questions, and for her careful reading of the book's first draft. María's love for her father—and her commitment to honoring his life's work—is deeply moving.

Alicia Carrasco Gutiérrez played a crucial role in this project, conducting nearly two dozen interviews with questions I emailed her from Canada. Alicia's enthusiastic work enabled this project to move forward with the speed both don Manuel and I desired.

Walter, Hilda, and Delia Llamojha Puklla shared loving memories about their father as well as their reflections and concerns about the book. Although I met her only once, doña Esther Honorata Puklla warmly welcomed me into her family's life and readily offered her thoughts about her husband's activism. Don Manuel's brothers Emilio, Víctor, and Alejandro also agreed to be interviewed for the project. I thank them all for opening their lives and homes to Alicia and me. I am also grateful to the many current and former members of the Peruvian Peasant Confederation who shared their memories of don Manuel and his work.

Funding for this project came from a University of Alberta Support for the Advancement of Scholarship grant and the Social Sciences and Humanities Research Council of Canada.

Archivists and librarians at the Archivo Regional de Ayacucho, Ayacucho's Proyecto Especial de Titulación de Tierras, the Biblioteca Nacional del Perú, the Centro de Información para la Memoria Colectiva y los Derechos Humanos, the Nettie Lee Benson Latin American collection at the University of Texas at Austin, and the Hoover Institution all provided support and access to crucial documents, periodicals, and recorded interviews. I thank Natacha Carroll for superb research assistance in the Biblioteca Nacional.

Ricardo Caro Cárdenas offered many insights, shared essential documents, and answered my dozens of questions about the Peruvian left. He also kindly arranged access to the Peruvian Peasant Confederation's archive. I am tremendously lucky to have such a generous and knowledgeable colleague and friend. I also benefited from many conversations about don Manuel's life and work with the historians Nelson Pereyra Chávez and Iván Caro.

Gladys McCormick read a very early draft of this book, and her critical feedback helped me craft a more accessible work. Susan L. Smith likewise offered helpful comments on earlier versions. Ileana Rodríguez-Silva helped me think through some of the major challenges this project posed, and she provided outstanding conceptual advice.

Florencia Mallon gave much generous guidance and thoughtful suggestions about the book's direction. I am exceptionally grateful for her ongoing support and friendship. Duke University Press's two anonymous reviewers pushed me to both broaden and deepen my analysis, and I thank them for their highly constructive feedback. Many thanks to Lydia Rose Rappoport-Hankins, Danielle Houtz, Martha Ramsey, and Lorien Olive for guiding the book to publication. I would also like to extend warm thanks to Gisela Fosado for her keen insights and terrific advice.

My parents, Ed and Andrea Heilman, gave me unceasing encouragement and support throughout this project. Ken Mah crafted the maps in this book, took hundreds of photographs in Austin, rescued my computer from certain death, and pushed me to keep moving forward. He is the very best husband a person could have. Our son Theo was born as I completed the final revisions for this book. I cannot wait to tell him all about don Manuel.

— JAYMIE PATRICIA HEILMAN

"Now Peru is mine!" So declared an indigenous teenager named Manuel Llamojha Mitma after he entered the Peruvian army in the late 1930s. A Quechua peasant from the impoverished highland department of Ayacucho, Llamojha was determined to bring socioeconomic justice to a country rife with sharp anti-indigenous prejudice and startling inequalities, and he soon grew into one of twentieth-century Peru's most creative and dedicated political activists. This testimonial biography offers the first extended exploration of Llamojha's life, ideas, and work, chronicling his struggles against indigenous oppression, territorial dispossession, and sociopolitical exclusion, all problems that he defines as legacies of the Spanish conquest.[1] Read together, Llamojha's recollections about his life offer a means for understanding Peru's—and, indeed, Latin America's—troubled twentieth-century history. Fundamental issues like racism, revolutionary politics, agrarian reform, and political violence figure prominently in Llamojha's narrative, with one man's extraordinary life reflecting the course of an equally extraordinary century.

Although Llamojha's stay in the military was short-lived, he dedicated his life to fighting on behalf of Peru's indigenous peasants (campesinos). He led major mobilizations for indigenous land rights in his home region of Ayacucho during the 1940s and 1950s, and he ran for national political office in 1962. That same year, he became secretary general of Peru's largest national peasant organization, the Confederación Campesina del Perú (Peruvian Peasant Confederation; CCP). Llamojha's activism took him to Cuba, China, and the Soviet Union in 1965, and during the 1970s he became embroiled in the bitter, divisive political quarrels that plagued the Peruvian left and fractured the CCP. In the 1980s, Llamojha was falsely accused of membership in the Peruvian Communist Party-Shining Path, a political party whose armed struggle plunged Peru into a twenty-year internal war that left over 69,000 Peruvians dead, the vast majority of whom were of rural, indigenous origins. That devastating conflict forced Llamojha to flee Ayacucho and live as an internal refugee in the city of Lima for nearly twenty years. The war also led to the permanent disappearance of his youngest son.

During many of our interviews, Llamojha wore a baseball cap embroidered with the iconic portrait of Che Guevara. Llamojha in a Che Guevara hat provides a striking image, for part of what makes Llamojha's recollections so valuable is that they help us see beyond Che, beyond the man who has come to symbolize twentieth-century political activism in Latin America.[2] The popular fascination with Che is easy to understand: this handsome young hero dedicated—and ultimately sacrificed—his life to the pursuit of revolutionary change. But Che was far from alone in his efforts, and his embrace of armed struggle represented only one particular form of revolutionary activism. Across Latin America, thousands of men and women likewise devoted their lives to pursuing fundamental political, social, and economic change, and their struggles to bring revolutionary transformations did not always involve the use of violence. Unlike Che Guevara, Llamojha never participated in guerrilla struggles; in our interviews he laughingly recalled that he had never even held a gun. Llamojha's activism instead involved writing, talking, and extensive efforts to mobilize indigenous peasants to press for socioeconomic justice and radical political transformation. And as an impoverished husband and father based in the Andean countryside, Llamojha did not have the kind of youthful urban virility and highly charged sexuality that—along with the ever-present beard—characterized the revolutionary masculinity of activists like Che.[3] Llamojha's recollections therefore allow us to reflect on both the many different shapes of activism in twentieth-century Latin America and the enduring legacies of those struggles.

Llamojha's life stories also help us to temper romantic visions of political activism. His recollections push us to look past simple narratives of heroic struggle and triumph as he shares memories of unjust imprisonments, torture, and the severe economic hardships linked to life as a political activist. His life

FIG. I.1 Llamojha, Concepción, 2013. Author photo.

stories also expose heated political disputes between revolutionary activists, fights that left him slandered and marginalized by his former political allies. And unlike those revolutionary fighters who died young in the throes of armed struggle, Llamojha survived, living through the horrifying internal war in his country that brought terrible losses for him and his family. He also had to confront the difficulties of aging, struggling to remain politically active and relevant as an elderly man.

Llamojha's life history chronicles the realities of anti-Indianism: an ideological system that casts indigenous peoples as inherently inferior to whites and as impediments to national progress and a system of practices that excludes indigenous people from full citizenship while exploiting their land and labor.[4] Anti-Indianism has long flourished in Peru, a country that is home to a large and diverse indigenous population; today, well over one-third of the country's population is indigenous.[5] Of the many different indigenous groups or nations living in Peru, peoples of Quechua ethnoracial heritage like Llamojha's are by far the most numerous, followed by the other main indigenous ethnic group living in the country's Andean sierra region, the Aymara. In addition, over sixty different indigenous ethnic groups live in Peru's lowland Amazon region. Despite the large number of indigenous people in Peru, anti-Indian racism has been—and remains—sharp there. The most indigenous regions of Peru's Andean sierra, the departments of Ancash, Apurímac, Ayacucho, Cuzco, Huancavelica, and Puno, were long known by the pejorative name mancha india (Indian stain), and the word indio (Indian) has long been a highly charged racial slur that simultaneously connotes backwardness, ignorance, and a latent potential for violence. Throughout this book Llamojha describes how such racism operated in his country, his home community, and even his own family. He spent his political career fighting against the consequences of anti-Indianism, leading mobilizations demanding indigenous peasants' land rights and national inclusion.

At its core, Llamojha's life history is about indigenous peasants' struggle for justice, in particular their fight for land. Across twentieth-century Latin America, campesinos from diverse regions and countries pressed for lands that they felt rightly belonged to them. The need for agrarian reform was particularly pressing in twentieth-century Peru, as Peru's agricultural land was heavily concentrated in the hands of a small landowning minority. In Llamojha's home department of Ayacucho in 1961, just 0.3 percent of all rural properties held 59.2 percent of the land, meaning that there was a gross disparity between large landed estates known as haciendas or latifundios and indigenous peasants' plots of land.[6] Ayacucho and the neighboring departments of Apurímac and Huancavelica formed the most impoverished area of Peru. The land campesinos owned was not only insufficient in quantity; it was often also quite poor in quality. As a result, indigenous peasants had barely enough land to meet their subsistence needs, and the food they produced was rarely varied enough to provide adequate nutrition.

To Llamojha, the problem of land is not just one of economic injustice; it is instead a problem that originated with the European conquest of Latin America. From the outset of the colonial period in the 1490s, many rural indigenous communities found their lands encroached on and even stolen by Spanish—or Portuguese, in the Brazilian case—colonizers who established large haciendas. The process of indigenous peasants' dispossession from their

MAP I.1 Peru

lands increased dramatically in scale and speed during the late 1800s, when now-independent Latin American nations became deeply enmeshed in the global market economy. Foreign demand for Latin American agricultural goods like coffee, sugar, tobacco, wool, and many other products led to a sustained assault on indigenous community lands by profit-hungry hacendados, the owners of private estates.[7] Countless indigenous peasants saw hacendados claim more and more community lands as their own, and many rural indigenous communities disappeared entirely, leaving community members to labor as landless peasants on haciendas. Although campesinos had long fought to defend their lands, using the courts, protests to government officials, and sometimes violence to protect their communities, the twentieth century witnessed unprecedented peasant mobilization demanding land. Campesinos filed complaints, staged protests, and even launched armed uprisings to demand the return of their lands. As a direct consequence of these efforts, governments in Mexico, Cuba, Guatemala, Bolivia, and Peru, among others, introduced agrarian reforms designed to redistribute land, expropriating hacienda lands for the benefit of campesinos.

Llamojha's life stories also chronicle one of the most profound shifts in twentieth-century Latin American history: the massive migration of men and women out of the countryside and into cities. Llamojha moved from his rural Andean community to the coastal capital city of Lima in the 1930s, at the beginning of an urbanization process that eventually transformed most Latin American countries. Power, social prestige, and wealth were overwhelmingly concentrated in Lima, a city long racialized as European, and many indigenous migrants faced wrenching discrimination and alienation when they arrived there. Yet those same migrants helped transform the capital city, changing its social, political, and economic dynamics through their labor, organizational efforts, and cultural practices.[8] Their arrival in Lima shaped—and was shaped by—the rise of major political parties like the Alianza Popular Revolucionaria Americana (American Popular Revolutionary Alliance; APRA) and the Communist Party, which offered radical new approaches to the many problems that plagued Peru.

Through Llamojha's experiences we can also see what it meant to be a political activist across the decades of the Cold War. Although he shares humorous recollections of his exploits against local hacendados and his daring escapes from police, he also reveals that he was routinely branded a communist and jailed on charges of subversion. Those charges were spurious: Llamojha worked closely with members of different branches of the Peruvian

Communist Party, but he never formally joined any political party and never self-identified as a communist. Llamojha's narrative shows that the Cold War was far more than an ideological and diplomatic fight between the United States and the Soviet Union. It was instead a broadly global conflict that had profound consequences in the everyday lives of Latin American citizens. Latin American states, elites, and sometimes even average men and women made accusations of communism to discredit individuals they deemed threatening and to justify their own—often violent—assertions of power. But, as Llamojha's account shows, the Cold War decades were also a time of enormous political creativity in Latin America, generating tremendous energy and excitement among activists and their sympathizers as they imagined, and fought for, revolutionary change.[9]

As Llamojha narrates his experiences of political activism in the 1960s and 1970s, he speaks of divisions and betrayals in Peru's left-wing political parties. Throughout much of twentieth-century Latin America, internecine conflicts between leftists led to heated confrontations, nasty invective, fractured parties, and countless political heartbreaks. In Peru these divides resulted in the bitter 1973 split of the CCP, the country's most important national campesino organization. In this book Llamojha shares anecdotes and opinions about several of the towering figures of the Peruvian left, and many of these stories are as sharply critical as they are humorous. What emerges is a portrait of Llamojha's steady political marginalization across the 1970s.

Llamojha's life stories also help us to understand the most devastating period of Peru's twentieth century: the 1980–2000 internal war, which began after the Peruvian Communist Party-Shining Path launched an armed struggle in May 1980. The resulting insurgency and state-sponsored counterinsurgency cost the lives of an estimated 69,280 Peruvians, most of them indigenous peasants. Strikingly, the Shining Path was responsible for the majority—54 percent—of these deaths.[10] In my book *Before the Shining Path*, I have argued that we need to understand the Shining Path's violence in its historical context. In the early days of the war, militants of the Shining Path took brutal and decisive action against abusive local authorities and wealthier peasants who had long exploited their poorer neighbors. Although indigenous peasants had long sought state intervention against these abusive figures—making heated and repeated complaints, often over the course of decades—these individuals remained in positions of power at the district level until Shining Path militants executed them. But the Shining Path did not stop there. Instead, party militants turned the same sort of violence against average indigenous peasants who were unwilling to wholly accept the Shining Path's mandates. In so doing, Shining Path activists essentially replicated old patterns set by abusive authorities and wealthier campesinos.[11]

We can see many of these same processes at work in the stories Llamojha narrates, including the Shining Path's assassination of a much-hated district official. Llamojha's connections to the years of violence are also intensely personal. From the 1980s—and indeed to this day—many of his enemies and rivals have accused him of belonging to the Shining Path. That false accusation came in part because the Shining Path tried to gain traction in the branch of the CCP that Llamojha led after the confederation's fracture in 1973. The accusation also came because one of the Shining Path's earliest armed attacks was directed against a hacienda that Llamojha had long challenged. Tragically for Llamojha and his family, that accusation appeared in one of the first and most influential studies of the Shining Path, Peruvian journalist Gustavo Gorriti's 1990 book *Sendero*, in which Gorriti mentioned a "clandestine meeting in the Ayacucho home of Shining Path peasant activist Manuel Llamojha Mitma."[12] Building off of Gorriti's book and influenced by other accusations I had heard, I too assumed that Llamojha had joined the Shining Path, and I wrote as much in *Before the Shining Path*. It is now clear that these claims were all mistaken; Llamojha never belonged to the Shining Path.

Peru's internal war upended Llamojha's life, forcing him to escape from Ayacucho and live as a displaced person in Lima for almost two decades. The war also generated the greatest tragedy Llamojha ever experienced: the disappearance of his son Herbert. Although Herbert Llamojha denied that he was a member of the Shining Path, he was present during one of the party's armed attacks and was consequently jailed on charges of assault and armed robbery. In March 1982, Shining Path militants stormed the Ayacucho jail where Herbert was imprisoned, aiming to free all the prisoners and thereby liberate jailed party members. Herbert was one of 304 prisoners who escaped.[13] But that is all we know. He might have been killed in the ensuing shootout, or he might have been arrested and then killed extrajudicially. It is also possible that he escaped and then lost his life elsewhere. No one knows. Herbert's disappearance is the central sorrow of Llamojha's life and an open wound that remains terribly painful for him, and for his family, to this day. Sadly, the traumas of political violence and the tragedy of disappearances were all too common in Latin America's twentieth century, as military regimes and nominal democracies conducted brutal dirty wars against ordinary citizens. Llamojha's devastating experiences of loss echo across the Latin American continent.

The Activist Intellectual

Llamojha is what Marxist thinker Antonio Gramsci termed an "organic intellectual"—someone who gives his or her social group self-awareness and who uses his work to educate, lead, and organize members of his class.[14] Llamojha utilized his writings, his ideas, and his words to inspire and mobilize indigenous peasants and to fight for their rights. Writing in particular was central to Llamojha's political career. In our interviews, he laughingly recalled going from community to community, his typewriter strapped to his back, so that he could compose protest letters on behalf of local indigenous peasants. The fact that he could read and write—and write so beautifully and effectively—allowed him to provide a crucial service to campesinos. Within his home department of Ayacucho during the 1940s, 1950s, and even 1960s, literacy rates in rural communities were startlingly low because of astonishing state neglect, as the Peruvian state failed to provide adequate educational opportunities in the Andean countryside. As late as 1961, 79.5 percent of the population over age fifteen living in rural Ayacucho were illiterate.[15] By drafting letters for illiterate indigenous peasants, Llamojha enabled them to participate in a political system expressly designed to exclude them. That exclusion resulted from the fact that until 1980, the right to vote was dependent on literacy, a requirement pointedly intended to disenfranchise rural indigenous people.[16]

Writing was more than just a functional skill for Llamojha. It was—and remains—central to his identity and close to his heart. Throughout our interviews, he spoke of his typewriter, his papers, and especially his books with tremendous affection. He despaired at the fact that soldiers seized his personal archive and book collection in 1982, and he even anthropomorphized the religious books confiscated by the courts in 1948, lamenting that his books were subject to life imprisonment. He spoke about how much he enjoyed reading, thinking, and writing, recalling that he even used to write poetry. Llamojha is also very much a historian. He fills his narratives with references to colonial times, to the Inka, and even to humanity's very first emergence on Earth, and he has written an unpublished book about the history of his home community, Concepción.[17] He remembers giving talks to university students in Lima, and in recent years many students from Ayacucho's San Cristóbal de Huamanga University have made the four-hour bus trip to Concepción to visit him and interview him about regional history.

Llamojha's work as an indigenous intellectual reveals his concerted efforts to decolonize knowledge. He labored to acquire the literacy and writing abilities that Peru's exclusionary state system tried to reserve for nonindigenous elites, and he flouted the boundaries of the expected life course for an indigenous peasant. In most of the political documents he wrote across the twentieth century, he boldly changed the names of Peruvian communities and districts to better reflect their precolonial Quechua origins. He did the same with his own name, rejecting the Hispanicized spelling of his surname (Llamocca) in favor of a spelling with Quechua orthography (Llamojha). And in many of his writings and speeches, he used historical analysis to expose the colonial origins of problems like indigenous poverty, land loss, and racism.

In Peru, a country rife with racist and classist assumptions equating indigeneity and peasant life with ignorance, many observers were taken aback by Llamojha's skills as a writer and intellectual. His talents seemed at odds with what many people expected from an indigenous peasant. One Ayacucho schoolteacher whom I met recounted being stunned, at first meeting Llamojha, that the man who had written such a powerful denunciation of the Peruvian government's proposed education reform was simply a "humble campesino."[18] In a 1962 letter an Ayacucho authority commented that Llamojha could not possibly have written two of the documents in question—documents he did in fact write—asserting that he "does not have that capacity to draw up said communiqués."[19] Llamojha tells similar stories in his narrative, laughingly recalling how officials did not believe he could be the notorious Manuel Llamojha.

The disconnect between people's assumptions and Llamojha's appearance partly explains why he was able to escape police so easily and so often. That disconnect can also help us make sense of how Llamojha portrays himself in his life stories. At several points in his account he makes bold statements about his importance, comparing himself to Jesus and casting himself as fundamental to campesinos' triumphs. But the man who makes such claims seems anything but egotistical or arrogant in person. He is warm and soft-spoken, quick with a joke and a smile, and full of wonder about the world and its past. He is also frequently self-deprecating. As his daughter María explained, "My dad is really humble, down to earth and charismatic. He's not like other leaders who have a really strong personality and are really loud and effusive. My dad is really quiet, really calm, he doesn't appear to have all the vitality that he actually has, the great ability to get angry about injustice."[20] One man who worked with him in the 1970s similarly commented that Llamojha was rather quiet and that they had to "pull words from him with a spoon."[21] Llamojha's grandiose claims thus seem less the words of an egotist than they do expressions of proud amazement at all that he was able to accomplish given his modest background. His assertions are also tinged with nostalgia: he is now an elderly man with failing eyesight and limited mobility, and he is remembering periods of his life when his power and prestige were much greater.

Llamojha's bold statements about his importance may also be a response to his obscure place in contemporary Peruvian national consciousness. Unlike other Peruvian political activists of the mid-twentieth century—Héctor Béjar, Hugo Blanco, Abimael Guzmán, and Luis de la Puente, among others—Llamojha's name is not well known in Peru today, and many have forgotten his struggles. Even leading members of the present-day CCP failed to recognize Llamojha's name when I asked them about him.[22] Yet Llamojha was one of Peru's most creative and esteemed twentieth-century political figures. He was also one of the only major twentieth-century Peruvian political leaders who was both indigenous and a peasant, setting him far apart from the wealthier and whiter Peruvian political activists whose names continue to resonate in Peru.

Campesinos and Indigeneity

Llamojha defines himself and those for whom he has long fought as campesinos, or peasants. In Latin America, *campesino* does not necessarily mean indigenous, as the racial and ethnic identities of men and women who call themselves peasants vary enormously across the continent. In Peru, there were and are impoverished agricultural laborers of African, Chinese, and mestizo (mixed European and indigenous) descent, as well as of indigenous origin, just as there have been many indigenous men and women whose economic lives were not defined by subsistence agriculture.

To Llamojha, however, to be a campesino is to belong to a rural community that originated with Peru's Inka. As he phrased it, "We have been here since the time of the Inka. We're natives [naturales] of America, of the continent." His understanding of what it means to be a campesino is one that melds ethnic, class, and historical identities, and he is both passionate and explicit about his indigeneity. He remembers angrily challenging his sister when she denied her indigenous origins, he utilized election propaganda that described him as "coming from the core of the Indian race," and he speaks repeatedly about the beauty and importance of Quechua, calling it "the Peruvian language."[23] Llamojha's activism is also profoundly anticolonial. In his speeches and writings, he staunchly denounced the genocidal violence of the Spanish conquest and the suffering imposed by centuries of colonialism. In his notebooks he chronicles the Inka history of his home region, and he describes precolonial Andean labor practices.[24]

To Llamojha, there is nothing "unethnic" about his campesino identity.[25] Far from a strictly class-based definition of self, Llamojha's formulation of *campesino* is instead a staunchly anticolonial identity that embraces a Quechua ancestry. It is also a term he deems far more fitting than "Indian," a label he characterizes as a foolish mistake of colonialism. He explained:

> **Discrimination began when the Spanish took America. They categorized all the natives of the continent as "Indians," as people of another country, another world. I always felt proud when they called me "Indian." When Christopher Columbus came to America, he thought that all the inhabitants of America were from India. So I was proud when they said "Indian" to me, because that meant I was from India!**

Llamojha's formulation of an indigenist campesino identity reveals the complexity of indigeneity in Peru's Andean region.[26] Andean community members' understanding of themselves have varied dramatically across time, between Andean regions, between communities, and even between individuals. And because of the crippling constraints of racism in Peru, most rural Andean community members reject descriptors like indigenous, Indian, native, Aymara, and Quechua, choosing instead to call themselves campesinos.[27] Yet many of these community members take much pride in their Andean social, economic, and cultural practices and histories.

The shift to the campesino identifier was a gradual one. Documents from Llamojha's home region, Ayacucho, show members of rural Andean communities still occasionally self-identifying as indigenous as late as the early 1960s. Llamojha himself described his community's transition away from the label indigenous:

> **We used to write "indigenous campesino community" because representatives of the high authorities came and said "you are an indigenous community." So we accepted that and started to write documents and memos, always writing "indigenous campesino community." But later, we wanted to suspend use of that word. "Why should we write that?" we asked.[28]**

Llamojha's comments are key: he talks about leaving a word behind, not about discarding an identity. For Llamojha, there is nothing contradictory about using the term campesino to mean a Quechua speaker living in a community descended from the Inka.[29] Today, influenced by shifting continental politics, international funding opportunities, and the elections of presidents of Andean origin, more Peruvian individuals are explicitly self-identifying as indigenous. But that shift is not about Peru "catching up" to neighboring Andean countries where citizens began mobilizing around explicitly indigenous identities during the 1980s.[30] As the late anthropologist Carlos Iván Degregori observed, "perhaps it is not a matter of being ahead or behind, but rather of the distinct forms through which ethnicity is expressed in different countries."[31] And in Peru, for much of the twentieth century, Andean people largely chose to express their ethnoracial identity through the term *campesino*.

Writing a Testimonial Biography

My first encounter with Llamojha occurred in the Ayacucho Regional Archive. As I was researching the region's 1960s political history, I found several letters and reports from regional authorities warning about a dangerous communist activist in their midst. I also found a public letter that this activist— Manuel Llamojha Mitma—had written, and I was moved by its power and eloquence. A portion of that letter reads as follows:

> For more than 400 years, we have been eagerly awaiting the dawn of justice. Enough is enough. For more than four centuries, we have been suffering the flagellation of barbaric injustice. Enough is enough. We are still living the tragic misery of our lives, cheated and deceived by those who represent bastard interests. Enough is enough. The *latifundista* [estate-owning] gentlemen continue to enrich themselves, exploiting our sweat and the wealth of our territory.[32]

As I continued my research I found more and more references to Llamojha, and I learned that he had done an interview with Peru's Comisión de la Verdad y Reconciliación (Truth and Reconciliation Commission; CVR) in 2002. When I finally met Llamojha in May 2011, I proposed that we work together on a book about his life. He readily agreed.

Llamojha and I had different motivations for producing this book.[33] I wanted to share his fascinating personal history and exceptionally rich stories with undergraduate students, knowing that his life history would be a powerful tool for exploring key issues in twentieth-century Latin American history. His stories also push us to consider the connections—and departures—between the revolutionary activism of the twentieth century and the "left turn" taken by many Latin American governments in the first decade of the twenty-first century.[34] I also wanted to make Llamojha's experiences and ideas better known to scholars of Peru, as he shares crucial insights into the history of Peru's left and the CCP. Llamojha had a separate—but complementary—set of motivations. He wanted to ensure that future generations in countries throughout the world understood the injustices faced by Peru's indigenous peasants. As he phrased it,

campesinos have fought so much and suffered so much, during colonial times and republican times, too. We need the future world to know about this, the suffering of the campesinos.

Llamojha also wanted to record and preserve the history of his beloved community, Concepción. Doing so was especially important to him given the anguish he continues to feel over the seizure and destruction of his immense document archive by Peruvian soldiers in 1982. After I provided a first draft of the book to him, Llamojha insisted that the physical copy remain in Concepción, as it held the community's history and should be available to community residents for consultation.

Different though they were, our motivations jointly necessitated the production of a highly readable book appropriate for a broad audience.[35] The book that resulted blends the conventions of biography and *testimonio*. Like a testimonio—a first-person narrative that shares a witness's experiences of a particular atrocity or injustice—this book privileges Llamojha's voice and life stories.[36] The book visually foregrounds his stories, presenting them in his standard typewriter font to give particular emphasis to his words. And like a testimonio, this work serves to denounce injustice and inspire others to action. But this book also departs significantly from the conventions of a testimonio and moves into the realm of biography. Because of the centrality of writing to Llamojha's political career and its deep personal importance to him, I have included excerpts of numerous documents written by him. In addition, I have provided historical context in each of the chapters, and I have included considerations of what others from the period wrote or said about Llamojha. Drawn from extensive archival research, these additions allow readers unfamiliar with Peruvian history to follow Llamojha's complex account of political work in the years from 1921 to the present. These additional materials also round out Llamojha's life history, helping to fill the thematic and temporal spaces that separate his many stories.[37] Yet in keeping with our shared desire to create a broadly accessible and highly readable book, I have confined historiographical discussion to the endnotes. This book bridges the methodological boundaries between testimonio and biography, and the result is what I deem a testimonial biography.[38] It recognizes Llamojha and me as coauthors, acknowledging the intellectual and creative work both of us performed and the editorial authority we shared.[39]

This testimonial biography is ultimately about much more than just one (extraordinary) individual's life. Testimonial biography offers an exceptional tool for analyzing continuities and changes over decades, for showing the complexities and contradictions of the past, and for showcasing the relationship between individuals and the social, cultural, and political contexts in which they operate.[40] Consideration of an individual life—with all its hardships, triumphs, and losses—also offers the reader a vivid and intense understanding of what it meant to live in a particular situation, place, and time.

In keeping with Llamojha's long history of composing formal legal documents, he and I signed an agreement before Concepción's justice of the peace. The document we signed recognized us as coauthors; granted permission for his life history stories, photographs, and drawings to be used in the book; agreed that any royalties would go to him; and allowed me to sign all paperwork for the book's publication. We also agreed that the book would be published in both English and Spanish, to best meet our dual goals for the book. In doing so, we answered the crucial questions that historian Florencia Mallon asks about research collaboration between nonindigenous academics and indigenous actors: "Who gets to talk about what, and in which language?"[41] This project is not about a North American scholar "giving voice" to a subaltern—Llamojha speaks just fine on his own, with seemingly inexhaustible intellectual energy, to all who want to listen. The book is instead about using the resources I have at my disposal to enable Llamojha to reach an audience well beyond those persons who visit him in Peru. The book is based on the mutual respect we have for each other as intellectuals and on our exchanges of ideas, documents, and knowledge.[42]

This testimonial biography was also shaped by the pressures and ravages of time. When we spoke about this book, Llamojha's primary concern was that it be completed as quickly as possible—a desire connected directly to the fact that he is in his nineties and acutely aware of his own mortality.

Anthropologist Barbara Myerhoff reflected on a similar issue in her study of elderly Jewish immigrants at a seniors' center in the United States. Noting these elderly men and women's determination to share their life stories, Myerhoff commented, "Again and again they attempted to show outsiders, as well as each other, who they were, why they mattered, what the nature of their past and present lives was. . . . Their extreme old age and sense of little time remaining intensified the desire to formulate a presentation of themselves."[43] Llamojha felt a similar sense of urgency about getting his story recorded and published, but our research plans were interrupted by tragedy. Just over a week after my first set of interviews with Llamojha in May 2011, his beloved wife, Esther, died unexpectedly. This was not the right moment to pursue more interviews, and I could not remain in Peru for an extended period, as the demands of family and my academic job meant I had to return to Canada.

The solution Llamojha and I found came through the participation of my longtime friend and research assistant Alicia Carrasco Gutiérrez in this project. Alicia carried out a series of follow-up interviews with Llamojha between October 2011 and July 2012, using lists of questions I emailed her from Canada. Alicia's participation in the project as a research assistant allowed the interviews with Llamojha to continue while I was in Canada.[44] She also interviewed three of his children and all of his surviving siblings, again using questions I sent her.[45] Llamojha and I then revisited the main themes of the book in a set of lengthy final interviews in May 2013, when I brought him the manuscript draft.

Llamojha's sense of urgency for completing this book also grew from his sadness and frustration over the failings of his memory. Although he shared amazingly detailed recollections of key events in his life—all the more astonishing given that he is in his nineties—he lamented the lapses in his memory that occasionally left him unable to answer my questions. He commented that sometimes he could not even remember his own name, and he wondered if someone had used witchcraft against him. His concerns about his decaying memory gave added weight to his desire to finish the book as quickly as possible. To supplement the life stories he shared during our interviews, and to relay his personal history in its richest detail, I have included segments of his 2002 interview with the CVR. For the sake of transparency, I explicitly signal any material that comes from that interview.[46]

Rather than narrating his life's course in a straightforward chronology, Llamojha shared dozens of stories about key moments in his life. As so many of us do, he often voiced slightly different versions of the same anecdotes in our interviews.[47] In many instances I've amalgamated those versions in an attempt to best reflect his gifts for storytelling and share the fullness of his experiences. I have also edited his stories to minimize repetition. This method has drawbacks: it hides the emphasis that repeated stories and frequently reiterated sentences offer, and it imposes chronological order on an account that jumped back and forth in time. But the advantage is a narrative that is both readable and complete.

Llamojha's recollections allow us to see what happened during his life as an activist. We get access to key events, individuals, and experiences spanning the decades of his political career. Even more important, his stories reveal what *mattered* during his years of struggle. His words show his ideas, his opinions, and his perspectives, building a much fuller and more complicated portrait of his life than would be accessible from written documents alone. Certainly, we should not read Llamojha's life stories as strictly literal narrations of the past: he is a man in his nineties, speaking about events that occurred many decades ago, and he routinely recalls long-ago conversations in what surely are not verbatim renderings. It is difficult to specify the exact dates of many of the events he describes, and a handful of his stories seem to border on the apocryphal. His life stories are best read as historical memories shaped by his past and present dreams and desires, sorrows and triumphs, and by the Peruvian realities that he tried so hard to transform. The sharing of these remembrances is at once a social, cultural, and political act that helps Llamojha make sense of all that he accomplished, endured, and witnessed.[48] As oral history scholar Alessandro Portelli phrases it, "oral sources tell us not just what people did, but what they wanted to do, what they believed they were doing, and what they now think they did."[49]

There is no doubt that my status as a white university professor from a wealthy country—and my research assistant Alicia Carrasco's status as a university-educated urban professional—meant that our interviews with Llamojha were shaped by significant power disparities.[50] Moreover, as the author of the first draft of this book, I made the first major decisions about what appears in these pages before taking a translated version of the book back to Llamojha and his family for feedback and revision. But it is also true that Llamojha brought his own priorities and agendas into our interviews, knowing that the interviews would form the basis of a book about his life. He clearly wanted to tell stories about his political life, and when Alicia and I tried to direct the conversation toward a discussion of his family life, asking questions about his wife, siblings, and children, he usually steered the conversation back onto a political track. His narrative decisions had nothing to do with sentiment; his deep love and affection for his family were readily apparent in his daily interactions with them. He also showed a dogged optimism in our interviews, insisting that he had no regrets about his work and minimizing the suffering he endured during his constant imprisonments, years of extreme economic hardships, and major political disappointments. His interview choices reflected his desire to craft a narrative of his struggles as a campesino leader, to inspire others to action, and to cement a legacy of his political work.[51] As he noted in one of our interviews, "You always have to be in the struggle. Until the very end."

"I'm Going to Be President of the Republic"
THE FORMATION OF AN ACTIVIST, 1921–1948

Seven years old and outraged at the theft of his family's livestock by a local landlord, a very young Manuel Llamojha Mitma proclaimed, "I'm going to be president of the republic, and I'm going to make the haciendas disappear!" This chapter considers Llamojha's formation as an activist, exploring how and why he chose to dedicate his life to a struggle for justice. His dreams and ambitions radically transgressed the boundaries of an indigenous peasant's expected life course. The constraints of anti-Indianism in Peru were so tight that many Peruvians deemed campesinos too backward and too ignorant to do anything other than grinding physical labor on the land.[1] Educational opportunities in rural Andean communities were also so grossly lacking that few indigenous peasants could realistically aspire to much more than a life of agricultural labor. The most ambitious and fortunate campesinos were sometimes able to enter positions of local authority—becoming district mayors or justices of the peace—and some were able to migrate to urban centers and find working-class jobs. But the goals Llamojha set for himself, including the priesthood, military leadership, and even the presidency, were ones definitively closed to indigenous peasants, and few Peruvians would have even imagined an Andean campesino having such ambitions. Such were the extreme limitations of life in Peru's rural indigenous communities during much of the twentieth century.

Llamojha was an exceptional child who became an extraordinary man, but there was much about his early life that would seem familiar to Latin Americans who grew up during the first half of the twentieth century. In the 1920s and 1930s, more Latin Americans lived in the countryside than in cities, and many shared Llamojha's experiences of grinding rural poverty, pronounced state disregard for the countryside, and hacienda abuses.[2] Impoverished Latin Americans often desperately wanted access to better schools and better teachers, longing for education, and in these pages Llamojha explains how he acquired his most important political tool: his literacy. Like Llamojha, tens of thousands of Latin Americans migrated from the countryside to urban centers in the first decades of the twentieth century, searching for better opportunities and better lives. Many faced terrible ethnoracial and class discrimination on their arrival in the city. Some joined burgeoning leftist political parties and organizations that promised to fight for socioeconomic justice and build more equitable nation-states. Llamojha himself turned to what soon became one of Peru's most important political parties: APRA.

Childhood

Born at the base of a tree on May 3, 1921, Llamojha began his life in the humblest of circumstances.

> My parents had gone to harvest wheat, potatoes, and that's how I was born, at the base of a tree.[3] When I was born, there was nothing. Just birds singing in the tree, while I was crying at its base. There weren't even any angels there to greet me. When Christ was born, angels came! But not for me; they didn't come for me. Not angels, and not the Three Wise Men either!

Situating the very start of his life on a plot of his family's farm land, a few kilometers away from the community of Concepción—a small town in what was then Cangallo province in the department of Ayacucho—Llamojha stressed his connection with rural Peru, his poverty, and the unremarkable beginning of his very remarkable life.[4]

The eldest of six children, he was born to indigenous peasant parents who were themselves from the region.[5] Like the overwhelming majority of campesinos in early twentieth-century Ayacucho, Llamojha's mother, Paulina Mitma Vásquez, spoke only the indigenous language Quechua. His father

FIG. 1.1 Concepción. Author photo.

was different. Although Quechua was his first language, Anselmo Llamojha Martínez spoke some Spanish, and he even knew how to read, something that was exceptional among indigenous peasants of the period. That rarity was a symptom of the Peruvian state's terrible neglect of rural Andean communities. Many communities, like Concepción, had no schools at all, and those few rural schools that did exist rarely taught past the earliest grades. Such schools also suffered from a lack of resources, and their teachers often had little more than basic literacy and numeracy skills.

> My father knew how to read, though not very well. He didn't have suffi-
> cient schooling, because back then, there were no schools in the Peruvian
> Andes. The hacendados prohibited it. Because there weren't any schools
> in rural towns, people would learn to read by paying someone who already
> knew how. My dad sold a young bull to someone so that he'd teach him
> everything. And later, to learn about the church and how to sing in church
> in Latin, he sold another bull to another person who was a cantor [church
> song leader] and who played the organ.

Anselmo Llamojha's path to literacy was one followed by other Andean campesinos privileged enough to have the means to privately fund literacy train-

ing.[6] Such peasants, however, were rare: most were so impoverished that they could not spare animals, crops, or cash to pay for an education. The Peruvian state's pointed abandon of the Andean countryside meant that it was not until the 1940s that the state initiated significant efforts to expand access to education there.[7] It was not until 1969 that education became compulsory for all Peruvian children, forcing the state to ensure access to schooling.[8] Some Andean communities were able to cobble together enough resources to establish schools in the 1920s, when Llamojha was a child, but as he notes, many such schools faced concerted opposition from hacendados who felt threatened by indigenous education, no doubt fearing that widespread literacy among campesinos would limit landlords' abilities to exploit them and gain access to their lands and resources.[9]

With his literacy and musical training, Llamojha's father then began assisting local priests with their duties.

> My father worked in the fields and he was an assistant in the church; he helped the priests say mass. He was also a cantor and he played the church's organ. They always called him to other *pueblos* [towns or communities], too, to get him to go and celebrate the patron saint festivals. As for my mother, people tell me she was just like me. She was really good to me.

Llamojha had much more conflicted memories of his father, a demanding and sometimes violent man.

> My dad didn't have patience for anything. For us, for kids. He wouldn't let us play at all. Not at all. When we were at home, he'd give us wool to spin. We had to spin wool until we got sleepy. He didn't let me do anything. We couldn't play when he was around. It was only when he was away that we could go and play for a while, run around. But when he was at home, not at all. Not for anything! He'd give us homework, or make us help in the kitchen, anything. We couldn't be lazy.
>
> If I was doing something, everything was fine. But if not, the whip! He wasn't just this way with me; he was the same with people on the street, kids out on the street. When he went out, no one could be out in the street playing. He'd get out his whip and chase the kids. He'd even whip their parents!
>
> "Why are your kids outside playing?" he'd say. The whole pueblo was afraid of my dad. And they respected him. That's what my dad was like.

MAP 1.1 Department of Ayacucho

FIG. 1.2 Paulina
Mitma Vásquez,
Llamojha's mother,
location and date
unknown. Photo
courtesy of Manuel
Llamojha Mitma.

Llamojha's father also provided young Manuel with what would soon become his most important skill: the ability to read and write.

> When I was about five years old, my dad taught me to read and write.
> First, my dad taught me the alphabet. After I learned the alphabet really
> well, he gave me homework from the Mantilla book; he made me finish it.
> Back then, Mantilla was the famous book.[10] You had to finish that book.
> Those who did so perfectly, who mastered Spanish, could be authorities.
> Also, the book *Mosaico*.[11] *Mosaico* was for learning to write. That's how it
> used to be.

Llamojha's father not only taught him to read and write but also pushed
him to study and improve. There were many reasons why Anselmo Llamojha
was so determined to educate his young son. Literacy enabled indigenous
peasants to gain access to positions of political authority in their home communities and districts, and it allowed them to personally examine the legal

documents that were a fixture of rural life—documents that often led to exploitation, as unscrupulous individuals routinely tricked illiterate men and women into signing unjust contracts and bad land deals. For males, literacy meant access to citizenship, as the right to vote was restricted to adult men able to read and write. Literacy also conveyed a tremendous amount of respect and dignity, as it correlated so closely with urbanism, modernity, and power in Peru.[12] Many indigenous people also valued literacy in its own right, treasuring the ability to communicate and learn through reading and writing.[13]

Because of his father's stern exactions, Llamojha was forced to turn his childhood labor responsibilities for tending the family's animals into a space for studying and learning.

> **My father gave me homework, and I'd go out to tend my sheep, but I had to take my book with me.**
>
> **"You have to study up to this part," he'd say.**
>
> **I studied, I wrote, I copied, so that it all entered into my head. I'd go home and he'd give me a test, and then he'd give me more homework for the next day. He taught me to read, little by little. We always lived in the countryside. So, when I would go out to tend to my sheep, I always went with my books. Before, because there wasn't a school, they didn't even sell notebooks in our community, or pencils either. So, I wrote on maguey leaves. *Hojepajpas* [the Quechua term for such leaves], we said. We wrote on the leaves with little sticks. Using little sticks, the writing comes out really clearly.**

As Llamojha recalled this period of his life, he drew a clear connection between his education and his political goals. He recalled, "I had a plan: to learn to read, and I wanted to be president of the republic! But first, I knew I must study." Llamojha's literacy also propelled him into his very first position of leadership.

> **Back then, no other boys knew how to read. Of all the adults in the pueblo, only four people knew how to read. Because I was the only boy in the pueblo who knew how to read, no one else, the kids followed me around. They also had their sheep, their cows. Every day, I went out with my sheep to watch them as they grazed, and kids followed me where I went, to the puna [high Andean plateau], so that I could teach them to read and write. Each boy brought a huge number of maguey leaves, and I taught them**

how to write the alphabet on those leaves. Every day they followed me! Poor little things.

I taught the boys to read, to write. And at night, I made them march in the plaza. I made them march in the plaza, made them do their military exercises!

The people, they liked this. We did these exercises, and later, my dad made me to go to church with these boys. Inside the church, I made them pray, I made them sing.

But, one day, while these boys and I were having fun in the puna, a fox took our sheep! There used to be a lot of foxes—not like now when there aren't any—and you had to be very careful. But because we were having fun, a fox took my sheep and theirs, too. So when I returned home in the afternoon: a whipping!

When Llamojha shared his life stories, he directly connected his life as an activist to an event that occurred in 1928, when he was just seven years old. This event involved the Ayrabamba hacienda, a large sugar-producing estate that bordered the community of Concepción. As was typical among landowners in the region, Ayrabamba's owner collected *hierbaje*, fees levied on indigenous community members for pasturing their animals on hacienda land. Hierbaje fees were often paid with animals rather than cash, and many peasants felt that these fees were highly unjust and that hacendados routinely used them to justify their illegal seizure of peasants' livestock. Those seizures also imperiled campesinos financially, as families depended on their animals for their very subsistence.[14]

I would have been seven years old. We lived in Kalabazayoj, about eighteen kilometers down from Concepción. We lived there in winter, in the rainy season, with our cattle. We had some sheep, too, but not many. Thirty sheep, more or less, and I guarded them.

The hacienda Ayrabamba, it's just down from here [Concepción]. The hacienda took all the cattle from the people, they rounded them up.

"Hierbaje!" they said.

So, when I was tending my sheep, a huge number of police and people from the hacienda appeared, gathering everyone's cattle, sheep, and hens. They came over to where I was and they took away all of my sheep, every last one of them. They took all of them and I got really upset. I went home to tell my parents, to inform them. My dad wasn't home, just my mom, and I told her, crying. My dad came home from the fields in the afternoon and he yelled at me.

"Why did you let them take the sheep?"

"What was I going to do? So many people came, and they took them," I said. But he whipped me anyway.

"You let them escape," he said.

The next day, my dad went to demand the sheep. The hacendada, her name was María Elodia Parodi, she didn't want to give them back, not one sheep.[15] She kept all of them, and six cows, too. And from there, my idea was born.

I swore, "One day, I'm going to be grown up, and I'm going to study, and I'm going to be an authority!" My plan was to study and become president.

"I'm going to be president of the republic, and I'm going to make the haciendas disappear!" I said.

This idea has stayed with me all my life. That is, once I was grown I would struggle against the hacendados, fight with the hacendados until the haciendas disappeared. And with this idea, I've fought, to the point of making the hacendados disappear.

The anger that seven-year-old Manuel Llamojha Mitma felt toward local hacendados was a sentiment shared by campesinos across Peru's Andes. Many of them felt terribly abused by landowners who unjustly seized their animals, encroached on and stole community lands, and forced them to perform unpaid labor services on haciendas. During the 1920s this anger coalesced into a massive rural movement for dramatic social, economic, and political change. Indigenous peasants sent innumerable petitions and letters, invaded haciendas to reclaim their lands, and in a few instances even staged armed uprisings to protest abuses and demand better treatment in Peru. Much of this mobilization was informed and directed by the Comité Pro-Derecho Indígena Tawantinsuyo (Tawantinsuyo Pro-Indigenous Rights Committee), until it was outlawed by President Leguía in 1927.[16]

Llamojha's anger was also shared by many members of his home community. In 1929 a number of indigenous peasants from Concepción filed a complaint before the Bureau of Indian Affairs in Lima, accusing the owner of the Ayrabamba hacienda, María Elodia Vassallo de Parodi, of a wide range of abuses.[17] Those abuses included her unjust seizure of community members' cattle, unfair fines for pasturing animals, and her attempts to claim ownership of a lake that community members used for irrigation.[18] The following year, four Concepción campesinos appealed to the foremost authority in the department of Ayacucho, the prefect, requesting urgent protection against this landowner. Their letter charged that she had ordered one hundred of her workers to raid Concepción. Those workers had then seized seventy head of cattle, forty horses, six hundred sheep, and two hundred goats, all on the claim of charging hierbaje. The campesinos wrote that the seizure of animals had been unwarranted and, worse still, had been carried out with violence and intimidation. Vassallo de Parodi's workers had fired gunshots into the air, flung rocks at community members, and even whipped some women and children. From the perspective of the men writing to the prefect, all of this was done "with the fundamental and premeditated end of appropriating the lands of the community."[19] Yet, as happened so often in rural Peru, these complaints and pleas brought no meaningful action from Peru's courts, government representatives, or politicians, who showed little interest in defending indigenous peasants.[20] Llamojha thus grew up in a community where hacendados' abuses were angrily discussed and challenged, but to little avail.

As he matured and thought more and more about his future, dreaming about becoming president, he also considered a different path: the priesthood.

I didn't like working in the fields. Instead, I wanted to be something else when I grew up. My intention was to become a priest. From the time I was little, when I was around five years old, I wanted to be a priest. I liked that. My dad played the organ and he taught me to play, and also how to read Latin, to celebrate mass, to help the priests. I learned all of this. And so, when I was bigger, ten years old, I started to assist with mass. I was really little, but I helped them celebrate mass.

I wanted to become a priest, and so when my father died in 1936, I went to Lima with this intention.

Llamojha's desire to become a priest reflected the fact that priests ranked among the most powerful and influential residents in rural indigenous communities. Priests were among the few individuals who knew how to read and write, and it was not unusual for them to assume a prominent role in local politics.[21] They also presided over the key events in Andean peasants' lives: baptizing them into the church, conducting marriages, and holding funeral masses. Priests' proximity to the word and instructions of God also meant that they commanded respect from peasants, most of whom were devoutly Catholic. Llamojha saw the admiration Concepción's campesinos had for the local priest and for his father, a church assistant, and he probably desired the same sort of admiration for himself. Llamojha is also a very spiritual man, as is shown in his frequent references to Christ in his recollections and writings.

Determined to become a priest, Llamojha left his home community of Concepción in 1936, when he was just fifteen, and made the long journey to Lima. That move to Lima was far from unusual: as many as 65,000 men and women migrated from Andean provinces to Lima between 1919 and 1931. They moved to the nation's capital because they understood that in their extremely centralized country, wealth, political power, and social opportunities were concentrated there. Prospects for education, employment, and social advancement were far greater there than in their home regions.[22] But in Lima, many of these migrants found themselves victims of significant race and class prejudice, scorned and exploited by wealthier and whiter Limeños (Lima residents) who disdainfully regarded them as backward, ignorant Indians. Llamojha experienced that treatment in his own extended family, as his cousin's Limeña wife believed she and her husband could cheat him, taking advantage of his labor while tricking him out of a salary.

> An uncle of mine took me, he brought me to Lima so I could study to become a priest. We arrived in Lima and then he left me, he abandoned me. I worked for two years. First, I went to the home of a relative who had a dairy business, Julio Calderón Llamojha, and I delivered milk in a wagon. I worked for two years, and he didn't pay me during those years. He told me he was sending my mom the money. Then, because he wasn't paying me, I spoke with my mom and she told me it was a lie.
>
> "He hasn't sent me any money at all!" she said to me.
>
> So, I talked to him. His wife was the one who did this, because she was a Limeña. I spoke to them and told them that I wanted to leave. They didn't want me to go, they wanted me to continue there, and they offered to pay me. But even then, they still didn't pay me! So I escaped, I escaped. Because I didn't find work, I had to sleep in cornfields. I looked for work for a month, and I didn't have anything to eat. Happily, I had a friend from the north, and he gave me 5 soles [Peru's monetary unit] when I told him about my situation. I used that money to eat until I could find a little bit of work.

Llamojha worked in Lima for a couple of years, until about 1938, when he decided to study for the priesthood. Having been told that the Convento de San Francisco (San Francisco Monastery) took in orphans and educated them, he decided to approach the priests living there.

> I went, all by myself, to introduce myself at the Convento de San Francisco. I spoke to a priest who came out to meet me when I knocked on the door.

FIG. 1.3 Llamojha, Lima, 1939. Photo courtesy of Manuel Llamojha Mitma.

"What do you want?" he asked.

"I've come to see if you'll take me. I want to be a priest."

"What level of schooling do you have?"

"I don't have any. I've never been to school," I said.

"How are you going to become a priest then? Come back here when you've finished your education. If you've never been to school, how are you going to become a priest?"

But I insisted. "But I want to be a priest! I'm already trained for this. I help celebrate mass, I do everything. I go from town to town, helping priests celebrate mass."

> "Do you know Latin?" He pulled out his Latin book. "All right, read!"
> So I read.
> "All right, sing!"
> So I sang.
> "It can't happen. To be a priest, you need a higher education."
> "But it's not necessary," I said. "I know everything. I know how to celebrate mass. I go to the pueblos where there aren't any priests, and I hold mass," I said to him.
> "How can you conduct mass? You're committing a crime!" he said to me.
> They didn't want to take me. They gave me three books in Latin and threw me out. With that, I left, and I lost my hope.

The priest's rejection of Llamojha was about much, much more than his lack of education: it was about his race and his class. In Peru, as throughout most of Latin America, the Catholic priesthood was largely reserved for middle- and upper-class men of European descent.[23] The notion that an Andean campesino would think himself a candidate for the priesthood most likely struck the priest as absurd, so he challenged the teenager on the grounds of his education, incorrectly assuming—as so many in Peru did—that to be indigenous was to be illiterate.[24]

But Llamojha was not discouraged for long. Instead, he came up with another plan: he decided to become a soldier.

> "There's time to study in the barracks, and I'll have food, everything," I said.
> I wanted to study, because I'd never gone to school. Sure, I knew how to read properly, but I wanted something more. So, I thought I'd join the military and study politics. I wanted to become a soldier so that I could make a revolution, an armed struggle, to make all the haciendas disappear. My intention was to form a government, become president of the republic, and put Peru in its place. There were so many abuses in Peru, so much injustice.
> I introduced myself at all the barracks, but none of them would take me. Not for anything!
> "You're just a youngster, and you don't have your papers," they'd say. I was so mad!

Llamojha's ideas about the military reflected the fact that recruits were provided with a rudimentary education—something the Peruvian military regarded as part of its heavily racialized "civilizing mission" for predominantly Quechua- and Aymara-speaking conscripts.[25] While some Andean men shared Llamojha's view that military service was a route toward education and upward socioeconomic mobility, his efforts to enlist were highly unusual. The most common route into the military was conscription, as all Peruvian men were required to do a period of compulsory military service. Only those with enough money to purchase exemptions were spared this obligatory service. But because military officials often fell short of their recruitment goals—due to exemptions and noncompliance—they frequently resorted to a forced recruitment practice known as the *leva*: seizing young men unable to produce their identity documents and taking them straight to the military barracks.[26] The leva overwhelmingly targeted rural indigenous men, and many Andean families angrily opposed the practice, as it wrenched young men away from their families, fields, and communities, where their labor, economic support, and social presence were sorely missed.[27] The practice of forced recruitment—this time, operating in the city—was how Llamojha was finally able to enter the military.

> I was walking around one day, down Abancay Avenue, and a number of soldiers were rounding up boys as recruits. They used to draft people like this. I stuck myself in among the boys so the soldiers would take me to the barracks, because they wouldn't take me when I went on my own. So, I put myself in among the group of recruits, without the soldiers realizing. And that's how they took me to the Santa Ana barracks.
>
> I was there for a month. They checked me out there. After examining me, they took me to Miraflores, to the San Martín cavalry. I was really happy.
>
> "Now Peru is mine!" I said.
>
> I was happy there. They gave me a horse; I had to wash my horse each day. They make you get up early there, when it's still dark out. They get the soldiers up, so that they can do exercises. I was always the very first one ready in the morning.

At the barracks, Llamojha once again began leading his peers. This time his followers were not school-age children but young men drafted into the military from departments in Peru's Andean sierra region. Those departments were overwhelmingly rural and indigenous, and the recruits were monolingual Quechua speakers. As Llamojha explained,

> When I had been there a month, they brought in some recruits from the sierra. There were about one hundred of them, and they didn't speak

Spanish. So I was put in charge of them. I was named to lead the exercises, to get them to do their exercises, speaking in Quechua. They were from haciendas and I spoke to them.

I said to them, "We have to make a revolution! We have to stay here to make a revolution. Once and for all, we have to save our campesino brothers who are like slaves on the haciendas!"

In his interview with the CVR, Llamojha further fleshed out this story:

The campesinos said, "Yes, yes. When we are on the haciendas, they make us suffer. They tie us up, they whip us."

We thought and we talked about this. "How are we going to save ourselves? We're suffering." So, this was my approach: take the presidential palace!

But Llamojha's plans to use his army career as a launching point for revolution fell apart, betrayed by the very skill that would later prove so central to his activist career: his writing. As he explained in one of our interviews,

Because I always walked around with my folder, I had all my writings, my plans in my folder. I wrote while I was in the barracks, but I really shouldn't have written things down.

I wrote, "Now I'm going to carry out a coup d'état. I'll get myself prepared here."

All my folders, my plans about how we were going to make a revolution, they were all underneath my pillow. One day, there was an inspection. They'd inspect the bed, do the cleaning, all of that. A sergeant who was doing the inspection found my folder; he went through it and found my plans, and he delivered it to the commander. In the barracks, General Porturas was in charge. My folder got delivered to him. The next day, he called me.

"You have plans here in the barracks for making revolution!"

They accused me of being an Aprista.

It is not surprising that the barracks commander associated Llamojha's plans for revolution with membership in APRA, which was Peru's most significant populist political party. Members of this party, known as Apristas, had launched a series of insurrections against the state in the early 1930s. The party was repeatedly outlawed and had an especially tense relationship with the Peruvian military.[28] Here again, assumptions based on race and class no doubt shaped others' perceptions of Llamojha: unable to imagine that an indigenous peasant could independently formulate his own plans for revolution, military officers simply assumed that he was carrying out the orders of a militant urban political party. They punished him accordingly and even sent him to El Frontón, a penal colony on an island off of Lima's coast that was one of Peru's most notorious prisons.

> They punished me for a month. They took away my shoes, and I spent the month sweeping the whole barracks shoeless, punished. I slept in a jail cell without a bed for one month. From there, they sent me to El Frontón prison. I was in El Frontón for three months, and then I got out. But I had nothing. I had to keep fighting, I had to be something. But I had failed. I could no longer be a soldier. I was sad. I couldn't be a priest. I just had to work, nothing more.

Although Llamojha was not a member of APRA during his time in the military, he considered joining the party shortly after his release from prison. He had likely met several Apristas while imprisoned in El Frontón, as the island jail housed numerous political prisoners.[29]

> I heard their propaganda. They always talked about the masses, about the campesinos. I met with some Apristas in Lima, but I just met with them, nothing more. I wanted to belong, I wanted to be one. APRA had only just emerged and at that time, I was in [the coastal city] Callao. So I went to their first assembly. I went to this meeting and I met [APRA founder] Haya de la Torre there. It was a giant meeting, and everyone had their white handkerchiefs. I took out my little handkerchief, too.
>
> "Let's see the handkerchiefs! With your left hands!" they said.
>
> But then I went to APRA's main office, and they started talking differently. I told them that we had problems with the hacendados and that we wanted them to help us in Concepción.
>
> The party said, "No, no, no. How are we supposed to help you against the hacendados?"
>
> "But the hacendados are taking our lands," I said.
>
> "No, we can't look into that!"
>
> "But the pueblo is abused by the hacendados," I said.
>
> "No, we don't do that."
>
> They weren't interested at all. So, I told them to go to hell!

Llamojha's negative experience with APRA reflected its tepid support for indigenous issues and community land struggles at the national level. While

APRA's regional branches were often highly attuned to local political needs, and sometimes even drew significant support from indigenous peasants, Haya de la Torre never pursued the issue of indigenous land rights in a meaningful way. Instead he argued for a program of anti-imperialism, nationalization, and regional rights.[30]

Although Llamojha quickly withdrew his support from APRA, he nonetheless continued his political education and development during the mid-1940s. His continuing political evolution owed partly to his work in Miraflores, a neighborhood that would ultimately become Lima's wealthiest residential district. He worked for a family that belonged to Peru's oligarchy—an elite so small and so disproportionately powerful in economic, social, and political terms that it was commonly referred to as Peru's "forty families."[31] The things Llamojha saw, heard, and read while working in Miraflores cemented his understandings of class and race inequalities and injustices in Peru. He explained that, following his release from El Frontón,

I found a job in a home on the other end of town. I worked in Miraflores in a home of the high bourgeoisie, of the great and powerful; the Pérez Figuerola family. I worked there as a butler for two years, with my black pants and white coat, with my bow tie. I dressed like this to serve them. It was a big house, because they were great and powerful millionaires. There were five of us guys, four girls, a cook, a tailor; one person for every job. I worked there for two years; I was very considerate.

And while I was there, I heard them talking. I was listening, you see. This family had three haciendas, and I learned about what it was like. They talked about people, about the Indians and the blacks who worked on the hacienda.

"This person didn't do his work, so we kicked him off the hacienda." They talked about all of this and I listened. I was recording it all in my mind.

"Your time is almost up!" I thought.

I know all of their secrets! I have read all of their codes. They didn't know that I was doing this; it was all in their libraries. I would go into a room to clean, and they'd stand up and leave. And from there, I'd take out all of their books and start to read all of their secrets. I have read all of their plans, what they have to do when there are strikes. I read all of this. I know how they manage Peru. Right now, currently, only eighty families dominate Peru. Eighty families of the high bourgeoisie. I know all of their secrets, their strategies! I moved to other houses, too. I was there until 1948.

The final key element for understanding Llamojha's emergence as an activist involves his work with other Lima-based migrants from his home community, Concepción. Together, in 1941 he and several of his fellow migrants formed a club named the Comité Pro-Comunidad Indígena de Concepción Chacamarca (Pro-Concepción Chacamarca Indian Community Committee).[32] That name reflected the club's earliest goal: getting official recognition of Concepción as an "indigenous community," a legal status that guaranteed community land rights and the right to elect a village council. Formal recognition as an indigenous community would be Concepción's most valuable tool in a fight against hacienda encroachment, as officially recognized indigenous community land was inalienable, that is, it could not legally be bought, sold, or appropriated.[33]

Many such migrant clubs formed in Lima during the 1930s and 1940s, as tens of thousands of migrants moved to Lima from the Andean sierra searching for work and education. These clubs often hosted social events for members, and they provided a sense of community and social support for Andean migrants as they struggled against the alienation and severe discrimination they faced in the nation's bustling capital city.[34] Many migrant clubs quickly became much more than social organizations; they became political advocates for their home communities. As Lima was the heart of Peru's political and economic system, these migrants were better positioned than Andean community members to lobby government officials, and they had more financial resources to dedicate to their home communities' legal struggles than did those who remained in the countryside. These migrant clubs ultimately provided the very sort of support for Andean communities that the Peruvian state so grievously failed to offer.

> We gathered there and we helped Concepción with everything. Those from Lima, they sacrificed a lot, to do everything.
>
> We fought, and the institution sustained the fight with money. Everybody contributed. They held parties to collect money. The institution fought a lot, to work things out with the hacendados, for travel fare, to receive visits here. The institution collaborated in everything, in the search for the pueblo's papers. Back then, we didn't have the pueblo's papers ready. So we worked to get Concepción its land title. The institution did everything. It also worked on the issues regarding the hacendados, to defend ourselves against the haciendas. That's how we fought hard to find justice.

I asked Llamojha what role he played in the migrant club.

FIG. 1.4 The Pro-Concepción Chacamarca Indian Community Committee, Lima, 1946. Llamojha is seated third from right. Photo courtesy of Manuel Llamojha Mitma.

All my life, I was secretary general! They never let me go! I was always named secretary, because I work with papers, I handled the papers.

The migrant club also played a major role in winning official recognition from the government for Concepción as an indigenous community. Acquiring formal recognition was a cumbersome and expensive process, as community members had to provide a census of their community's population, a map of the community's lands and borders, and its official land titles.

We started the process in 1942. We started filing papers with the ministry for the community's official recognition. Of course, it was already a community. It always had been. But it lacked legal recognition.

The community finally won official recognition in 1944. Llamojha told his CVR interviewers that the migrant club also helped Concepción fight against local hacendados. When his interviewers asked what this fight involved, he explained:

> **It was about the borders, because the haciendas advanced and occupied. The Ayrabamba hacienda occupied sixteen hundred hectares of our land. Ayrabamba is really small, it only has 380 hectares, just sugar-growing plains. But Ayrabamba wanted to take our lands right from the peaks, where there are twenty-eight agricultural plots. They took them from us, and they made us pay rent, on our own land! But we fought hard. This fight against all the hacendados began in '43. But it didn't go anywhere [at first] because the main leaders of Concepción sold themselves out to the hacendados.**

As secretary general of Concepción's migrant club, Llamojha also challenged local authorities who he believed worked against Concepción's interests. In 1946 he was one of forty-eight Concepción community members to sign a letter to the director of Indian affairs. Though we cannot know it for certain—and he himself is unsure—he most likely wrote this letter. The text carries his particular style, and he was one of the few members of the club able to write with both ease and grace. The letter complained that Juan Zea, Concepción's *personero* (official legal representative), had been abusing his powers and should be removed from his post. As the letter phrased it, "because he has committed grave offenses, the Indians no longer have the least amount of confidence in him and yearn for him to be replaced by the person who ends up being voted for in the elections. This is justice."[35]

Seven months later, over one hundred Concepción community members, including Llamojha, signed their names to a letter repeating the calls for Zea's ouster from the personero position. This letter reiterated the complaint that he had not fulfilled his duties, and it added new charges, claiming that he had forced Concepción community members to pay him cash and had seized their animals by force. The letter even accused him of attempted homicide, asserting that he had attempted to kill his niece when she objected to his unwarranted seizure of goods. The same letter also accused him of becoming an "unconditional and submissive servant" of the hacendada Elodia Vassallo de Parodi.[36]

Zea was not the only abusive authority against whom Llamojha and his fellow community members protested. As secretary general of the migrant club, Llamojha, together with the club's president and accountant, composed a letter to Cangallo's subprefect in February 1947. The letter denounced the actions of Concepción's lieutenant governor, Grimaldo Castillo. They wrote: "The pueblo finds Castillo repugnant because he is a despot and never does what is good for the pueblo. He just responds to the hacendados' dictatorial orders. The pueblo asks that he be replaced by someone who would be elected."[37] The demand, in essence, was twofold: first, that Castillo should be removed, and second, that Concepción residents should have the right to choose their own lieutenant governor rather than simply accept the individuals appointed to the position by regional authorities.

Complaints against abusive authorities were a constant in Peru's rural Andean communities during the twentieth century. Indigenous peasants often felt abused and mistreated by district authorities who seemed more interested in their own private gain than in the interests of the community. It was particularly upsetting that these authorities were appointed rather than elected into their positions of power. Rural residents had no say over whom the regional authorities chose to govern them at the local district level.[38] The most they could do was send letters of protest denouncing particularly abusive figures. Regional and national authorities rarely heeded those complaints, and it was not unusual for abusive district authorities to remain in positions of power for years, even decades.[39] It is not then surprising to learn that the Concepción migrant club's demands for Grimaldo Castillo's removal were left unanswered. He would remain a prominent and vexing figure in Llamojha's political life for decades to come, holding positions of power at the district level until he was assassinated by the Shining Path in the 1980s.

Llamojha left Lima in 1948, returned to Concepción, and began a period of active and direct involvement in rural struggles. Reflecting on why he left Lima, he explained:

A commission came from Concepción and my institution in Lima named two of us. That's why I came back to Concepción. They sent us to investigate the hacendados' abuses against us, and I remained here with my campesinos. What's more, the other pueblos didn't leave me alone. Campesinos always brought me to their communities, to teach them how to fight against the hacendados.

Llamojha's return to Ayacucho in 1948 launched the next phase of his political career.

TWO

"I Made the Hacendados Tremble"
DEFENDING JHAJHAMARKA CAMPESINOS, 1948–1952

Remembering his struggles against local landlords, Llamojha exclaimed, "I made the hacendados tremble!" This chapter considers his first major action as a rural activist: his work to defend campesinos who lived and worked on the Jhajhamarka hacienda. The Jhajhamarka hacienda, bordering Concepción, became the site of a prominent conflict between its owners and the campesinos who labored on its land.[1] The conflict was especially significant because of its timing; it occurred at a moment that historian Eric Hobsbawm has referred to as Peru's "great rural awakening"—a period of peasant activism that remains decidedly understudied by historians.[2] Llamojha's detractors responded to his work on the Jhajhamarka hacienda by resorting to an effective tool of political slander: they branded him a communist. Although he was not a member of the Peruvian Communist Party, his opponents cast his work as that of a communist in an effort to delegitimize his efforts to win socioeconomic justice. The year 1948 marks the start of these struggles and counterstruggles.

Llamojha's experiences in Jhajhamarka show the abuses and degradation that many Latin American peasants endured on haciendas. Jhajhamarka's campesinos lost community lands because of trickery; they were forced to perform servile labor; and they were subjected to terrible violence, beaten by hacendados and tied up, as Llamojha phrases it, "like pigs." But he also chronicles the many different ways campesinos fought for their land and for better treatment, forming a union, going on strike, and even committing a murder. Their major push for their land rights came during the early moments of the global Cold War, with the world increasingly divided into communist and anticommunist factions, and their community's struggle was shaped by that international conflict. Hacendados, government officials, and soldiers mobilized the language of anticommunism against campesino activists, creating a strong interplay between the local and international processes of the Cold War.[3] Llamojha's stories also show that activists' lives are not defined exclusively by political work and struggle: 1948, the year he began working with Jhajhamarka campesinos, was also the year he met and married Esther Honorata Puklla.

The Return to Concepción

After Llamojha returned to Concepción from Lima in 1948, sought out by his fellow community members to investigate Concepción's problems with local hacendados, they insisted that he stay.

> The community members wouldn't let me leave.
> They said to me, "Stay in Concepción. Don't go back to Lima!"
> I met my wife that year, when I was back in the pueblo. We didn't speak at first; I just saw her from afar.
> My mom bugged me about her. "You have to marry her, no one else. If not her, then no one."

In rural Andean communities, it was common for families to negotiate marriages. So Llamojha visited Esther's aunt, María Puklla, to ask for permission to marry.

> I fell in love with Esther and she insisted that we get married immediately. Because she was an orphan, she only had her aunt, her dad's sister. So, I went to talk to her aunt. My mom went with me. And her aunt accepted!
> "Sure! Get married already!" her aunt said. She made us choose a date right then and there.
> We chose a date and we got married in a civil ceremony first. We had a Catholic ceremony later.

Jhajhamarka's History

Soon after his return to Concepción, Llamojha began working with indigenous peasants from the nearby Jhajhamarka hacienda. Before proceeding with his recollections about that struggle, we need to pause and reflect on an issue of orthography. Although the name Jhajhamarka is officially spelled, using the letter *c*, as Ccaccamarca, Llamojha always uses the Quechua orthography—Jhajhamarka—and he wanted to use this spelling throughout this book. Jhajhamarka is a much better phonetic match to the name; we shared a laugh about how the name is definitely *not* pronounced, with hard *C* sounds, as "Kakamarka." But Llamojha's spelling is not just about sound; it is about historical accuracy, anticolonial sentiment, and an embrace of Peru's indigenous Quechua heritage. Noting that he often changed the spelling of place-names in documents he wrote—showing Ccaccamarca as Jhajhamarka, the province of Vilcashuamán as Wilka Uma—I asked Llamojha to explain his practice. He began his explanation with Wilka Uma.

> Wilka is something sacred, sacrosanct. And it's not Huamán, it's Uma. Wilka Uma. That means "Sacred Head" [in Quechua]. Vilcashuamán was the principal region in the time of the Inka. Then, in the colonial period, they started to ruin the name. The name of the province is Wilka Uma. For Jhajhamarka, "Jhajha" means a fallen rock, from a hill. "Marka" means pueblo.

In a 2011 document Llamojha stressed the need for the phonetic spelling of place-names and noted that "RUNA SIMI [Quechua; literally, 'language of the people'] should be properly written and spoken, without letting oneself be dragged down by the influence of the writing and pronunciation style that the Spaniards imposed."[4]

When our conversation turned to the Jhajhamarka hacienda, Llamojha extended his story all the way back to the colonial period, couching his narrative in deep historical context.

> Jhajhamarka had been a hacienda since colonial times. I'm writing its history, about how it used to be. In those times, it was an *obraje* [colonial factory, usually for making clothing] and a commercial center for slaves. Indian slaves cost 300 pesos and black slaves cost 500 pesos. The hacendados brought them there and kept them in a jail, where they punished them.

MAP 2.1 Province of Vilcashuamán

When Llamojha shared similar details with his CVR interviewers, he told them that he had discovered all of this information while searching for historical documents in Peru's National Archive in 1958. As he phrased it,

I read it, and that's how I know. If I hadn't read it, I wouldn't know!

As Llamojha continued his description of Jhajhamarka, he explained that after Peru transitioned from colonialism to independence in the 1820s, Jhajhamarka's owner died without heirs and left the hacienda to the Convento de Santa Teresa (Santa Teresa Convent). Such bequests were not unusual: convents were major landowners in both the colonial and republican periods in Peru.[5] This convent then rented out the hacienda to different administrators, who ran it. In the late nineteenth or early twentieth century, an individual named Benigno Cárdenas became the new administrator.

A man named Benigno Cárdenas rented the Jhajhamarka hacienda for three lifetimes. Back then, they used to lease for lifetimes, and each lifetime lasted fifty years. Benigno Cárdenas rented it for three lifetimes. Benigno Cárdenas was a really abusive man on the hacienda.

Llamojha offered more details about Benigno Cárdenas to his CVR interviewers, using the label *gamonal*, a common Peruvian term for an especially abusive rural strongman, often—but not always—a hacendado.[6]

That gamonal would sit in his doorway every day, all day long. All of those who passed by had to approach him and greet him. They came up to him, and they had to kiss his hand. If they didn't approach him as they were supposed to, right away, he would grab them right there and strike them with his whip. He whipped them and then put them in the hacienda jail.

The campesinos couldn't endure his abuses any more, because if any little cow, any little animal, got close to the hacienda house, he would seize it and not return it to its owner. He'd say that it was his good fortune, that God was great, and that it was his good luck.

Llamojha continued his story about Benigno Cárdenas, framing it as an example of solidarity and activism in an indigenous community.

The only road, the *camino real*, passed right in front of the hacienda's door. People would come from different places and pass by there to head up into the hills. Benigno Cárdenas would sit in his doorway and monitor all the travelers. He'd inspect their cargo, the things they were carrying,

and people had to have documents from the authorities. He'd keep all the cargo and animals of those who didn't have permission from the authorities of [the nearby communities] Chumbes or Concepción.

So, the pueblo of Jhajhamarka decided to free itself from this hacendado, by any means necessary. The campesinos killed him in 1917, because they couldn't endure it any more. Nine people agreed to kill him, just those nine, so as not to compromise the pueblo. They didn't care if they went to jail or not.

One night, these nine men positioned themselves along the road, one here, another one over there.

One of these men went into the hacienda house and said, "Señor! Señor! There are nine thieves on the road, cattle rustlers! Let's go!"

The campesino got the hacendado up out of bed and they left the hacienda. From there, they went along a big path. Then, one campesino jumped out from over here, another from over there. They grabbed Benigno Cárdenas by the scruff of his neck and they killed him right there. They hung him with a sling made from llama skin. The campesinos showed me all these places, and how the killing was done. They took me to show me what happened, and how they left the hacendado hanging there.

Those nine people took sole responsibility, to protect the masses from blame. They went to the authorities and they said, "We killed him."

Only those nine people were detained. "We did it on our own," they said. These campesinos went to jail, twenty-five years in El Frontón, and they died there, in El Frontón. Only one survived. He finished his twenty-five years and got out. But a few days after he arrived at his house, he died, too. That's how things were back then.

Unfortunately, as Llamojha explained in our interviews, the abuses on the Jhajhamarka hacienda continued for two more generations.

Benigno's sons went on committing abuses. These two sons, Antonio and Alonso, one was a lawyer, the other was a doctor. These two sons, they wanted to formalize the documents. Because Jhajhamarka was the property of the Convento de Santa Teresa, they were nothing more than tenants. They wanted to purchase the property, and so they forced Jhajhamarka's campesinos to give them 130 bulls. They used those 130 bulls to buy the hacienda from the nuns of the Convento de Santa Teresa.[7]

One of them said to the campesinos, "I am selling my hacienda. Give me 130 bulls so that you can be Jhajhamarka's owners." But this was a trick.

The Cárdenas brothers were actually buying the hacienda and they bought it with the campesinos' 130 bulls. That's how they took possession of the Jhajhamarka hacienda.

And the people, the workers, the Cárdenas brothers treated them like slaves. The brothers rented the campesinos out to other sugar-producing haciendas, and then they took the campesinos' salaries. They didn't give those salaries to the peasant workers.

These two brothers, they each had a son. Their sons' names were Ernesto and Carlos; they were the last owners of Jhajhamarka. They were really barbarous, too. They had a room where they abused and killed peasants. This room dated all the way back to the time of slavery. In slave times, peasants were branded with irons, just like cattle, on their backs. And that still existed in Jhajhamarka; they branded the campesinos with hot irons. I learned about this, and I even saw it, too. So, Jhajhamarka's campesinos rose up in 1947. And in '48, I came back from Lima. When Jhajhamarka's campesinos found out that I was here, they came and took me to Jhajhamarka.

Fighting for Jhajhamarka

I asked Llamojha how Jhajhamarka's campesinos knew that he could help them. The answer revolved around the migrant clubs in Lima.

We started working together in Lima. They had an organization in Lima, an association [migrant club], just like we had. They always held parties, and they invited us to go. So, I met them, and they got to know me. And so when I returned to Concepción, they immediately called on me to go to Jhajhamarka.

I had a relative here, on my wife's side, whose name was Leoncio Fernández. He never abandoned me, ever. When they took me to Jhajhamarka, he went with me.

"I can't let you go alone. I have to help you," he said. So, each time Jhajhamarka called on me, the two of us went. He was really good to me; he was like my brother. He never left me. He accompanied me everywhere.

Together, the two men worked to organize Jhajhamarka campesinos. Leoncio Fernández also helped Llamojha in a crucial material way: he bought him his first typewriter.

FIG. 2.1 Jhajhamarka peasants, Jhajhamarka, 1949. Courtesy of Proyecto Especial de Titulación de Tierras, Ayacucho.

Leoncio Fernández said, "You'll work with this!"

He had bought the typewriter in Lima, secondhand. It was really old, but it served me well.

We held assemblies to explain to folks how they should confront the owners. After a few days, I returned to Concepción. Then the next week, the Jhajhamarka campesinos called me back. They came to Concepción with a commission, and they brought me back to Jhajhamarka on their horses, to continue fighting, to continue writing documents and complaints. Jhajhamarka was the worst hell. It was slavery! This is what we fought against.

In July 1948, Llamojha helped Jhajhamarka campesinos form a union. Given that Peruvian government authorities and the courts failed to provide them with adequate support in their struggles against hacendados, neglecting to take punitive action or even actively siding with abusers, many campesinos began to form unions in the mid-twentieth century. They hoped that they could use their unions to defend themselves, their rights, and their lands. Sometimes these unions formed with the help of urban political activists; often campesinos took action on their own initiative. Although the Jhajhamarka union was not the first such organization in Peru's Andean region, it was certainly one of the earliest.[8]

Without question, Jhajhamarka campesinos benefited from propitious timing when they founded their union in July 1948. Just a few months later, in October, General Manuel Odría seized national power in a coup. In the repression that followed, many political activists were jailed, and many organizations, including the CCP, had to cease operations. It would have been much harder to form the Jhajhamarka union under such circumstances. Llamojha described the formation of the union.

> I organized a tenants' union and we began the struggle. I started to draw up documents. I went with my typewriter. I drew up documents and got peasants to sign them. I always walked around with my typewriter, I wrote petitions, and got all the people to sign. The documents said, "a series of abuses are committed on this hacienda, so the people want the hacendados to retreat. If they don't, the pueblo will take charge." And then I took the documents to Lima myself, to deliver them to the ministry. I always did this, because the national government would readily order an investigation, whereas if you just presented your documents in Ayacucho, no one would investigate. So, I took documents directly to the ministry, to the government itself. That's what I did, to the point that I made the hacendados tremble!

I asked Llamojha about how he drew up these complex legal documents, doing so without the aid of a lawyer.

> I worried about this a lot. From the time I learned to read, I struggled to learn how to write formal requests, memos. There was a book called *Mosaico* and it explained how to do this. There were examples of memos, requests, denunciations. That book *Mosaico* had everything, and that's how I learned to draft memos.

Llamojha even crafted the elaborate stamps that graced the signature lines of many documents, adding authority to his letters.

> You make the stamps from rubber balls, it turns out nicely. It's easy to carve. I'd break a Gillette shaving razor into little pieces and then tie the pieces to a little stick, and then use this to carve.

He then personally delivered these documents, unwilling to go through the regional hierarchy of provincial and departmental officials.

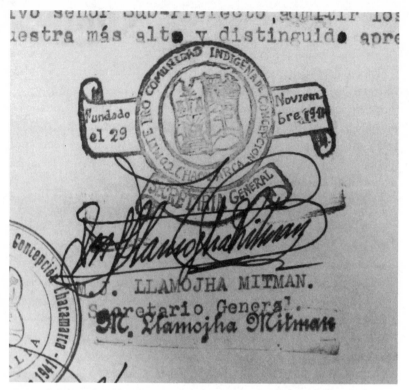

FIG. 2.2 Stamp produced by Llamojha. Courtesy of Ayacucho Regional Archive.

I presented all the denunciations against the hacendados, against the abuses they committed, directly to Lima. I would go to the government itself, to the presidential palace, and leave the denunciations at the document reception office. Or I'd go to the ministries. I'd never present a denunciation in Ayacucho to the lower authorities, because they never paid attention, they never brought justice. I'd go directly to Lima instead. From Lima, they'd order the prefect or the subprefect to investigate the abuses the hacendados committed.

Llamojha's comments reflect the realities of Peru's highly centralized political system. With political power concentrated in Lima, it made sense for him to skip over relatively powerless regional authorities and take his complaints directly to the Lima-based ministries and government offices that had the authority to order investigations. In addition, many regional authorities were so closely connected to Ayacucho hacendados—by friendship, family ties, shared social status—that they were unlikely to take action against even the most abusive landowners.[9]

Most of Llamojha's writings about Jhajhamarka are hidden from view: he helped the hacienda's residents compose letters, but he didn't affix his own name to these documents. For years, he kept his own personal archive, retaining a copy of every document he prepared. But soldiers seized that archive of invaluable papers during the violence of the 1980s, and it has almost certainly been destroyed. So the historian can only guess which of the many letters of complaint filling Ayacucho's archives were written by Llamojha. One such document probably—but not certainly—written by him was a March 1948 letter to the Bureau of Indian Affairs.[10] In this lengthy letter, a number of Jhajhamarka campesinos complain that they are treated "as if we were slaves." They describe the unremunerated labor burdens placed on young children, women, and the elderly; they denounce the paltry salaries men receive; and they detail the hacendados' routine seizure of tenants' livestock. As the letter phrases it, "the wealth of these hacendados continues to increase, under the inhumane and slave-like exploitation of the Indians."[11] The letter also decries the hacendados' violence against campesinos and asks that the hacienda's lands be distributed among its tenants.[12]

Whether or not that particular letter was written by Llamojha, it is clear that he wrote most of the documents that were sent from Jhajhamarka during the late 1940s and the early 1950s. Even those unsympathetic to Llamojha stressed his role as a scribe. One police investigator wrote that Llamojha "was the one in charge of drafting memos or any other document that would be directed to the authorities." The investigator added that as only Llamojha and another activist named Moisés Ayala were literate, they alone knew the contents of the letters Llamojha typed. As such, Llamojha was able to make "completely unfounded complaints" and accused Ernesto Cárdenas of "completely absurd things."[13] Those complaints fit into a much larger pattern of hacendados and regional authorities blaming "indios leídos" (literate Indians) for stirring up trouble over landownership and indigenous peasants' rights in the early twentieth century.[14] Driving home the importance of Llamojha's writing, the investigator confiscated Llamojha's documents as well as his pencil, his stamps and stamp pad, and, of course, his typewriter.[15] Llamojha recalled:

The typewriter remained with the judge in the Cangallo court. When I got out of jail, I asked for my typewriter back. They said, "Bring us the receipt!" They wanted proof that I hadn't stolen the machine.

> Leoncio Fernández had to go to Lima to ask for the receipt, and then we
> went together to Cangallo to claim our little machine.
>
> Leoncio said, "We always have to go together, damn it! I am not going
> to let you go alone."

Jhajhamarka campesinos had many reasons to look to Llamojha for help.
His literacy and knowledge of Peru's governing system were invaluable resources for them. By serving as a scribe for largely illiterate Jhajhamarka
campesinos, Llamojha enabled them to engage a political and legal system
that was otherwise closed to them. It was not unusual for literate campesinos
to assume such roles in their communities, composing petitions and letters
for their neighbors and relatives.[16] A letter signed by seventeen Jhajhamarka
campesinos explained: "Manuel Llamocca, even though he is not a tenant
on the hacienda, helps us with our complaints . . . and we sought him out
because, as the majority of us are illiterate, we always need educated people
who can write for us."[17] The same letter decried the fact that Llamojha had
recently been arrested and badly beaten.

While most of the documents Llamojha wrote do not bear his name, one of
the most important documents produced in Jhajhamarka does: he authored
and signed the "Act of the Foundation of the Sharecroppers Union of the
Ccaccamarca (Jhajhamarca) Hacienda," which recorded the establishment
of the Jhajhamarka tenants' union in 1948. This document is worth quoting
at length:

> In the pueblo of Huampurque, part of the Jhajhamarca estate, the share-
> croppers of said hacienda gathered in the home of Mr. Benedicto Prado.
> They utilized the abilities granted by Article 62 of the National Constitution
> with the goal of reaching a unanimous agreement to incorporate all of the
> sharecroppers of the Jhajhamarca hacienda who live as victims of abuses
> and long orphaned from light and justice under an inhumane and cruel
> yoke, without knowing the path of liberty and social justice enjoyed by
> men in Peru. Gathered together, the Indian sharecroppers stated that they
> yearn for justice and man's right to live free from the chains of oppression.
>
> The delegation of the community of Concepción de Chakamarka, which
> went to said place after being invited by the aforementioned sharecrop-
> pers, having clearly heard these Indians' unanimous statement, proposed
> the formation of a *sharecroppers' union*. The union would be the central
> base for supporting all the community members or sharecroppers of said
> hacienda against the injustices committed by the hacendados Carlos and

FIG. 2.3 Jhajhamarka peasants, Jhajhamarka, early 1950s. Courtesy of Proyecto Especial de Titulación de Tierras, Ayacucho.

Ernesto Cárdenas who, without any sort of consideration, inhumanely usufruct the Indians' work. Those in attendance were in agreement with the Concepción delegates' proposal, and they felt it advisable to establish the union immediately.[18]

This document is revealing in many different ways. Its reference to a specific article of the Peruvian constitution is a common feature of many of Llamojha's writings. He explained:

> I always walked around with the Peruvian political constitution. And I had the civil and penal codes. When I wrote documents, I always had to mention the key articles. I always had to write, "This article says this; it protects the peasantry." That's how I pestered the authorities.

A second feature of the document that demands attention is Llamojha's use of the term *yanaconas* (sharecroppers). At first glance, Llamojha's use of the label seems a curious choice: the term was most commonly used for workers on large commercial plantations, usually on the Peruvian coast. Campesinos like those in Jhajhamarka—indigenous peasants who held lands in usufruct in exchange for unpaid labor on a hacienda—were usually referred to as *colonos* (tenant farmers).[19] Even a police investigator sent to Jhajhamarka commented that "the condition of sharecropping does not exist on said estate, but rather tenants."[20] Yet the decision to label the organization a "sharecroppers union" was no accident. Using the term *sharecroppers* allowed Llamojha to insert Jhajhamarka peasants into the framework of the new Ley de Yanaconaje (Sharecropping Law). This 1947 law protected sharecroppers from eviction, promised better working conditions, and made written contracts mandatory.[21]

Llamojha's work with Jhajhamarka campesinos garnered much attention from the hacendados Ernesto and Carlos Cárdenas and from regional authorities sympathetic to the landowners. A police investigator sent to Jhajhamarka charged that Llamojha, "in his eagerness to cause every sort of difficulty for the hacienda's owners, made the Indian tenants believe that they would obtain the possession of the estate by forming a Sharecroppers Union. To that end, he gathered all the people of Jhajhamarka together and proceeded to form a supposed union."[22] The investigator insisted that such an act was illegal, as the campesinos had neither sought nor received authorization from the proper authorities.[23] He accused Llamojha of cheating Jhajhamarka campesinos of money by means of a "visibly malicious" claim of collecting funds for the hacienda's purchase.[24] A civil guard corporal, in turn, accused Llamojha and his fellow activist Moisés Ayala of threatening the lives of the Cárdenas brothers and using intimidation "to usurp their lands."[25]

Many of the documents I encountered—including the letter quoted above—mentioned Moisés Ayala, a peasant activist from the nearby La Colpa hacienda. I asked Llamojha to tell me about him.

Yes, Moisés Ayala. He's the one who started to organize the struggle in Jhajhamarka, in 1947. In '48, with me, we continued the fight together. But when they started to take us prisoner, he backed down. He wouldn't get involved.

Llamojha also spoke at length about the repression that led Ayala to retreat. It was both brutal and dehumanizing, treating Llamojha, Ayala, and Jhajhamarka campesinos like animals rather than people.

We began the struggle in January, and in the month of May, the police came here and detained me; they arrested fifteen people. The hacendados had made a written denunciation against me, saying that I had threatened their lives. The police arrived when we were in an assembly. But they didn't grab us right then; they came at night instead. The campesinos had fallen asleep, because they'd started to drink after the assembly. I

was tipsy, too, and I fell asleep, using my typewriter as my pillow! When I woke up, they had taken my typewriter, and they were tying me up with straps used for pigs. They grabbed me by the neck and then they took me.

The two Cárdenases were there, and one of them started to beat me on the path. Because it was night, nobody could see anything in the dark. They took sixteen of us prisoner, tied us up like pigs. On the path, the hacendado started to hit me. A civil guard—he was a really good guy—jumped to my defense.

He yelled at the hacendado, "You're being abusive! Why do you have to hit him? He's a prisoner! You have no reason to raise your hand against him!"

We arrived at the hacienda house and they put the fifteen others in the hallway of the hacienda house. They put me in the jail where they used to put slaves, just a tiny room. They had hooks on the wall. In colonial times, they'd hang slaves from the hooks and they'd brand them on the back with a hot iron. I saw the branding iron hanging on the wall. I thought maybe they were going to brand me! That's where they kept me. I was detained for four days in there.

The hacendado ordered the civil guards not to give me food or a bed. But there was a really good guard, he was from Andahuaylas. At night, he brought me a mattress, food.

"Don't worry, I'm here," he said.

He brought me the mattress and food at eleven or twelve at night. Then, early, at four or five in the morning, he came to get the mattress back.

"Give me your mattress! The *patrón* [landlord] is going to come," he said. I gave it back to him, and then I was left on the floor, shivering. The landlord came at six or seven. He came and he opened the window.

"And? How are you? Did you sleep well?"

"Yes, I slept well." He didn't know that I'd slept on a bed!

This recollection introduces us to two sympathetic policemen, or civil guards. Such figures pop up again and again in Llamojha's life stories. There are two explanations for this recurrent theme. One has to do with his persona: he is a warm, relatively soft-spoken man, full of stories and laughter. He is also quite short in stature, even in comparison to other Andean men. It is not hard to imagine that he inspired a great deal of sympathy, even in the individuals responsible for arresting or guarding him. The second explanation has to do with politics: like many persons sympathetic to socialist ideas, Llamojha probably saw policemen as members of the working class and thus as potential allies in the broader class struggle against the capitalist elite. His life stories thus serve to emphasize that point.

We were there [in the hacienda house] for four days, and on the fifth day, they transferred all the prisoners to Ayacucho. We stayed in the police station in Ayacucho for twelve days while they took our statements. Each statement took almost the whole day, and there were lots of us. The accusation that the Jhajhamarka hacendados made against me was that I was passing myself off as a priest, and that I walked from pueblo to pueblo, marrying and baptizing people. They had captured me in Jhajhamarka with my Latin, Spanish, and Quechua religious books. So, I was interrogated about this every day. And on the last day, they took me to the Ayacucho bishopric.

Three officials took me in chains. It was funny. Each time I remember it, it makes me laugh. They brought me before the bishop in chains!

They presented me to the bishop.

"Mr. Bishop, we're bringing you an individual who has passed himself off as a priest."

The bishop looked at me. "You passed yourself off as a priest?"

"No, not me."

"Where's your cassock?"

"I don't have a cassock!"

The bishop looked at all my books. "Why do you have these books? Where did you take them from?"

"They're my books! I'm a cantor and I play the organ. I always travel through pueblos, I play the organ. I help priests celebrate mass. That's why I walk around with my books. I walk through all the pueblos, I lead processions in fiestas," I said to him.

"You lead processions?"

"Yes, I lead processions. When there are no priests, I lead."

He thought for a moment.

He gave me my book. "All right, let's see. Read Latin!"

So, I read Latin.

"All right, sing!"

So, I sang in Latin. I read correctly in Latin, there was no problem. Then, another book.

"All right, sing in Latin!"

I sang. Then, another book, too. "Let's see, sing a mass!" I sang and I sang. Then, he took out an organ, a small, portable one.

"Let's see, play for me!"

So I played.

And then the bishop said to the police, "He is a cantor and a musician. Why did you bring him to me?" I had passed all the tests!

But they kept my books. My books are still imprisoned by the courts. When they took me prisoner in Jhajhamarka with my books, they took me with everything, and <u>my books are still in the court.</u> They're under life imprisonment!

When Llamojha talked about Jhajhamarka in our interviews, he emphasized that the charges against him centered on accusations of impersonating a priest. Those accusations are preserved in archival documents. The regional inspector for the Bureau of Indian Affairs asserted: "to attract sympathies, he [Llamojha] pretends to be the parish priest of Vischongo, he keeps a special religious book, he expedites baptismal certificates, and he makes all the Indians believe that the estate will be divided up."[26] A police investigator made the same accusation, <u>claiming that Llamojha tried to deceive Jhajhamarka's peasants</u> by carrying around books for mass, issuing baptismal certificates, and passing himself off as a priest. Because of these efforts, the investigator asserted, "<u>the majority of the Indians blindly obey the instructions they receive to obstruct or somehow bring about damage to the owners of the hacienda.</u>"[27]

The archives also show that these charges against Llamojha were not entirely spurious. Nested between letters and documents about the Jhajhamarka case lies a handwritten letter from "Manuel J. Llamojha Mitman, Parish Priest of the Doctrine of Vischongo, of the Vicariate of Cangallo, of the Dioceses of Ayacucho." The letter certifies the existence of a young man's baptismal certificate in the parish archive, and the certificate is signed with Llamojha's name, with the word "PARROCO" (parish priest) stamped under it. If someone faked don Manuel's looping, elegant handwriting and intricate signature, they did an exceptionally good job.[28] Although Llamojha's maternal surname, Mitma, is misspelled as "Mitman," he often added this *n* to his name during the 1940s, likely reflecting an experiment with Quechua orthography. When I shared this document with Llamojha and asked if he had ever forged baptism certificates for campesinos in need, he laughingly admitted it. He replied,

<u>Yes, if they couldn't find them and urgently needed them, I'd make them.</u> I did wedding certificates, other documents for matters with the ministry. That's what my life was like. I saved many people this way.

Llamojha also very much conceptualized himself as a religious man and carried out many of the roles linked with the priesthood.

> **Christ fought this way, too.** That's why he was crucified. He taught about the struggle, about how we should struggle. I followed that teaching. I went around to the pueblos, always teaching catechism. Like Christ, I made people pray and I led religious processions. So, the hacendados denounced me, saying I was trying to pass myself off as a priest.

Although the archival record includes charges against Llamojha for impersonating a priest, they are overshadowed by the accusations that he was a communist. Here, context is especially important. As noted, in 1948 Peruvians found themselves living in the international situation of the Cold War, with increasing tensions between communist and anticommunist regimes and their sympathizers. General Manuel Odría outlawed Peru's Communist Party after the October 1948 coup, and anticommunism became a versatile tool in Peru. Churchmen, Peru's economic elites, and even average citizens used accusations of communism to tarnish reputations and dismiss demands for socioeconomic justice. Members of the increasingly conservative APRA likewise voiced sharp anticommunist sentiment, distinguishing themselves from communists to try to bolster their own power.[29] Llamojha's critics used the ideas of the Cold War against him, framing his actions in Jhajhamarka as those of a determined Communist Party militant.

A police investigator charged that Llamojha and Ayala carried out clandestine meetings on the Jhajhamarka hacienda, instructing tenants on the "hostile attitudes that they should adopt against the landlords" and misleading the tenants to believe that they would be able to evict the hacendados. The investigator stressed that Llamojha and Ayala's goals were "inspired by the 'Communist Party'" and that they were attempting to mislead Jhajhamarka's indigenous peasants, "maliciously trying to confuse Community with Communism."[30] The same investigator argued that the two men's "communist ideas" had led them to "inculcate subversive actions in Indians' minds, like not recognizing legal norms and absenteeism at work."[31]

A civil guard corporal made similar assertions, accusing Llamojha, Ayala, and a Jhajhamarka campesino named Teodoro Illanéz of "obeying orders and directives of communist bosses in Lima."[32] This corporal reported that he and the hacendado Carlos Cárdenas had unwittingly interrupted a meeting of over fifty Jhajhamarka tenants, led by Llamojha and a campesino named Manuel Huaytalla. The corporal reported that the meeting's participants were drunk and reacted insolently, so he and Cárdenas quickly left. Then, the corporal reported, "they once again started to insult us, threatening to kill us, and at the same time saying *vivas* [long live!] to the Communist Party. It is known that Manuel Llamocca, Manuel Huaytalla, and Moisés Ayala are agents sent by Lima communists."[33] Even the regional inspector for the Bureau of Indian Affairs levied these sorts of accusations. He characterized Llamojha as a "communist agitator and propagandist of anarchist tendencies." He added that Jhajhamarka was an "estate where communists make a pernicious labor against the rights of property and social peace."[34]

There is no compelling evidence that Llamojha actually belonged to the Communist Party at this point in time. He insisted in our interviews that he never belonged to any political party. Moreover, the Communist Party was relatively weak in Ayacucho and throughout Peru during the 1940s.[35] The most damning "evidence" of Llamojha's communist sympathies came from two typed letters supposedly found among his possessions.[36] The first is addressed to Cupertino de la Cruz, a Jhajhamarka resident living in Lima. It reads:

COPY

Ccaccamarca, May 1st 1948

Mr. Cupertino de la Cruz:
Lima.

On a special task for our *comuneros* [community members], I am informing you that we have advanced our labors significantly, and we will soon be a pueblo, because we have named our authorities and also named our delegates, such as Antonio Prado, Bruno Prado, Modesto Lahuana, Hipólito Lahuana, Alejandro Cisneros, Marcelo Cisneros and others that I will soon send you. Now, my friend, the people are ready to act against the Cárdenas brothers in active form, for we are determined to hang them and repeat the heroic attitude of our ancestors and in this way impose our communist desires, for which the party will congratulate us. Do not forget to continue the efforts with our friends and continue the tasks. Long live our party! We will see you soon, when we receive you in our pueblo, Ccaccamarca.

(Signed)
Manuel J. Llamocca Mitma[37]

The next letter, dated just one week later, was addressed to Llamojha's fellow activist in Jhajhamarka, Moisés Ayala.

(COPY)

Ccaccamarca, May 8, 1948

Mr. Moises Ayala.
Ayacucho:

Dear brother Moises:

As you have not written me anything of the commission we have given you, we are sending you this card to find out if you have achieved what we thought about regarding Bernardina Cisneros and if you have seen our communist friends in Ayacucho. I ask because I am advancing our work a great deal and believe that within a few days, we will be yelling out a *viva* to our party with our other brothers, and already in our pueblo of Ccaccamarca.

Ernesto's brother has arrived with two civil guards. He appeared at our location the other night, but we made him run. I mocked them and all the people applauded me, celebrating my conduct.

Send me news and some propaganda to continue my work.

Until soon, brother.
M. Llamocca Mitan

These letters are fakes. Not only do they lack the usual grace and style of Llamojha's writing; they also use the traditional spelling of Jhajhamarka.[38] Even more telling, the letters actually misspell Llamojha's surname. When I shared copies of these letters with him, he commented:

I couldn't talk about politics like that. I wouldn't talk like that. Maybe it was from Castillo, or Raúl Agüero, to implicate me. Or maybe Joaquín Chávez.

Those men were abusive authorities in Concepción, and Llamojha had protracted conflicts with them. In other documents from the 1940s, Llamojha also stressed the apolitical nature of the sharecroppers' union. He wrote that the union "at its core, does not treat questions of partisan politics, which can be the cause of divisionism in the social organization."[39]

The very existence of these fake letters, however, is revealing. They show both the determination and perhaps even the desperation of the Cárdenas hacendados and their allies in their fight against Llamojha. These letters also show that his opponents felt accusations of communism were the most effective means of discrediting him; they could just as easily have composed letters describing his plans for personal enrichment and gain. "Communist" was an easy and effective accusation to hurl against him, and he faced it repeatedly over the long course of his political career. Further, by casting him and Ayala as communists, hacendados and authorities were relying on established, racialized tropes about "outside agitators" generating trouble among naïve indigenous peasants, tropes that effectively dismissed Jhajhamarka campesinos' agency and their desires for significant socioeconomic change.

When Llamojha shared his stories about Jhajhamarka, he repeatedly mentioned a person named Luis Medina.

> Luis Medina was a person who was half deaf, but he headed the struggle. He was an illiterate man, but he was very brave. He didn't pay attention to anyone, not even the police! He ordered the police around.
>
> He was the delegate whom we sent from Jhajhamarka with petitions to present in Lima. On his way back, they detained him at one of the checkpoints and they brought him to the Ayacucho jail where we were.
>
> The next day, the police freed him.
>
> The police said, "Get out of here already! You're free!"
>
> But he didn't want to leave. "I will leave with them," he said.
>
> He didn't want to leave for anything! So the police lifted him up and threw him in the street. Two police grabbed his legs, and others grabbed his hands, taking him, carrying him in the air to the streets.
>
> He came back. "I will not leave! I'll only leave together with them!" he said.
>
> We finally said, "Go! Leave! Better yet, because they're going to take us to Cangallo, you'll have to bring us food."

Llamojha's comment about food reflected the fact that in most Peruvian jails, prisoners had to rely on outside friends and relatives to bring them their daily meals. He recalled the conditions in the Cangallo jail:

> After the bishop's, they made me return to jail, and then they transferred all of us to the Cangallo jail. I was in jail six months, alone now. The rest had been released. They accused me of being a communist priest. That's what it said in the accusation, in the file. "Communist priest, to be captured," it said.

FIG. 2.4 Luis Medina (center), Jhajhamarka, 1952. Photo courtesy of Manuel Llamojha Mitma.

I was treated well in the Cangallo jail. There was a guard, he was like a brother to me. Right there, he brought me his table, he lent me his typewriter. Using his typewriter, I wrote up defenses for the prisoners. I wrote documents requesting their freedom. Some were in there for no good reason, because of slander. I sent these documents to Cangallo authorities, others went to Ayacucho.

After six months, someone came from Jhajhamarka. He got me out, paying bail. I think he paid 120 soles to get me out on bail. He got me out and took me to Jhajhamarka. There, I began to prepare more documents, I got people to sign them, and then I left for Lima. I took these papers to the ministry and presented them, so that they would come to Jhajhamarka to investigate. With this struggle, we lowered the hacendados' morale.

The fight for Jhajhamarka wound down after an extended strike in which campesinos withheld their labor services from the Cárdenas hacendados. This strike proved a major economic blow to the landlords.

I proposed to the campesinos that they go on strike, that nobody go to work on the hacienda. So, they carried out a strike. That strike lasted one year. The hacendados didn't have anyone to work for them, the campesinos were working for themselves. So the Cárdenas brothers withdrew. They went to Lima and the campesinos took possession of the hacienda.

The campesinos took it without purchasing it. The pueblo was left with the hacienda, and they have it to this day. I got a piece, too. They gave me an alfalfa field.

The strike Llamojha described began around 1951, and he worked actively with Jhajhamarka campesinos until 1952. Although the Cárdenas hacendados effectively abandoned the Jhajhamarka hacienda in the late 1950s, leaving its tenants in control, the community's legal standing remained ambiguous and contested until 1977, when the government formally recognized its status as an official campesino community.[40] While the struggle for Jhajhamarka began to wind down in the 1950s, fights over land rights and hacendado abuses began exploding in other parts of Peru's Andean sierra. Llamojha was well positioned to play a leading role in those struggles because of the important experience he had gained in the fight for Jhajhamarka. His work there marked the starting point of his labors as a campesino activist.

THREE

"Jail Was Like My Home"

FIGHTING FOR CONCEPCIÓN, 1952–1961

"I was always in the struggle," Llamojha asserted. "I didn't abandon it, even for a day." From 1952 until 1961, he dedicated himself to defending his indigenous community from the abuses of local hacendados and district authorities. During these years, he would often tie his typewriter to his back and walk to nearby communities to assist them in their own struggles for land. His help was sorely needed, as conflicts between indigenous peasants and hacendados were growing more and more common—and more and more heated—across Peru's Andean sierra region during the late 1950s. Peasants in Cuzco's La Convención Valley, for example, formed a union and then went on strike, demanding much greater control over the lands they worked. In 1959 one of the most serious land conflicts to that date exploded in the central Andean region Pasco, when campesinos seized a portion of a hacienda they felt rightfully belonged to them. Numerous other land invasions—or land recuperations, as sympathizers called them—followed.[1]

Llamojha plunged into the work of defending Concepción by seeking election to his community's village council. He quickly became embroiled in a series of heated conflicts with district and regional authorities and with the hacendados who encroached on Concepción's lands. He used his talents as a writer throughout these struggles, and his enemies repeatedly tried to turn his intellectual work against him, accusing him of duplicity, forgery, and even counterfeiting money. Until Peru transitioned back to democracy in 1956, he fought these battles in a national context of authoritarian military rule, but his experiences show that *local* authoritarianism was just as significant. He repeatedly confronted district-level government authorities who racially denigrated him and his supporters as upstart Indians, even though these authorities were themselves of rural, indigenous origins.

Llamojha's stories about the 1950s—a particularly underresearched decade in Latin American history—expose some of the painful personal costs of political activism.[2] Although he made many daring escapes from the police, he also endured repeated imprisonments and terrible mistreatment. He was forced to go into hiding and even had to fake his own death. And he did not bear those difficulties alone: his family was devastated each time he was jailed, his children and wife missed him terribly when he traveled away from home or was in hiding, and they suffered financially because his activist work carried no salary. Llamojha himself rarely speaks of the difficulties associated with activism, stressing instead the virtue of complete dedication to the search for social justice. That complete devotion, however, generated its own significant troubles.

Positions of Authority

In 1950, while the struggle for Jhajhamarka was ongoing, Llamojha and doña Esther witnessed the birth of their first child, Hilda.

> During my wife's pregnancy, I went to work on a hacienda near here.[3] When I came back, she gave birth. I wanted a little boy, but we had a girl. Two years later, my son [Walter] was born.

Shortly thereafter Llamojha moved back to Lima, and he remained there until 1955.

> After three years in Concepción, I returned to Lima. I had to go back and present documents to the ministry. And I stayed in Lima, working at the central railway station. I called my wife to come, too.
>
> I started off as a mechanic's assistant at the railway station, but then they moved me to the document reception office, and I worked there as an assistant to the secretary. I would have kept working there, except that we were in a mess with the hacendados. The struggle had started in Concepción and I was worried.

Community authorities in Concepción weren't interested. Sure, they took an interest at first, but then they got frightened by the threat of jail, and they stopped fighting. The first leaders who were named in 1944 weren't good for anything. Worse still, one of them betrayed the pueblo and joined with the Ayrabamba hacienda. Others entered the community presidency, but then they couldn't leave their chores, because to fight, you have to leave everything and devote yourself to the struggle.

That's why I came back. We were in Lima for three and a half years. Then, we went back to Concepción again. I had to come back and lead the struggle.

On his return to Concepción in 1955, Llamojha began working alongside his local allies to organize elections for a new village council (*junta comunal*). Community members would vote for the village council, and a representative from the Bureau of Indian Affairs would then ratify the election and formally appoint the chosen authorities: a community president, a secretary, and a *personero legal*, or indigenous community legal representative.[4] The personero legal acted on behalf of community members in all official matters, representing the community in legal disputes and petitions for government intervention. It was the ideal position for Llamojha, given his talents for composing legal documents and writing compelling letters of protest.

The personero is the one who represents Concepción, the community. He represents them before the authorities. Back then, the ministry used to name them. The ministry would send commissions to preside over the elections for personero.

The right to elect village councils was one of the most important benefits held by officially recognized indigenous communities. In a national context of widespread disenfranchisement because of exclusionary literacy requirements, and in a highly centralized system where departmental, provincial, and district authorities were appointed rather than elected, the elections for village councils were unusually participatory in the Peruvian context. All male heads of families—regardless of their literacy—were allowed to vote.[5] The first step in convening elections for the village council was to form a provisional directing junta to organize and oversee the elections.

I came back here to Concepción in '55, and we began the struggle. Without me, the people didn't move. The people were united. There were only three *malditos* [damned ones] who served the hacendados. I returned and organized the masses here, in the community.

The very next day after I arrived, four people came from the Ayrabamba hacienda.

They came to my house and said, "How can we possibly be so disorganized? We are going to form an association."

I said to them, "There's no need to form an organization; the community is already officially recognized. What we really have to do is get the community to name a provisional directing junta."

We signed an agreement and pledged to fight until the end. That's what we did! These people followed through, and they didn't abandon me. Once we had formed the junta, we agreed to spend one week summoning everyone. For one week, they ran about, calling on people to attend the assembly.

As Llamojha spoke about this assembly and the provisional directing junta, he offered more detail about the three men he often described as being "against the community."

These three people weren't even from the pueblo. This is the hacendados' secret. Back then, the hacendados dominated all the pueblos. They're the ones who put their people into power. Their secret agents, one could say. In collusion with government authorities, the hacendados would impose people from other places on each pueblo. These three people: Joaquín Chávez was from Huanta, Raúl Agüero was from Andahuaylas. The other one, Grimaldo Castillo, his dad was from Huamanga.[6] They were the bosses and eternal authorities. They never left their posts: governor, judge, municipal agent. These men, not any others, were always the authorities.

They're the ones who informed to the municipalities, to the provinces. They were against the pueblo, servants of the hacendados. They were the ones who told the hacendados how many cattle there were in the community. They [Castillo, Agüero, and Chávez] informed the province so that the province could charge people fees. I didn't have even a single cow, but they reported that I had fifty-three cows! And then authorities came to charge me. That's how it was. They did all of this; they were incredible. They were really against the pueblo.

They said very clearly, "We have to screw the pueblo." That's how these three talked. That's how they were.

Llamojha's description of these three men reflects a common experience in rural Peru during the twentieth century. Unlike the elected indigenous community authorities, positions of formal government authority at the district level—posts like that of governor, lieutenant governor, justice of the peace, and municipal agent—were all appointed rather than elected posts until 1963.[7] The department prefect placed individuals in power, often ignoring community members' desires, and it was in his power to appoint individuals from outside the local district, as frequently occurred. More often than not, these appointed district authorities were among the wealthiest residents of the area. Even though they were commonly of rural, indigenous descent, their marginally greater wealth, their literacy, and their privileged position of power led them to self-identify as "non-Indian" and pejoratively racialize average community members as "Indians." Complaints against highly abusive district authorities fill Ayacucho's archives, but provincial, departmental, and national authorities rarely paid attention to these protests and frequently re-appointed the same men. Campesinos' frustration with these abusive district authorities stands out as one of the key features of twentieth-century politics in rural Ayacucho.[8]

Llamojha recalled how Concepción's three abusive district authorities, Castillo, Agüero, and Chávez, angrily resisted community members' efforts to elect a new personero legal:

In the first assembly, we gathered and we asked them to come, but they didn't want to go.

They said, "We haven't called this assembly! Why would we go to an assembly of Indians?"

Well, fine. We gladly carried out our meeting. After that, we named our provisional directing junta. Then, with the new provisional junta, we formally requested that the election of a personero legal be carried out by ministerial order.

We communicated with Lima, and the ministry replied, saying, "On this day, this date, the inspector of Indian affairs will come. He will preside over the election."

The Ayacucho inspector of Indian affairs communicated with us, answering from Ayacucho. His letter said, "This memo has reached us. The Ayacucho inspector of Indian affairs is going to come on such-and-such day."

Because he was governor, Agüero got the letter.

"Who do you think you are, calling the inspector?" he asked. "There's no chance he will come, no chance he'll pay attention to you! I am the one who has to call him to come! He is going to stay at my house. You don't even have a place to house him!"

He read the memo, threw it on the floor, and started to crush it with his foot. He started to stomp on the memo! I left. That night, I informed the provisional junta in an assembly. Demetrio Gutiérrez was there. He was an employee of the Ayrabamba hacienda, but he fought for Concepción. He was really gutsy!

"Caramba! How could the governor do this? We have to denounce the governor," Demetrio Gutiérrez said. Then he said, "I have a house! We are going to have the inspector stay there. How could that damned governor say we don't have a house?"

On the appointed day, we sent a delegation to Pampa Cangallo to meet the inspector. On the way here, the delegation told the inspector what these three district authorities were like.

Because the inspector had been told about what life in the pueblo was like, he said, "I will have our authorities, the _envarados_ [customary indigenous authorities who enforced moral order in indigenous communities], here alongside me."

The envarados were the local police, the pueblo's police.[9]

The next day, the inspector was eating breakfast with the envarados at his side. The envarados were there with their _bastones_ [ceremonial staffs of authority]. When they were eating their breakfast, these three authorities came through the front door.

"Mr. Inspector! How can you be here in this house? You should have come to my house!" the governor said.

"Mr. Governor, I am in a house; I'm not in the street. I'm in a house, with my police at my side. So, Mr. Governor, please wait for me outside, because I am going to finish my breakfast."

The inspector then went the town hall, accompanied by the envarados. It was lovely! They got to the town hall and they started to put the names of the candidates for personero legal on the chalk board. There I was, number one. Governor Agüero came from his house when I was leading the vote.

He said, "Mr. Inspector! I cannot permit this Indian to become the legal representative! This Indian doesn't know how to read, he isn't even from the pueblo. I don't know where he came from."

The inspector told him to go to hell! "Mr. Governor! You are in charge in your house, not here! Go home!"

So, the governor left in a rage. He entered his home and he grabbed a chair, threw it to the ground, and started to stamp his feet in rage. The inspector had put these three authorities in their place.

This is how the election was. I won the election, as legal representative. Those three men were enraged.

In many communities, these kinds of abusive district authorities ranked among the wealthiest local peasants, owning larger plots of land than their neighbors or melding agricultural work with other forms of paid employment, like teaching positions or store ownership. When I asked Llamojha if this was the case with Castillo, Agüero, and Chávez, he said no. Instead, what set these men apart from their neighbors was their schooling.

It was that they had an education—Agüero had a high-school education, Chávez just had elementary, and Castillo had just four years of elementary. Castillo thought of himself as being like God around here, as being of a superior race. He thought he was better than all the people from here, and that's why he treated us like Indians. He thought ill of us, and that's why the pueblo didn't get along well with him, or with the three of them.

Noting his frequent mentions of anti-indigenous prejudice, I asked Llamojha if racism was a major problem in the 1940s, 1950s, and 1960s.

Yes, it was serious, both here in the pueblo itself and on the haciendas. The dominant ones, the hacendados, treated us in the worst way, insulting us.
"Indians! Outlaw Indians!" they'd say. That's how they treated us.
They always said that we were of different blood, of a different race.

Llamojha also explained that such racist ideas even worked their way into his own family. He described his sister Donatilda:

She was very cold.
She would say to me, "What are you involved in? The people, the Indians, what are they going to do for you?"
"You're Indian, too!" I'd say.
She was white, really white-skinned. When she was little, my dad really liked her, he didn't ever want her to cry. That's why she lived so proudly. She didn't even want to look at us.

Despite the concerted opposition of Concepción's three abusive district authorities, Llamojha began serving as Concepción's personero legal in 1956. He described his duties:

As personero legal, I had to represent the community and go to the authorities, to the ministries, bringing reports about the community, because it was in a fight with neighboring hacendados over our borders. I complained that the authorities shouldn't support the hacendados who had taken over sixteen hundred hectares of land belonging to Concepción. I always acted in defense of all the pueblos that belonged to the province of Vilcashuamán; I walked around everywhere.

As personero, I started to fight against the hacendados' abuses. I presented the denunciations myself. I didn't need a lawyer, because I had trained myself well. Buying books, reading the laws, I learned everything and I composed the documents myself.

As personero legal, Llamojha actively defended Concepción's indigenous peasants in their conflicts with the neighboring hacendados Elodia Vassallo de Parodi, her son César Parodi, Alfonso Martinelli, Juan Echegaray, and Abel Alfaro. Each of these hacendados encroached on Concepción's lands, forced Concepción's campesinos to work hacienda lands and labor in hacienda homes without payment, and unjustly seized community members' animals. The kinds of abuses they perpetrated were commonplace among hacendados of the era. Llamojha had much to say about these landowners. Note that Llamojha mentions campesinos referring to these hacendados as papá (father) and, in Elodia Vassallo de Parodi's case, mamá (mother). Those labels reflected long-standing patterns of deferential respect and, more important, indigenous peasants' attempts to evoke feelings of paternalism (or maternalism) in hacendados and thereby limit abuses.

Elodia was the principal leader of the hacendados, the strongest force. Eight days after my first election as personero, she sent me a letter from Ayrabamba saying, "Now that you are legal representative, we are going to come to an agreement. First, you have to go to Lima and sign a document."

She had made the first two Concepción personeros sign a ministerial document promising to send people to work on the Ayrabamba hacienda for free for one month. The whole community, all the community members, had to work. The women had to go and do domestic service in the hacienda's house. These papers in the ministry said all of this. The personero who started new in the post had to sign this document. Elodia sent me a letter saying this.

She also tried to buy me off. She sent that letter with a bag of oranges and six bottles of aguardiente [sugarcane alcohol]. And she promised to buy me a house and find me work in a government ministry.

I answered the letter saying, "Ma'am, we do not live on the hacienda. We live in our community. No one is going to go to work for free. You have to pay. You have to follow through with your duty. In addition, you should not carry out hierbaje. This has been prohibited," I said.

So she presented a denunciation against Concepción, saying that the Indians of Concepción and Jhajhamarka had invaded Ayrabamba to destroy it. She claimed that the house was completely gone and that there was no sugarcane left, that we had burned everything.

It was a lie. So, I went to Lima to present a denunciation against Ayrabamba. When I was about to return, I found out there was an order for my arrest. There were all sorts of checkpoints with orders to arrest me, so I couldn't go back to Concepción. So I sent a telegram to my mom, to my wife, and to a relative who was in Ayacucho, saying that I had died. They believed it was true!

I sent that telegram in order to be able to travel freely! Here in Concepción, they rang the church bells for my death and they held a wake with my clothing [a traditional Andean religious practice known as the *pacha vela*]. I had a cousin in Ayacucho, he got my death announced on the radio. All the court authorities found out and they believed that I was dead, so they lifted the order for my arrest! So I came back in peace. You have to carry out these kinds of intrigues!

When I arrived, those three people who were against me, they informed Ayrabamba, the hacienda.

They said, "The dead man has been resuscitated!"

"Ask the authorities to capture him!"

So, they presented a document to the authorities in Vischongo, saying that the dead man had come back to life! Vischongo then informed the Cangallo subprefecture, saying that the dead man had been resurrected! Elodia likewise filed a complaint against me, denouncing me for actions against the public faith.

The denunciations from the hacendada Elodia Vassallo de Parodi were so serious that Llamojha had to contact lawyers, an action that cost him a significant amount of money. He recalled that the lawyers told him:

"There is an order for your capture! The situation is grave! You have to hide in Lima for seven years!" they said to me.

"Why would I hide for seven years? I haven't done anything."

"But your mamá Elodia has denounced you, saying that you have destroyed the hacienda house. So, you have to go into hiding for seven years. We can't get you out. Anyway, the court is closed until the 18th of March," they said. "So, if you want to turn yourself over to the court, you have to hide until they reopen."

So, I went to Huanta.

After a few months of hiding in the northern Ayacucho city of Huanta, Llamojha went to the city of Ayacucho to present himself before the courts. The story he narrates of this experience reveals his frustration with Peru's notoriously slow criminal justice system. It was not unusual for trials to drag on for years, and court inaction sometimes left accused individuals stuck in wretched jails for extended periods, even years, without convictions.[10] Llamojha tried to circumvent a long preliminary wait in jail by simply going straight to the courts.

When they opened the court, I went to turn myself in. The denunciation was serious.

"I've come because of the denunciation." I said.

"Go turn yourself in at the police post!"

"But here is the denunciation. The arrest order came from here, so that's why I've come."

"Go turn yourself in at the police post, so they can arrest you!"

I didn't want to go. I went to the court daily, for four or five days, but nothing happened! They didn't want to take my statement.

"Go to the police post! Go to the police post," they said to me.

It was a Friday afternoon; it was five o'clock and everyone was getting ready to leave. I entered the court and said, "Please take my statement. Today is Friday, and I have to leave the city."

"Go on, go turn yourself in at the police post."

"Why would I turn myself in there, when I have the denunciation right here?"

Because they didn't want to do it, because they were getting ready to leave, I said, "Fine, then, sir. I am going to leave a deposition, please allow me to use the typewriter." So, I sat down at the typewriter and put in the paper to write a deposition.

"You! Who are you to grab the typewriter?"

"You won't attend to me, so I have to do it myself!"

"Fine. Go and get your lawyer."

I went down and got my lawyer. He started to take my statement in relation to the denunciation. I gave my statement about the invasion of Ayrabamba. It took a long time, from five until eight o'clock at night. I explained what had happened with the false denunciation about the destruction of the Ayrabamba hacienda. I clarified all of this. After that, it was eight at night, and they sent me to jail.

As Llamojha continued his story, he highlighted his own morality and honor, stressing that he did not evade imprisonment despite his obvious opportunity to do so.

Because it was already nighttime, they sent me to look for the police.

"Go, look for police who can take you to the jail!"

So I went and looked. There weren't any close by. I found a police officer down at the corner.

"Come! They're calling for you in the court," I said.

"What are they calling me for?"

"I don't know," I said.

At the court, they said, "Take this young man to jail." They gave him a document and he took me to jail.

Then the policeman said to me, "You came and got me for this! Why didn't you escape?"

"Why would I escape?"

Llamojha remained imprisoned for a month, and he returned to Concepción on his release, probably in early 1958.[11] To get back to Concepción, he needed to find a vehicle headed in that direction, or he would face a very long, grueling walk that would take several days to complete. As he told the story of his return, describing a subterfuge involving Elodia Vassallo's son, César Parodi, he emphasized both his cunning and the helpful collaboration of others, two key themes that run through many of his stories.

I was in jail a month in the Ayacucho prison. They went and investigated, but they didn't find any evidence of an invasion in Ayrabamba. Instead, they found that everything was in order—the house and the cane fields were still there—so I was set free.

I left the jail to come back to Concepción, but there was no way to get back home. Ayrabamba's chauffeur was in Ayacucho, and he saw me and asked me, "What are you doing here?"

I said to him, "I'm leaving jail, but I don't have any way to get back. The car left without me."

"Here's the Ayrabamba car. Let's go," he said to me. But the owner [César Parodi] was there.

"The owner is going to see me!" I said.

"He won't see you. You'll ride on top and I'll cover you with a canopy. He's going to go inside the car so he won't see you."

So, I climbed up and they took me to Ayrabamba. When we arrived in Ayrabamba, the owner got out and then I came down from on top of the car. He didn't see me!

After the conflict with Elodia Vassallo de Parodi, an even more serious dispute erupted in April 1959 with the hacendado Abel Alfaro, owner of the Mejorada hacienda. Llamojha described Alfaro:

He was really liked by the pueblo. Everything was very good and the pueblo was fine with him. But then he started to plant a piece of land that belonged to Concepción. He wanted to take over the terrain from this zone, so he plowed it with seven teams of oxen and planted wheat. The whole community rose up.

The women were the bravest. The women immediately got involved and demanded that the people uproot this planting. We uprooted it and planted barley. So Alfaro started a lawsuit, accusing us of an armed attack.

Alfaro brought five police officers to his hacienda. That night, one of the hacienda workers came to warn me.

This worker came and told me, "Alfaro has brought police; they're going to come and capture you tomorrow."

In the morning, while I was watching, the police came down to Concepción on horseback. Back behind this house, there is a big tree, a *molle* tree, and I climbed it. The police entered our house, looked around, got the kids out of bed, and the kids started crying, screaming. The police broke everything that they found. Everything. They even threw the table onto the floor. They climbed the hill to look for me, but they couldn't find me.

They went from house to house, they went all the way up the hill, but I was hidden in my tree. At three that afternoon, they left the governor's house and they entered a store on the corner and started drinking.

I was really angry, so I climbed down from my tree and went to go and ring the church bell, so that people would come out of their homes and start to gather. I turned up the street and a woman saw me.

"Here he is! He's escaping!" she said.

It wasn't the police who came, but Alfaro himself. He came with his horse. I had gone into the church tower to ring the bell, and he climbed up the tower behind me. Inside the tower, he pulled me from behind when I was climbing up the stairs. He pulled me down, and he grabbed me, kicking me. Then, he got on his horse and he started to trample me. At that moment, three women appeared. They pulled him off me. They defended me, these three women.

From there, I ran over to the cornfield. I thought to myself, "If I hide here, they're going to find me."

I decided to go over the fence but as I was climbing up it, two police came. I got down off of the fence and I stayed there.

"They're going to grab me," I said.

The police turned around, they passed me, and I greeted them. They passed right in front of me, because they didn't know who I was!

So many police were looking for me, going from house to house. Everyone got mad.

"Why do you have to come in here?" they said to the police. "He doesn't live here. He must be in Lima." The women said this. Women are the ones who always participate in the struggle. Without the woman, there can be no triumph!

Women not only participated in this 1959 dispute with the hacendado Alfaro, they were also targeted for arrest by police forces.

A total of thirteen women and three men were jailed. Alfaro accused them of armed attack. The police were pursuing me in the pueblo, and because they couldn't find me, they started to seize the women.

The arrested included Llamojha's mother, his wife, Esther, and his two-year-old son Herbert.[12] In a letter Llamojha wrote to an Ayacucho senator, he described how police officers broke into numerous peasant homes at three o'clock in the morning. When they found women sleeping alone in their homes, the officers attempted to rape them. The officers next seized fourteen people: seven women and five men, a baby and a toddler.[13] Ten of those detainees—including doña Esther and the very young Herbert—were then transferred to the city of Ayacucho, forced to walk there on foot, "carrying their bags and children on their backs." The officers subjected the detainees to "beatings and kicks," and several elderly women fell down as they struggled to walk. All of the detained were accused of "attack by armed force."[14]

Following these arrests, Llamojha wanted to meet with his fellow community members to decide on an appropriate response to this police violence, but it was difficult to arrange such a meeting without attracting the police's attention. He credited a local female peasant with finding the needed solution.

> I was hidden in the hills with the community president and we decided to go to Lima. We had to meet with the rest of the community, but there were forty police officers in Concepción, and they wouldn't let anyone go out at night. But there was a woman who always intervened bravely in Concepción. Celia Cuba.
>
> She took action. Caramba! We couldn't hold a meeting in the pueblo, so she decided to carry out the meeting in the cemetery. It was a trick!
>
> She went to the police and said, "A baby has died, and we're going to bury him at night."
>
> The tradition here is to hold a burial with music, with a harp, a violin, and the ringing of the church bells. The police agreed, and so everyone came out for the meeting that night. The community president and I were hidden in the puna, and we came down to the cemetery. They came, carrying a coffin and singing. They'd prepared a baby's coffin. The police didn't intervene. She'd left a case of beer for the police to drink!
>
> We held the meeting in the cemetery and I consulted with the masses. After that, the community president and I left for Lima.
>
> We had to go on foot, because we couldn't pass through the police checkpoints on the road. My brother Emilio went with us. He brought his little horse to carry food for the journey. We had to walk for fifteen days to get to Ica.

Llamojha, his brother Emilio, and the community president had very little money between the three of them. They were forced to abandon Emilio's horse as they walked, unable to bring the animal along once they made the decision to catch a ride on a passing truck.[15] By the time they got to the department of Ica—the halfway point of the journey—they had only enough money to send one man on to Lima. Llamojha made that trip while his brother Emilio and the community president remained behind, finding temporary work that would finance their trip back home to Concepción. Llamojha explained that they arrived first in Ica.

> The next day, I left for Lima. Once I arrived in Lima, I started to run around, presenting documents. My complaints were published in newspapers, in *El Comercio*, in *La Crónica*. And that's how we got the female prisoners out of jail.

Llamojha's ideas about women deserve close attention, for he expressed contradictory ideas about gender and women's roles in our interviews. He staunchly opposed his wife's desire to find paid employment outside the home, and he even jokingly threatened her with physical violence. Yet throughout his stories he voiced tremendous respect for women. He recognized Elodia Vassallo de Parodi as the leading force among local hacendados, and he routinely celebrated the role of women as rural activists. Referencing women's reactions to a canceled meeting in 1962, Llamojha remembered peasant women saying:

> "You men, why are you retreating? Why? You are cowards! You don't have pants! Lend us your pants and we'll put them on, and we'll make them respect us!" The women gave us courage.[16]

Certainly, some of that praise may been have related to the fact that his interviewers, Alicia and I, were female. But Llamojha also made such declarations in highly public settings. In a public speech in November 2011, he recalled the work of two women who pressed the village council to fight for Concepción's legal transformation into a provincial district, a feat accomplished in 1954:

> They were the ones who were the driving force. They were like mothers to all of us guys who were dawdling, pulling us by the ears. My ears hurt to this day! Back in those times, women were the ones who made the village council move forward, who made us fight and work for the creation of the district.

Llamojha's descriptions of female activists reflected the fact that campesina women often took a prominent role in rural politics during the mid-twentieth century. Andean women routinely marched at the forefront of the groups of peasants who seized hacienda lands—a strategy based on the calculation that soldiers and police would be less likely to use violence against women than men—and they voiced strong opinions about their communities' problems.[17] Yet women in Peru's rural Andean communities also faced terrible problems of domestic violence and systematic subordination in community affairs.[18] Sexism and respect often operated simultaneously, and Llamojha's stories reveal as much.

Personal Costs

After hearing about Llamojha's activities in the 1950s, I asked him what his happiest times were in those years. He answered:

> I didn't have any happy moments in those years, because I was pursued all the time. From the moment I started, I never relaxed. I didn't give up. Other authorities started to struggle, but they stopped when they were threatened with jail. But not me. I continued, doing what I felt like. Why would I give up?

I followed up by asking what his most difficult moments were during the 1950s.

> When the police started chasing me, defending the hacendados. Because of the hacendados' complaints, the police pursued me. I could never stay here in the house, hardly at all, because I was always running. I never gave up. Each year I went to jail two or three times. Jail was like my home! The hacendados denounced me, and I was hunted everywhere in Peru. The police came at every moment to look for me, to take me prisoner.

One of the many denunciations Llamojha faced related directly to the events of April 1959. The hacendado Abel Alfaro informed Ayacucho's prefect that the police had entered Concepción to investigate death threats that Concepción residents had made against him. By Alfaro's telling, Llamojha then goaded Concepción residents into an armed attack. Alfaro wrote:

> The community, under the instigation of the ringleader don Manuel Llamocca Mitma, rose up against the Police Commission, numbering more than 150 people, surprising the four members [of the police], mistreating them, detaining them for more than twelve hours. In this same circumstance, the community members yelled out and decided to kill me. . . . They lamented that I hadn't gone with the commission, because they would have killed me immediately, but they decided to do that on the first opportunity.[19]

Although the hacendado's version of events had little basis in fact, Peruvian authorities heeded it, and Llamojha had to go into hiding once again. Numerous documents from the latter half of 1959 describe him as a fugitive wanted on charges of "attack by armed force."[20]

Although Llamojha evaded arrest for a time, he was eventually captured and placed in jail. *Sierra*, a Lima newspaper written by Andean migrants in the capital and attentive to issues involving Peru's southern Andes, forcefully denounced this arrest in a story titled "Imprisoned for Defending His Pueblo." After outlining the groundless nature of the charges against Llamojha, *Sierra*'s writers made a public call to Ayacucho's political, judicial, and police authorities: "Your support for the unjust pretensions of the hacendados against the rights of an entire pueblo like Concepción is stimulating a deep resentment among the indigenous population, whose results could be bloody. . . . It is time to intervene and fulfill your duty, in keeping with the law, to act in favor of the humble and destitute pueblo, pressing for justice."[21]

Conditions in jail were extremely difficult, and Llamojha told of being tortured in prison.

> I remember that once, before they took me to Lima, there were around twenty of us imprisoned in the police headquarters. An official was hitting us. They threw us on the ground and they walked around, beating us with a stick. They even walked on top of us, while we writhed in pain.

But Llamojha rarely dwelled on his own persecution during our interviews. Wanting to stress his triumphs as an activist, he instead answered questions about imprisonment with stories about his own ingenuity or the solidarity of police and prison guards. He cast himself as an affable trickster, able at times to earn the sympathies of those paid to punish him. As he continued his answer to the question about his most difficult moments in the 1950s, he spun his reply into one of these ingenuity/solidarity tales.

> The police who didn't know who I was couldn't catch me.
>
> They'd arrive in the community and ask me, "Do you know Manuel Llamojha?"
>
> "Yes, but he's not here," I'd say. "He must be over there, walking around in the hills. He's out with his sheep."
>
> And so they'd take me along! "Let's go! Help us look for him. You know him," they'd say.
>
> I went up into the hills with the police, to search for myself! And when we looked in the bushes, we didn't find me!
>
> "He's not here anymore! Where could he have gone? He must surely be in another pueblo, because he walks around in other towns," I'd say.
>
> The hacendados always denounced me, and they made the police hunt me down. But then the police realized what was going on, and they didn't

pursue me as much. The police received arrest orders to come and capture me. Sometimes they got lazy about coming here, and they'd send me a telegram from Cangallo!

"There is an arrest order against you. Turn yourself in," they'd say to me.

"Turn yourself in! If you don't, we'll come and get you."

I would go, I'd show up, and they'd let me sleep in their houses. The next day: to court.

"Here. We've captured him," they'd say.

Each year, I'd go to jail three times. The police knew who I was, and so they were actually considerate. At night, they'd let me out of prison.

"Go on! Go for a walk in the streets," they'd say.

They'd let me out at nine, I'd leave and go for a stroll in the streets, and then, at eleven at night, I'd return to go to sleep in the jail.

I have sacrificed much for my pueblo. Always imprisoned; every year in jail. But the hacendados didn't manage to frighten me. They didn't scare me.

Llamojha's stories about jail also emphasized how he turned prisons into sites of activism. As he described his monthlong imprisonment in 1958 over the fictitious assault on the Ayrabamba hacienda, he commented:

I arrived at the jail, and all those imprisoned, all the convicts, they already knew me and so they greeted me with applause! When I was in jail, I helped them with their documents, their requests, and that's why all the prisoners knew me. This time, too, I arrived and they clapped. The next day, they asked me to draw up their papers, their documents, requesting their release.

The conditions in Peruvian jails were abysmal. Prisoners suffered from severe overcrowding and poor sanitation and were dependent on family and friends to provide them with enough food to allow their survival. Even basic necessities, including water, were often in short supply.[22] Prisoners generally lacked the financial resources needed to hire good lawyers, making Llamojha's services as a scribe all the more valuable to them. In response to questions about conditions in jail, he again replied in a way that minimized his own suffering and instead highlighted his continuing activism.

In jail, sure, there is mistreatment against those prisoners who behave badly. And in the jail, if you don't have family, there is no one to bring you food. I never suffered for lack of food, because I always wrote up documents for the prisoners and so they'd make me eat. I prepared defense documents. And the judges, the police, they started to complain.

They'd say, "He wants to be in control here!"

Documents stored in Ayacucho's archives similarly show the ways Llamojha continued his struggles from jail, lobbying for prisoners' rights. He penned a lengthy letter of protest while imprisoned in March 1957.[23] The letter demonstrates his jail activism just as it exposes the horrific conditions prisoners endured, as well as the realities of the corruption in the Peruvian judicial system. A portion of the letter read:

> Our situation as prisoners grows more terrible and deplorable each day, because in addition to being deprived of our liberty, we find ourselves deprived of basics like water and other primordial life necessities . . . our stomachs should not be punished in this inhumane way because of the lack of water in the jail. Because of this, many of us have fallen ill.[24]

The letter further charged that three prisoners had died of starvation and urged the president of Ayacucho's Supreme Court to ensure that prisoners' basic needs were met. Not stopping there, Llamojha's letter went on to accuse a provincial court judge of corruption, charging that he kept some individuals imprisoned unjustly while he released other prisoners after they paid him hefty bribes.[25] Such corruption was far from unusual in the Peruvian justice system.[26]

Llamojha also used the discussion of prison to highlight campesinos' enduring support for him. Rather than emphasizing his own victimization and suffering, his jail stories stress peasants' devotion. He told his cVR interviewers that while he was imprisoned,

> three people from Santa Rosa de Ccochamarca [a community in the district of Concepción] came to the court.
>
> They said to the judge, "Lock us up instead! We need him in our pueblo, let him go!"
>
> The judge said, "Why would I lock you up? You haven't committed any crime."
>
> "He has work to do in the pueblo! Let him out!"
>
> They came from [the nearby hacienda of] Pomacocha, too. They took turns coming to see me in jail, when I was detained in the province. They brought me food. The campesinos never abandoned me.

The consequences of Llamojha's activism stretched beyond his constant imprisonment. Some of the costs of his struggles were more literal: his work as an activist did not bring a steady income. I asked him how he earned a living during his years as an activist.

Working in the fields, nothing more. But I didn't have much time to work, because they took me prisoner all the time, all the time.

It was also difficult for Llamojha to find temporary paid employment on nearby haciendas—something many Concepción campesinos relied on for money. He explained:

The hacendados didn't trust me. They'd throw me out. Ayrabamba was the worst; they didn't let me work there.

When I'd go out to travel around the countryside, my wife was always here [in Concepción] with the kids. I'd come back and sometimes, the pueblos would have given me food and I'd bring it to my family. Sometimes I'd be given a little goat and I'd bring it home. That made her happy.

Llamojha was sometimes able to earn money by getting casual office work in the city of Ayacucho.

I worked from time to time. They always gave me work, as a casual job. There were several lawyers who always gave me temporary work in their offices.[27] Because I was a typist, they gave me papers to copy.

I often worked for a man who was a congressional deputy; he's dead now. I don't remember his name. When I came to Ayacucho, they always gave me a little bit of work, even if it was just for a week, sometimes for a month.

An additional factor complicating Llamojha's life involved travel. From the time he began working with Jhajhamarka campesinos in 1948, his dedication to indigenous peasants and their struggles meant that he was frequently away from his home and his family. He helped campesinos in other communities organize, he assisted them in preparing letters of protest and legal documents, and he traveled to Lima to petition government officials on their behalf.

I was Concepción's representative and I was a union representative for various haciendas. The campesinos from the haciendas, they always came and took me to their communities. Sometimes on horse, sometimes on foot. They named me as their representative, and I went from place to

FIG. 3.1 Manuel Llamojha (left), Ayacucho, date unknown. Photo courtesy of Manuel Llamojha Mitma.

place this way. The peasants didn't leave me alone. Campesinos called me everywhere, because of the haciendas' abuses. So I went around with my typewriter. Wherever I arrived, I prepared complaints, documents, and presented them to department authorities and to the government itself. Sometimes, I traveled to Lima and presented these documents in the government palace. The government palace was my home!

Llamojha also spent a great deal of time preparing maps for communities in the Vilcashuamán region, as they were required to present detailed maps of their territory before they could receive government recognition as official indigenous communities. They also needed those maps for use in court, to defend their lands against encroachment by surrounding haciendas.

You make maps with special paper, and it has to be with India ink. All the pueblos asked me to make their maps. I measured with a rope, so that all of the distances would come out exactly right. I'd walk around the entire community and up all the hills using a ten-meter-long rope, showing how far it was from the ground to the top of the hill, all of that. That's why all of the communities got their recognition easily. No authority rejected my maps, because they were done exactly the same way engineers would do them.

Llamojha recalled that he was taking measurements in one community when three delegates from another community approached him.

"Can you come to our community and draw up a map?" they asked me.

"Sure. You name me and I'll go."

They returned to their community and informed a community assembly that I would be making the map.

"What's he going to do?" asked some other community members. "He doesn't know how to do it. He doesn't have a helmet, he doesn't have boots [the standard gear of agricultural engineers]!"

So they hired a teacher from Vilcashuamán instead. He agreed to make the map in exchange for a bull. But he made the map like a schoolboy would, a doodle on cardboard, nothing more. He also prepared the memo himself, requesting recognition for the community, but he didn't do it the way lawyers would. They presented the request to the ministry and the ministry rejected it. So they came back to me.

I went and I spent two days walking across all the hills. You have to measure the distances, the elevations, the paths, all of that, the way engineers do. I followed all of these rules and the community got recognized. I got recognition for all of the communities that belong to Vilcashuamán.

Llamojha's work with campesinos from other communities carried a significant personal cost: it meant that he was regularly away from home and his family had to make do without him. The dual realities of his time away from home—time when he could have been laboring on the family's agricultural plots—and his unpaid work as an activist placed significant financial burdens on his wife and children. I broached the subject of family finances by asking him whether or not his wife, Esther, found paid employment when the family lived in Lima during the early 1950s.

No, not at first. Then something happened and she left and went to work in a house. I was looking for her. She came back after a month.

"Where were you? Should I hit you?" I asked.

FIG. 3.2 Map drawn by Llamojha.

"I was in a house, working." When she came back, she'd brought me some underwear that she had purchased.

"I brought you some underwear. Put it on."

"But what were you doing in another house? Who took you there?" I asked.

"I looked for the job myself."

"But why would you look for it, when you have a life here at home?"

"I wanted to work."

"You escaped!" I said.

She worked for three months in that house. She only came back home once a month. But after three months, she didn't go back to work.

"I'll stay here now." And that's how we spent our life. We understood each other.

I met doña Esther Puklla only once, just over a week before she died, suddenly and unexpectedly, from an aneurysm. She struck me as a woman of sharp wit and quick intelligence. There was much affection between husband and wife. When Llamojha tried on a new hat I had brought him as a gift, doña Esther commented that he looked very handsome and laughingly wondered if some other woman would now steal him away from her.

But in our brief conversations, she noted the hardships she suffered because of her husband's activism. He was absent from their home for long stretches, whether because he was in prison, in other parts of the country working with peasants, in hiding, or even—in 1965—abroad. He was routinely away for months at a time, leaving her alone with their five children. Two of his daughters later told me that they did not see much of their father during their childhood and that their mother was the one who essentially raised them. Llamojha's daughter Hilda recalled, "We almost didn't see him. He'd come and go, come and go. We practically didn't see him; we were just with my mother. He'd always disappear. Sometimes he'd come after a year, after six months, he'd appear. It was like he was a visitor. One day he was here then the next he disappeared."[28]

Doña Esther's life was rendered even more difficult by the family's financial hardships. Besides the brief stint of domestic service Llamojha describes in this chapter, she worked in the family's fields and sold agricultural goods to the nearby Ayrabamba hacienda. Their children also had to work from a young age, something that was not unusual among impoverished Peruvian families, in both the countryside and cities. When my research assistant Alicia Carrasco asked Llamojha's son Walter what his father had done for a living, Walter answered, "My dad spent more of his time organizing people. My mom had a lot of patience with this. We worked with my mom in the fields, we lived doing this. From the time I was a little boy, I went to work on other peoples' fields, to work with harvests, with plantings. That's how we lived." He later added, "We always had trouble with money."[29]

Llamojha's constant imprisonments only added to the family's difficulties. His daughter Hilda recalled how difficult it was when her father was imprisoned. When asked what those times had been like, she answered, "very sad. We grew up alone." She recalled staying in the house with her younger brother Walter, tending to him while her mother went to the Ayrabamba hacienda to sell coca, alcohol, and fruit. "I was left to care for the animals," she recalled, "the chickens and pigs."[30]

As already mentioned, doña Esther was herself a target of repression—

FIG. 3.3 Esther Honorata Puklla, Concepción, 2011. Photo by Alicia Carrasco Gutiérrez.

jailed when police could not find her husband. She also suffered the repeated trauma of seeing her husband imprisoned. Walter recalled, "When I was a boy, I overheard my grandmother Paulina Mitma and my mother talking. They talked and cried, asking why my father had been detained and imprisoned. And they just had to wait until he would be released."[31] Llamojha's brother Emilio recalled how Manuel's imprisonments affected their mother. "She felt it so strongly. My mother would always say to me, 'Go visit your brother.' She always visited him." Llamojha's brother Víctor similarly recalled, "The poor thing always went on foot. I'd say to her, 'Mom, don't go anymore.'"[32]

Police harassment affected Llamojha's children, too. Walter recalled how one evening when he was little, a community member stopped by the house and told Llamojha that the police were looking for him. "My dad said to us, 'When the police come, you're going to tell them that I went to Lima by airplane. That's what you're going to say when they come to look for me.' And then he went and hid. The police came on horseback, they came to the patio. I looked at the police and I wasn't scared. They started to search through the house, from corner to corner. And when they asked me where my dad was, I told them he had gone to Lima in an airplane."[33]

Llamojha's younger siblings were also impacted by his activism. Although his sisters Natividad and Donatilda do not figure prominently in his stories or in the archival record—both women died of cancer, Natividad in 1966, Donatilda in 1997—his brothers Emilio and Víctor themselves assumed leadership positions in Concepción between the 1960s and 1980s. Emilio, four years younger than Manuel, was one of several candidates nominated for governor of Concepción in 1961 and by the middle of the 1960s was serving as Concepción's district mayor.[34] As he reflected on his relationship with Emilio, Llamojha commented:

He's my younger brother, and he never abandoned me. He always went around with me.

Llamojha had a much more complicated relationship with his brother Víctor, fifteen years his junior, and the tensions between the two men had tragic consequences in the 1980s. Víctor likewise took an active role in Concepción's politics, serving several times as governor, justice of the peace, mayor, and community president.[35] Llamojha also has a half-brother, Alejandro Alarcón, born in 1944, eight years after Llamojha's father died. Llamojha speaks with much affection about his youngest sibling. As Llamojha phrased it:

He's the best one of us all.

Despite all the familial challenges and hardships brought on by Llamojha's activism, doña Esther largely supported her husband's struggles. Walter recalled, "She understood. So did my grandmother, . . . She always understood my father's work, and she never complained. Well, sure, there were moments when she complained, but she had to understand."[36] Llamojha's daughter Hilda said much the same. "Sometimes she complained, sometimes she said he was doing good things. 'He's doing all this for a good reason,' she'd say."[37] Llamojha offered a similar perspective. When asked what doña Esther thought of his life as a leader, he replied:

> She was happy, because she struggled, too. She too was taken prisoner. She agreed with the struggle because we all suffered the hacendados' mistreatment. When I was hidden in the puna, she brought me food. She always accompanied me, and she never abandoned me. That's how we spent our lives: in the struggle.

The Power and Perils of Writing

One of Llamojha's most important tools as an activist was his writing. During his years as personero, he wrote dozens of letters decrying the abuses of the hacendados whose estates surrounded Concepción. These excerpts from two of his letters give a feel for both his writing style and the substance of his complaints.

Mr. Constitutional President of the Republic, Dr. Manuel Prado. . . .

In use of the faculty conferred by Article 60 of the Political Constitution of Peru, permit me to direct myself to the Nation's Supreme Head of State, soliciting that your Dispatch dictate orders so that the Ayacucho and Cangallo political authorities give ample and true guarantees to the inhabitants of the district of Concepción, who have been and are victims of the outrages and exactions contrary to justice. Those abuses are perpetrated by the owners of the bordering landholdings, such as Mr. Abel Alfaro Pacheco of the Mejorada Estate and Mrs. María E. vda. de Parodi of the San Germán de Ayrabamba hacienda.[38] Trying to usurp the communal terrains of the community I represent, they seize the comuneros' animals. Mr. Alfaro commits these acts frequently, even daily, with the cattle that pasture within our demarcated lands. He does this on his whim and caprice, with the goal of imposing fines upon the owners, without showing consideration or even compassion for the humble and defenseless Indians' tears. . . .

It is the public and well-known truth that the inhabitants of the district I represent are victims of abuses and outrages. They are lugging the crucifix of their tragedy under a black cloak of oblivion, and still the doors of justice will not open for them. For this reason, many of them, unable to continue supporting the weight of adversity that destiny has imposed upon them, have found themselves forced to abandon their lands because of their poverty and migrate to this country's capital in search of their daily bread to sustain their offspring.

As such: I implore you to accept my petition and order the respective authority to give ample guarantees to Concepción's inhabitants so that they will not be harassed by these men. Concepción's community members can no longer continue living in permanent anxiety, threatened by the storms of gratuitous suffering. This is justice.[39]

With phrases like "the crucifix of their tragedy" and "their daily bread," Llamojha infused his letters with references to Christianity. In a letter that followed the 1959 police assault on Concepción, he wrote to the director of Indian affairs using his ideas, his words, and his typewriter to contest Peru's highly unfair political system:

The pueblo, threatened by abusive storms, presented various memos before administrative authorities, asking that they be granted personal as well as patrimonial guarantees. They also asked for the hacendado Alfaro to abstain from invading the communal lands bordering his "Mejorada" estate and unjustly seizing community members' animals in order to charge them money . . . but, unfortunately, we have not merited the grace of being protected with justice, nor have we even been provided with guarantees. Instead, today the residents of the pueblo in general are feeling harassed with hostility by the police Mr. Alfaro brought from Ayacucho. And this is the reason that compels us to appear before you, Mr. Director, in demand of justice.[40]

No doubt because of the very power of Llamojha's words, unsympathetic government authorities and local hacendados tried to use his writing skills against him, routinely accusing him of writing lies or composing falsified documents. As noted, those denunciations fit into a common historical practice of regional Andean elites blaming "indios leídos" (literate Indians) for fomenting troubles in the countryside.[41] These accusations also resonated with an especially common complaint voiced by indigenous peasants themselves: that *tinterillos* (shyster scribes) abused their literacy for personal gain, tricking illiterate campesinos into signing falsified documents. Those fraudulent documents cheated indigenous peasants of resources, committed them to actions they did not want to take, and slandered individuals they actually supported.[42] Government officials and hacendados mobilized these ideas to try to discredit Llamojha.

In a 1958 letter, Cangallo's subprefect asserted that all the complaints Llamojha had raised in a letter to the Peruvian president were unfounded.[43] Ayacucho's prefect, in turn, wrote the director general of government to inform him that the complaint Llamojha had sent was "completely false" and that none of the hacendados Llamojha had denounced had committed abuses. The prefect also charged that Llamojha enjoyed living a life of ease and that whenever he fell short of money to "live lazily" in Lima, "he comes to Concepción to promote conflicts and alarm the members of the community by making them believe that the aforementioned neighboring hacendados want to take away their animals and try to make them work on their estates without the due remuneration." Llamojha's goal, the prefect maintained, was to encourage community members to "gather together a bag of money so that he can travel to the capital of the republic, promising them that he will denounce these 'imaginary' facts to the President of the Republic and to the Minister of Government."[44]

The accusations against Llamojha sometimes bordered on the absurd. In one such case he was accused of "crimes against the public faith" in making counterfeit money. The "money" in question was clearly nothing more than the drawings of a schoolchild.[45]

> A boy from the school was playing, making drawings. He was happy with just one color, doodles. Back then, there used to be markets where they gather cattle for sale. This boy went there and tried to pass this money off, buying something. [The hacendado Abel] Alfaro was there. He called the boy to the side and said, "Tell them that Llamojha gave it to you."
>
> Then Alfaro loudly asked, "Who gave it to you?"
>
> "Llamojha gave it to me," the boy said.
>
> The two of us were imprisoned. I was in jail for a month. The boy for eight months.

FIG. 3.4 Counterfeit bills used as evidence against Llamojha. Courtesy of Ayacucho Regional Archive.

The counterfeit money case was only one of the forgery charges Llamojha faced. Others were legion, and they carried serious consequences. He was imprisoned for nearly seven months in 1957, charged with forgery, usurpation of authority, and crimes against public peace for forging birth certificates and municipal documents.[46] While he did—as he laughingly admitted—occasionally forge birth and marriage certificates for desperate campesinos, most of the forgery charges against him were grossly exaggerated if not entirely fictitious. The hacendado Abel Alfaro informed police in August 1959 that a letter of complaint sent by two Concepción campesinos had to be a fake, as there were no such persons in the community. Alfaro's conclusion was that the letter "must be one of so many works of craftiness and wickedness" perpetrated by Llamojha.[47]

Accusations of forgery also figured in local hacendados' efforts to have national authorities revoke Llamojha's status as Concepción's personero legal. The hacendados Abel Alfaro and Alfonso Martinelli began their effort to oust him from his role as personero in June 1958. In a letter to the minister of labor and Indian affairs, Alfaro and Martinelli decried Llamojha's "lack of moral suitability" for the post of personero, calling him a "known agitator and inciter who has a long criminal record."[48] As evidence, the two hacendados referred to his previous imprisonments and included copies of a police report claiming that he was inciting local campesinos to invade a hacienda. In addition to several other accusations, their letter also claimed that he had forged a receipt.[49] The letter achieved its desired effect. A subsequent government letter referred to the hacendados' charges and repeated a specious police claim that Llamojha resided permanently in Lima, rendering him unable to serve as personero.[50] Action was swift: on July 22, 1958, Ministerial Resolution 251 officially removed Llamojha from his post as personero.[51]

I was named personero numerous times. The hacendados always tried to annul my election. They presented denunciations to get my election annulled, but the community always named me again. They only named me. The struggle is really lovely when the masses are united.

Concepción's campesinos angrily contested Llamojha's removal. In a letter to the minister of labor and Indian affairs, over one hundred Concepción peasants declared that "the whole community makes our energetic protest against the wicked maneuvers" of the hacendados Alfaro and Martinelli leading the Bureau of Indian Affairs to have "unduly dictated the revocation of the mandate of our Personero Legal the Indian Manuel J. Llamocca Mitma." The letter stressed that Llamojha had done nothing wrong and emphasized that as the community had elected him, only the community had the right to remove him. The letter further asserted that the hacendados Alfaro and Martinelli had orchestrated his removal so as to "be able to continue committing seizures of animals and usurpation of communal terrains."[52] Passionate statements of support for Llamojha also came from Lima. Seventy-five members of the Concepción migrant club petitioned the director general of Indian affairs, denouncing the fact that Llamojha had been ousted because of a complaint "formulated by the gamonales, exploiters, usurpers, abusers" who utilized "unfounded slanders, with unreliable and untrue documents . . . because they see that [Llamojha] is moral and he doesn't permit them to perpetrate abuses against the Indians he represents."[53]

I told Llamojha about these documents and asked him to speak some more about how local hacendados pressed higher authorities to revoke his personero status. He shared the following story about how local hacendados arranged for a new community election, hoping that Concepción's campesinos would elect someone else to the post of personero.

The high boss of the Ayacucho police, the Cangallo subprefect, and the Ayacucho inspector of Indian affairs, all of them came, and with seven police on top of that. A huge number of people came.

The plaza was completely packed with people. Demetrio Gutiérrez was

there, too. He was an employee of the Ayrabamba hacienda, but he never did anything in their favor. Instead, he acted for Concepción. He walked around the plaza talking to people, explaining to them why they should vote for me and not for others.

The hacendado from Pacomarca, Juan Echegaray, came after him. He walked among the people, telling them not to vote for me. I was in the doorway of the town hall, and he came, making insinuations. I was standing, just like this, and there was a woman sitting down beside me. The owner of Pacomarca approached her.

He spoke to the woman in Quechua, "Hey, woman! You shouldn't vote for Llamojha!"[54]

The woman answered in Quechua, "That's how we're going to vote, sir."

"Listen, woman, damn it! He's worthless!"

"Well, then we'll vote for him until he's worth something!"

Enraged, the hacendado went into the town hall. The voting started, and everyone voted for me. 380. 380 voted for me, fewer voted for the others, and I ended up elected. So the hacendados presented a document requesting that my election be annulled. They annulled my victory, and once again there were elections.

Ayacucho authorities continued to use accusations of forgery and trickery to cast doubt on Llamojha's actual popularity in Concepción.[55] Despite these accusations, he continually won reelection as personero. In June 1960, Concepción campesinos once again voted for a personero legal and chose Llamojha by an overwhelming majority: 356 of 532 votes. His next closest competitor won only seventy votes.[56] The migrant newspaper *Sierra* reported Llamojha's victory, noting that it had come despite the fact that the hacendados had offered free cane alcohol for every vote against him.[57] Local hacendados, however, refused to accept the vote. Abel Alfaro Pacheco and Juan Echegaray pressed Cangallo's subprefect to hold another election; the hacendados also pressured—and even bribed—community members to vote against Llamojha.[58] Yet he won that election, too.[59]

Such displays of support notwithstanding, Peruvian government officials still refused to accept Llamojha's reelection. Determined to get his reelection as personero ratified, Concepción's campesinos looked in a new direction: they petitioned Peru's largest national campesino organization, the CCP, for help. Their August 1960 letter stated that as they were "fearful of once again being victims of a cunning ploy, we turn to this great campesino institution, begging that you protect us from this class of outrages and coercion that is being used against the sovereign will of a community."[60] The CCP answered this 1960 petition, lobbying the minister of labor and Indian affairs to ratify Llamojha's election.[61] This letter foretold a major political turn in Llamojha's political life: just two years later, he was elected secretary general of the CCP.

FOUR

For Justice, Land, and Liberty

NATIONAL AND INTERNATIONAL LEADERSHIP, 1961–1968

Greeted at the airport by a cheering delegation carrying flowers and flags, Manuel Llamojha arrived in China in 1965 at the height of his political prominence. The 1960s brought a series of major triumphs for him: he helped lead Ayacucho's most famous land struggle, he ran for a seat in Peru's national congress, and he was elected leader of the CCP. His work even moved onto the global stage, as he received and accepted a series of international invitations, traveling to Cuba, the Soviet Union, and China as a representative of Peru and its peasantry. But the 1960s were also years of terrifying Cold War repression in Peru. Llamojha was jailed and tortured in a 1963 military campaign against leftists, and he was incarcerated for a full year after his return from China, accused of being a dangerous communist.

The 1960s proved to be a dramatic decade for Latin American leftists. The 1959 Cuban Revolution inspired and emboldened many men and women— especially the young—leading them to believe that revolutionary change was a real possibility. Many became active in leftist politics, pushing established parties to transform or founding entirely new parties. Some traveled abroad, visiting socialist and communist countries to deepen their political educations and build global support for their efforts at home. A few joined guerrilla fronts, aiming to realize revolution through armed struggle. This vigorous political activism, and the prospect of a revolution along Cuban lines, terrified many in the military, in the government, and in the Catholic Church, just as it frightened many citizens—rich, middling, and even some poor—who feared that the traditional order was under attack. In the context of the global Cold War, many Latin American leftists found themselves harassed, jailed, and sometimes even killed by their governments. Throughout much of Latin America, then, the experience of the 1960s was characterized as much by incredible political excitement and energy as by fear and biting repression.[1]

Without question the 1960s were turbulent years in Peru, and Llamojha jumped into his national role during a particularly tumultuous period in Peru's history. Elected secretary general of the CCP in 1962, he headed Peru's largest campesino organization at precisely the moment when agrarian struggles reached a climax in the country. Many members of Peru's military believed that agrarian reform was the only solution to these troubles, and when it appeared that the reformist presidential candidate—a young architect named Fernando Belaúnde Terry—was going to lose the 1962 election to the now-conservative APRA, forestalling any chance of agrarian reform, the military took action. Soldiers seized power in a military coup in July 1962.[2] Shortly thereafter, the military government introduced regional agrarian reform, targeting Cuzco's La Convención Valley, where agrarian conflict had sparked national concerns. Peruvians returned to the polls in June 1963, and this time Belaúnde won.[3]

Belaúnde had made agrarian reform central to his energetic election campaign, and campesinos throughout Peru's Andean sierra took him at his word. Many peasants were so excited about the prospect of agrarian reform—and so determined to see it become a reality—that they began a wave of land invasions on the very day of Belaúnde's inauguration, seizing hacienda land. More and more land invasions followed, affecting almost every department in Peru's Andean sierra. Ultimately, as many as 300,000 campesinos took part in these land seizures.[4] Tens of thousands of campesinos also joined rural unions and federations of unions, bringing unprecedented levels of organization to the countryside. President Belaúnde responded with a mix of violence and reform. He deployed special assault troops to evict land invaders by force, and in 1964 he introduced a limited agrarian reform law.[5] Belaúnde again turned to military force when three guerrilla fronts launched armed struggles in 1965, ordering a massive military assault that left an estimated eight thousand rural, indigenous Peruvians dead.[6] Llamojha lived, worked, and struggled in this highly charged political climate.

Fighting for Pomacocha

Llamojha began the 1960s by participating in several prominent rural conflicts in the province of Cangallo, broadening his reputation as an important political activist. The best known of those countryside struggles was the fight for the Pomacocha hacienda.[7]

> Pomacocha was a hell. It was a hacienda owned by the nuns of the Convento de Santa Clara, and there were always wicked abuses there. Pomacocha began to organize in '60 through the residents in Lima, and they started to organize in the community, too. So in '61 they called me, and with Alberto Izarra, we started to orient the people, holding meetings. We also started to present documents where we pressed for Pomacocha to be declared a community, a pueblo.

Alberto Izarra was a young Pomacocha man who was studying law at the University of San Marcos in Lima and had begun working with the CCP at the end of the 1950s. Llamojha worked closely with Izarra and a number of other Pomacocha-born university students.

> We organized the people. The people there, they are really brave. The women especially. The administrators of the hacienda were from the area itself and they abused their brothers. So one night, a group of women organized and they took these two administrators from their room. They stripped the administrators naked in the plaza, they tied them up with rope, and they made them get on donkeys. They made them get on two donkeys, naked! They tied them to the donkeys with ropes and took them to the puna. From Pomacocha, it's about three kilometers to the puna. They left them there with all their things in the puna, naked.

By ousting the estate's administrators, Pomacocha's indigenous peasants effectively seized the hacienda. That seizure occurred in October 1961. Casting the invasion as a strike against the legacies of colonialism, Llamojha told his CVR interviewers:

> We took it in '61, in October. On the 12th of October, in memory of Columbus!

The Pomacocha seizure garnered a tremendous amount of attention from regional authorities and the media, with many proclaiming the hacienda's takeover to be the work of communist militants. Llamojha described some of that reaction when he spoke about his encounter with Ayacucho's Bishop

Otoniel Alcedo, who traveled to Concepción in the hopes of negotiating the return of Pomacocha's lands to the Convento de Santa Clara. Llamojha's story emphasizes the disconnect between his reputation as a powerful political leader and his appearance as a humble Andean campesino. Once again, he far exceeded people's racialized expectations of what an indigenous peasant could accomplish.

> Otoniel Alcedo came here [to Concepción] and he went to Juan Zea's house. I was in the fields and when I got back to my home, they called me to Zea's house.
>
> The bishop looked at me and said, "You're Manuel Llamojha?"
>
> "Yes, that's me."
>
> "But how can that be? The hacendados describe you as a lion, but now I see you and you look like an angel!"

Because Llamojha played a role in Pomacocha's seizure, regional authorities were quick to accuse him of encouraging other land invasions in Ayacucho, and his notoriety grew significantly.[8] In April 1962 a civil guard blamed him for the seizure of a hacienda in nearby Vilcashuamán. The guard reported that several campesinos had informed him that "they had received an order from the President of the Peasantry of Pomacocha, Manuel Llamocca Mitma," commanding them to invade the hacienda.[9] A Cangallo hacendado subsequently complained that Llamojha had visited his hacienda and generated problems with his indigenous peasant tenants.[10] Cangallo's subprefect, in turn, reported that Llamojha was "of the COMMUNIST partisan tendency" and that "being a current member of the National Confederation of Campesinos of Peru [sic], he habitually makes visits to districts with the end of agitating the masses to get them to carry out invasions."[11] These complaints show how regional authorities used Llamojha as a political scapegoat, blaming upheaval on just one activist as a means to minimize the scale of campesinos' anger and circumvent deeper reflection on the legitimacy of their concerns. Labeling Llamojha a communist served a similar purpose: it obscured his social justice motivations by casting him as someone driven solely by the mandates of a much-feared political party.

Llamojha also poured much of his energy into organizing Ayacucho campesinos at the provincial level, working to establish the Federación Campesina Provincial de Cangallo (Cangallo Provincial Peasant Federation). Llamojha planned to launch that federation in March 1962, at what was to be called the First Convention of Campesinos from the Province of Cangallo.[12] Llamojha and his fellow convention organizers sent personalized invitations to community personeros throughout Cangallo, urging them to send delegations to the convention. Those invitations featured Llamojha's eloquent outrage at the devastating socioeconomic legacies of colonial oppression. One such invitation explained:

> The cruel and terrible tragedies that we are suffering are now unbearable. We have been humiliated for more than 400 years of pain and misery, awaiting the miracle, the grace and the will of the landowning oligarchy.... Each day the price of basic life necessities rises, to the point that the poor cannot acquire vital foods for the sustenance of our homes. Numerous infants suffer from hunger and cold, waiting for the miserable pieces of stale bread that their parents have to get at the cost of sweat and tears. Practically thousands of innocent babies are condemned to die of hunger. The poor, by the grace of those who oppress us, do not have the right to life nor to health.

The invitation closed with a series of exhortations:

FOR JUSTICE, LAND, AND LIBERTY
FOR THE ECONOMIC LIBERATION OF OUR FATHERLAND
FOR THE PROVINCIAL UNION OF CANGALLO
FOR THE STUDENT-WORKER-PEASANT FRONT OF CANGALLO PROVINCE
LAND OR DEATH
JUSTICE OR REVOLUTION
LONG LIVE CHRIST THE KING[13]

The language in these documents conveyed the political spirit of the early 1960s: a sense of righteous indignation; a readiness to make bold, aggressive demands of the state; and an insistence that change must come immediately. Similar documents were authored by countless other activists throughout Peru and Latin America, and "Land or Death" was the often-repeated motto of Peruvian rural mobilizations. But Llamojha was always his own man: adding the phrase "Long Live Christ the King" was something most activists of the period would not have done, as they usually eschewed traditional Christian convictions in favor of Marxism's staunchly materialist visions.[14]

The planned congress generated considerable anxiety among Ayacucho authorities, and those authorities used the Cold War specter of communism to justify their drastic actions. Cangallo's subprefect asserted that the use of phrases like "Land or Death" in the invitations was proof that Llamojha and the other congress organizers were "nothing but instruments who are carrying out orders," obeying outside directives "of international character." Here, "international character" was synonymous with international communism. The subprefect also asserted that the invitation's high quality—it was printed at a professional print shop—confirmed the involvement of outsiders, as "MANUEL LLAMOCCA MITMA is not in any condition to spend a single cent from his private wealth, because he doesn't have any income and he does not have any known job, particularly for the printing of propaganda."[15]

Ayacucho's prefect quickly banned the congress, justifying his decision by insisting that its true goals were "purely demagogic and of a political character."[16] Civil guards then arrested Llamojha, claiming that he had several leftist leaflets in his possession and had been witnessed painting leftist graffiti in Pomacocha.[17] Several weeks after his arrest, civil guards forced him to affix his signature to a document that identified him as "the Communist leader Manuel Llamocca Mitma." In signing that document, he agreed to abstain from organizing political meetings unless he had formal legal authorization to do so.[18]

Llamojha's arrest on March 28, 1962, came one day after the major Peruvian newspaper *Expreso* published a lengthy story sympathetic to the canceled congress and featuring an interview with Llamojha himself. The article's bold headline read "PEASANT CONVENTION AGAINST SLAVE-LIKE FORMS OF LABOR," and in the interview, Llamojha explained: "There is neither politics nor communism behind our movement. It is a genuine action of communities that want the government to protect them from atrocious abuses that hacendados commit against them."[19] This lengthy article was extremely embarrassing for Ayacucho's top authorities. Because the story's writers portrayed Llamojha as a humble, devoutly Christian, self-educated campesino upset by extreme suffering in the countryside, the article made the prefect look like an uncaring reactionary when he deemed Llamojha a radical extremist. Worse still, the article led national authorities to send the prefect a series of highly critical telegrams that chastised him for his actions in the countryside.[20] It is hardly surprising, then, that Llamojha was arrested the very day after this story was printed. Although the *Expreso* story triggered his arrest, it also offered him national political exposure. Much more such attention soon followed.

Onto the National Stage

In 1962, Llamojha made his first (and only) foray into formal electoral politics: he ran for Peru's Chamber of Deputies as a candidate for the Frente de Liberación Nacional (National Liberation Front; FLN). The FLN was an electoral front created by the Peruvian Communist Party in 1960, designed to group together progressive forces for the 1962 presidential and congressional elections.[21] Llamojha clearly did not have sufficient financial resources to mount a major election campaign. The only piece of pro-Llamojha election propaganda I found in the archives was a simple handbill, typed rather than professionally printed. It said:

MANUEL LLAMOJHA MITMA

PEASANT CANDIDATE FOR DEPUTY FOR THE

DEPARTMENT OF AYACUCHO

MANUEL LLAMOJHA MITMA, authentic son of the heroic province of Cangallo, has been unanimously proclaimed by the pueblos of this area as candidate for deputy, to carry the voice of the peasantry to the National Parliament. A genuine son of the great masses of workers of the countryside, he has a trajectory of struggle in defense of campesino interests to his credit. He has also struggled concretely for Agrarian Reform, which means land for he who works it. His life is consecrated to fight for the demands of the indigenous peasantry, forgotten by the laws and vilely exploited by gamonales. Campesinos . . . are now determined to fight for their demands in the ballot boxes as one step in this fight. And for that, they have chosen a campesino who has come from the core of the Indian race, a man like Llamojha Mitma, who has demonstrated his spirit of struggle and sacrifice for their interests. Victim of slander, falsehoods, and intrigues, Llamojha has suffered unjust imprisonment many times, but he always carries forward the flags of campesino demands: Land and Liberty; Progress and the Struggle for National Liberation.

The Ayacucho National Liberation Front has included him in its list of candidates and as such, Llamojha Mitma will also struggle for the proposals of this revolutionary movement, adapted to our historic moment. Llamojha, in this sense, is the one chosen to represent his oppressed brothers for, as a member of the Confederación Campesina del Perú, he is also fighting for the organization of the peasantry. He likewise fights for every work of regional progress, as our province is one of the most forgotten ones of the country and we have the right to have our voice heard and demand action for the popular good.

Citizen, campesino, worker, artisan, small industrialist, intellectual, men and women, vote for MANUEL LLAMOJHA MITMA, guarantor of revolutionary struggle and of popular fervor.

LONG LIVE THE AGRARIAN REFORM AND NATIONAL LIBERATION!

Cangallo, February 1962[22]

I shared this document with Llamojha and asked him if he had wanted to enter Peru's congress.

Yes, to be a deputy. I didn't get enough votes. It was at the last minute, too. The campesinos in Lima proposed me.

"You should run, because you have ties with all the people, with the high-ranking people in the court. You should run!" they said to me.

So, I ran. Maybe I would have won, but here in Concepción, there were three elements, damned ones [the abusive district authorities Grimaldo Castillo, Raúl Agüero, and Joaquín Chávez], and they started to denounce me. They sent messages everywhere, saying that I was a stranger, that I was a fugitive who walked around, that I was an illiterate. They presented documents and denunciations against me, and for that reason, there wasn't enough of a vote. Sure, there were some votes, but it wasn't sufficient.

Although Llamojha today insists that he never belonged to a communist party and never self-identified as a communist, Ayacucho authorities took his congressional run as further evidence of his communist activities.[23] A November 1962 police report on him asserted: "Manuel Llamocca Mitma is an active militant of the Frente de Liberación Nacional (F.L.N.), and as such, is developing an intense campaign in favor of communism among the campesinos of the Province of Cangallo." The report noted that Llamojha "dedicates himself to making a political campaign in favor of his Party . . . pursuing as his principal objective the formation of Workers' Unions on these haciendas, demanding a salary increase." The report closed with the comment that Llamojha "maintains tight ties with the principal leaders of communism and *fidelism* [devotion to Cuba's Fidel Castro] in the Capital of the Republic."[24]

The year 1962 was crucial for Llamojha. His failed congressional run was followed by a major political victory: he was elected secretary general of the CCP. Founded in 1947, the CCP aimed to represent all of Peru's campesinos and fight for their political, economic, and social welfare. The CCP's work had only barely begun when General Manuel Odría seized control of Peru in his 1948 coup. That coup initiated a period of significant political repression in Peru, and the CCP had to suspend all of its activities and efforts. It was only in the late 1950s, after the restoration of civilian rule and a return to democracy in 1956, that activists began efforts to revive the CCP. It was not until July 1962, however, that the peasant organization was large or strong enough to hold a national convention, its Second National Peasant Congress. At that convention, Llamojha was elected secretary general.[25] He became the second such leader in the confederation's history.

> There was a national congress in Lima in '62, and in this congress they named me secretary general of the Confederación Campesina del Perú. That is, president. They named me because I always attended the meetings, representing Ayacucho and my pueblo. After that, they never let me go. Not for anything. They always appointed me in the congresses.

I asked Llamojha if his election had surprised him.

> No. People had already been talking to me about it.
> "You have to be secretary! Because you're the only one who goes from pueblo to pueblo. You know what the peasantry's struggle is like," they said.
> I still didn't want to do it, but they obligated me. "It has to be you," they said.

Llamojha added that one of the individuals who pressed him to accept the nomination was Saturnino Paredes, one of the most important figures in Peru's twentieth-century left. Paredes was a lawyer from the department of Ancash, and he came from an Andean peasant family.[26] At the time of the 1962 CCP congress, he was a prominent member of the Peruvian Communist Party and had served as legal advisor to the CCP since its revival in the late 1950s. In 1964, Paredes and several of his political allies broke from the pro-Soviet members of the Peruvian Communist Party and founded a rival Peruvian Communist Party that proclaimed support for communist China. The 1964 divide of the Peruvian Communist Party mirrored the larger Sino-Soviet split and reflected major ideological differences in Peru.[27] Members of the pro-Soviet party, known after the divide as the Partido Comunista del Perú-Unidad (Peruvian Communist Party-Unity), regarded the urban working class as the key revolutionary group and advocated a gradualist approach toward revolution that did not rule out cooperation with the state. Those belonging to Paredes's pro-China party, the Partido Comunista del Perú-Bandera Roja (Peruvian Communist Party-Red Flag), cast peasants as the true revolutionaries and rejected the possibility of statist collaboration.[28] Llamojha described how he met Paredes:

> I met him in 1946, I believe. My institution [the migrant club] in Lima was looking for a lawyer. We had found one already, but he didn't look after us well. So, some campesinos recommended that we go to see Paredes, because he was like a campesino, he knew what the countryside was like. So we went and he oriented us in what we should do, he advised us. He became Concepción's legal advisor.

Llamojha also told his CVR interviewers:

> Paredes always called me when he was in Ayacucho. He communicated with me, to get me to go to meetings of the Confederación [Campesina del Perú] before I was a member. So, I always went to the assemblies.

Llamojha's relationship with Paredes was crucial for Llamojha's activist career. It was in large part due to the two men's friendship that Llamojha began working with the CCP, and it is doubtful that he would have become the CCP's secretary general without Paredes's support. Paredes was simply that important a figure in the CCP and in the Peruvian left.[29] And the ultimate break between the two men would have perilous consequences for Llamojha's political career.

Participants in the 1962 CCP congress that elected Llamojha secretary general considered a range of issues. He explained:

> It was always about the peasantry: how to guide them, how to fight against feudalism, against the hacendados. How to fight and be united so as to be able to triumph.

At the congress, participants discussed Peruvian campesinos' socioeconomic situation, the shape of a "Radical Agrarian Reform," and the need for a worker-peasant alliance. Delegates also explored peasants' constitutional and electoral rights.[30] Participants ultimately approved a lengthy document outlining the CCP's statutes and its declaration of principles. That document affirmed:

The fundamental objective of the Confederación Campesina del Perú is the consistent struggle for the liberation of the peasantry from oppression and the exploitation of the latifundio, through the suppression of the semifeudal system of production in the countryside and the elimination of servitude, through the delivery of land to the campesinos who work it.[31]

Beyond calling for agrarian reform, the CCP also lobbied on behalf of Peruvian campesinos.[32] As CCP legal advisor, Paredes traveled to La Convención Valley in Cuzco in December 1962. Between 1958 and 1962, campesinos in the region had struggled to take control of the hacienda lands they worked. Together with prominent Trotskyist activist Hugo Blanco—the man who ultimately became twentieth-century Peru's most (in)famous rural activist—the area's campesinos seized so much hacienda land that the military government sent detachments of civil guards into the region in October 1962.[33] Paredes met with peasants from the beleaguered region and spoke out against state repression.[34] Llamojha himself began working with La Convención campesinos during the 1960s, probably sometime after Hugo Blanco's high-profile arrest in May 1963, as the two men did not meet until the 1970s.

While he criticized Hugo Blanco during our interviews, Llamojha always spoke very highly of La Convención campesinos themselves, particularly about those from the area of Quillabamba, where the struggles over land were especially heated.

For me, Quillabamba campesinos were the most united, the strongest. I was there with them, in the constant fight with the hacendados, back when the haciendas still existed.

We carried out assemblies, meetings about the abuses that the hacendados were committing. There was a hacendado, Romainville, who had a really big estate, and he was selling the hacienda. He had set the estate's value to include the residents: two thousand adults; fifteen hundred kids. That's how the hacienda was appraised! I arrived in time and I immediately prepared a document and got the communities of this sector to sign. I returned to Lima and presented it straight to the government. That's why the pueblos respected me. When there was an issue, they'd call me here. Cuzco called me. I was in Cuzco a lot, in Quillabamba. Quillabamba is my pueblo. They love me a lot. I defended the struggle, you see. That's how it was.

"You have to come! You have to come!" they'd say. They'd send a commission to bring me. They wouldn't leave me alone.

Llamojha also worked on behalf of peasants in other parts of Peru. Together with the Pomacocha lawyer and CCP activist Alberto Izarra, Llamojha urged campesinos in the department of Huancavelica to attend the First Congress of Comuneros and Campesinos of Huancavelica. Their open letter asserted:

> Campesinos and community members of Huancavelica: remember the blood that has spilled, the blood of campesinos spilled by the hundreds and thousands in recent times. Remember that at this moment, hundreds of campesinos are agonizing in jail for having fought for our cause. Remember the persecutions and sufferings that we undergo each day because of the big landlords and the police force at their service. Let us advance along the path shown us by [eighteenth-century indigenous leaders] Túpac Amaru, Atusparia, and all the martyrs of the Agrarian Reform, recovering our lands and permanently liquidating the latifundio and the servitude that we suffer. Let us march united as class brothers, and in this way we will win.[35]

By invoking key historical figures like Túpac Amaru and Atusparia, Llamojha was using history to inspire indigenous peasants and remind them of all that their predecessors had accomplished. The letter also shows an unmistakable outrage at the violence, exploitation, and abuse campesinos were enduring and reveals a staunch determination to fight for change.

Just as he labored to organize Huancavelica campesinos, Llamojha worked with peasants across much of the country, including the departments of Piura, Cuzco, Ancash, and Junín.[36]

As secretary general, I had to travel all across Peru. People called me from everywhere to hold assemblies. In every place, there were always abuses by hacendados. So they called me, and I went to all the areas of Peru to carry out departmental and provincial assemblies, congresses. I've seen all of Peru. All the campesinos called on me. Many times in many places. I went by foot; one day's walk, two days' walk, on foot. That's how the peasants brought me to hold assemblies, congresses, to inform them about the campesino movement of Peru.

When I went to their pueblos, peasants waited for me outside their towns, and when I approached they'd greet me with a harp, with a flag, and with music, with trumpets. They received me like I was God!

Llamojha's work as secretary general of the CCP was dramatic and exciting, but it also generated significant problems for him. Most basically, he earned no income for the days and months he spent working on campesinos' behalf. I asked him if he earned a salary as secretary general of the CCP.

No, you don't earn anything there. Instead, you have to sacrifice yourself. Sure, the campesinos paid your bus fare when they summoned you to different pueblos. They'd pay for a return trip, but nothing more. You don't earn anything, you just have to struggle. Struggle to liberate the campesinos from the clutches of the gamonales. I fought hard.

Llamojha's work as secretary general of the CCP also meant that he was targeted for arrest by Peru's 1962–1963 military government. In January 1963, it arrested and imprisoned more than eight hundred—and perhaps as many as two thousand—leftist political activists, peasants, students, and union leaders, including Llamojha, claiming that a communist conspiracy was afoot in Peru. The mass arrests were a classic example of Cold War political oppression in Latin America: no actual communist conspiracy existed; the government was using repression to try to dampen revolutionary fervor.[37] Llamojha spoke at length about this arrest to his CVR interviewers. His stories again emphasize the theme of surprise, stressing authorities' shock at the disparity between his reputation and his humble appearance as an indigenous peasant.

They made us get in the vehicle, and they brought me here [to the city of Ayacucho]. In the truck, they tied our hands to the handrails, and they brought us . . . rain started to attack us. And so they brought me here, completely sopping wet.

A fellow community member lived on Grau Avenue, and so I said to the commander, "Please, take me via Grau Avenue. I have a relative there, I'm going to let him know what's happening." So, they took me. I went with a guard and knocked on his door.

"I've been taken prisoner. Please bring me some clothes," I said.

They took me to the precinct on Garcilaso de la Vega Street. And there I was. I arrived sopping wet. There was a Sergeant Ochoa there, who used to work in the Concepción police post. He was really good to me.

"They've brought you like this?" So, he went out and he brought me a fourth of cognac and a cup of coffee. I drank down that whole fourth!

Then, a short while later, an order came for [Sergeant] Ochoa. There was no other civil guard, because they'd all left with orders. He was alone.

"Something is happening," he said to me. And then he locked me up in the cell, in the dark.

Later that night, at midnight, the raid began. Two generals came in, and they called to Ochoa.

"Ochoa, bring out the prisoner." And so he brought me out. They didn't believe it was me.

"I told you to bring Llamojha out."

"Well, it's him."

"How can this be him?"

I showed my identity documents.

"It's him! Look, here he is! This is who the hacendados are afraid of! Put the handcuffs on him." They looked for them, but there weren't any.

"Then use a rope."

Nothing. There wasn't even rope, because all of the civil guards had left, they'd gone to capture prisoners, political activists, and they'd taken all of their equipment with them. So, because there weren't handcuffs or rope, they ordered six soldiers to arm themselves, six soldiers got ready. The generals took me by the arms.

And when they were getting themselves ready, a guard who knew me—because I was constantly being taken prisoner—said, "but General, we don't need to take him with rope. We don't need anything. He can go on his own. You just tell him to go to a certain place, and he'll go on his own. You don't need to take him as a prisoner."

"How are we going to let him go alone? He's the high-ranking leader around here, number one in all Peru. How are we going to send him on his own?"

So, two generals took me by the arms. Three soldiers were in front with their machine guns, and three soldiers behind, too. They took me like this from the precinct over to the precinct in front of the market.

When I entered, there were a lot of political prisoners there. They'd brought a lot of people, it was completely full. So, I went in to greet them, but the guards wouldn't let me. They took me to a cell. The others were just in a room. I was the only one in a cell, they didn't put me with the others. I was in that cell for three nights. Sure, my relatives brought me stuff, they brought me a mattress to sleep on. But I wasn't allowed to sleep. The generals would come in, they'd come up to the cell door, and, from behind the bars, they'd force me to get up.

"Get up! Stand up with your hands behind your head!" they'd say.

They'd have me against the wall, and then they'd go, and I was so tired

I'd fall back into bed. But they'd come back again and get me up. It was like this all night. They tortured me; for three nights it was like this.

After three days, they brought us out and they took us to Lima.

In one of our interviews, Llamojha further explained:

They sent me to Lima in a helicopter together with other political prisoners, and we arrived at the Republican Guard barracks. At that time, I was secretary general of the Confederación Campesina del Perú and there had been propaganda in Peru saying that the top Peruvian leader had been detained. So, everyone got off the helicopter and I got off last.

As we got off, the people asked, "Where is the leader of the peasantry?"

"He's at the back. He's coming."

I got off and they asked, "*You* are the peasant leader?"

"I'm the leader."

We laughed!

"You're supposed to be enormous!"

Then, I got in the car and they took all of the accused to the barracks. That's life.

Llamojha told his CVR interviewers:

They took us to the Republican Guard barracks. We were there a month. They sent some to El Sepa [the Colonia Penal Agrícola del Sepa, a penal colony in the Amazon], others to El Frontón. The others they sent back, paying their way.

I said, "I'm not going to go. I'm going to stay in Lima." I didn't want to go back, because I had work to do in Lima.

The leader of the barracks was General Bedoya, an Ayacuchan. He talked to us in Quechua, and to say goodbye to us, for our goodbye meal, he said, "We have to make two pots of *mondongo* [tripe soup], Ayacucho style."

And he served all of the prisoners. He served us himself. He divvied out the food for us. He was a good guy.

Llamojha's stories about his 1963 arrest again offer a complex portrayal of soldiers and civil guards. He shows some of these men as pointedly abusive torturers and casts others as sympathetic men who trusted him and treated him kindly.

Shortly after his release from prison he returned to Ayacucho, and there he had an encounter with the leading presidential candidate, Fernando Belaúnde Terry. Belaúnde waged an energetic presidential election campaign, traversing Peru as no previous candidate had ever done, and that campaign brought him to the Ayacucho town of Pampa Cangallo.[38] Llamojha described meeting Belaúnde:

> He said to me, "Where are you from? Are you from here?"
>
> "No, I'm from Concepción."
>
> "Then what are you doing here?"
>
> "I've come to greet you."
>
> "You've come with this group to greet me?"
>
> "Yes."
>
> Then, we all got in the same car with Belaúnde to go to Cangallo. We got out in Cangallo and went to the main plaza for a meeting. Many people were waiting, and there I was.
>
> Those who knew me said, "You've changed your politics! Now you're a Belaúndista [Belaúnde supporter]! You're no longer a social activist!"

Llamojha was still very much a social activist, however, and he staunchly criticized the Belaúnde regime and especially its disappointing 1964 agrarian reform. The combination of a recalcitrant congress, hacendado opposition, the agrarian reform law's complexity, and Belaúnde's competing priorities meant that the law failed to meet the needs of the vast majority of Peru's peasants.[39] Llamojha offered a sharp criticism of Belaúnde's agrarian reform in an October 1964 letter that he wrote with several other leaders of the CCP. The letter called Belaúnde's reform the "Law of Agrarian Fraud" and denounced its failure to pursue the complete liquidation of haciendas and failure to challenge the "voracious oppression and exploitation by the great landowners." The letter closed with the slogans "LAND FOR HE WHO WORKS IT. LAND, FREEDOM AND JUSTICE. LAND OR DEATH, WE WILL WIN."[40] For Llamojha, only radical, peasant-directed agrarian reform would be sufficient.

International Travels

The drama and excitement of Llamojha's political work reached a new high in 1965, when he received an invitation to travel to Cuba. That trip then led to subsequent travels to the Soviet Union and China. His overseas travels were major transformative experiences in his life—a life that began in the humblest of circumstances, in an impoverished indigenous community.[41] Though they were astonishing for him, such international travels were actually fairly common among Peruvian and other Latin American political activists. Another prominent member of the CCP, Pelayo Oré Chávez, traveled to Albania, Cuba, Czechoslovakia, and the Soviet Union during the 1960s and 1970s.[42] Documents from the US Central Intelligence Agency claim that hundreds of Peruvians traveled to Cuba, China, and even North Korea for political training during the 1960s.[43] Enough Peruvian students were studying at the Patrice Lumumba University in Moscow, in turn, that they formed a Peruvian student organization on the campus in 1966.[44] The Peruvian government actively condemned such travels and explicitly prohibited visits to communist bloc countries.[45]

Llamojha's travels—all funded by the governments of the host countries— began with his trip to Cuba in 1965. He told his CVR interviewers:

Cuba invited me for a big meeting, a worldwide meeting, of the worldwide union of the workers of the world. I went to Cuba by invitation. For this worldwide meeting, tickets came for five delegates from Peru. They didn't get their passports, though. At that time, travel was prohibited. You had to take an oath that you wouldn't go to any of the fourteen socialist countries that existed at that time. It was difficult to get a passport, so the others got discouraged. People from five departments were supposed to go, with me representing Ayacucho.

I went, just in case, to the Ministry [to try to get a passport]. But they asked for my baptismal certificate, and I didn't have it . . . so I prepared a certificate myself. I made my own baptismal certificate, and I took it with me to the Ministry.

They asked me, "Where are you traveling to?"

"To the United States," I said.

"Do you have family there?"

"Yes, I do."

Happily, at that time, a relative of mine who was in the United States had sent me a letter. The letter said, "Get yourself ready, and I'll send you money for your ticket, so you can work here."

I presented this, and with this, staying really quiet, they gave me a passport. Sure, they made me sign a sworn statement that I wouldn't go to Cuba, or to other places.

Llamojha shared many stories about his time in Cuba during our interviews.

I participated in a great meeting of delegations from many countries. The Cuban government surely wanted to inform everyone about Cuba's situation.

I would guess there were about four thousand people in the meetings. There were delegates from all the countries of the Americas, from Europe, from China. There were a lot of delegates. Some countries had three delegates. Twelve went from Chile, fourteen went from Argentina. Many countries had five delegates. From the other countries, as many as twelve delegates went. They paid for their whole trip, the whole round trip. But I was the only one from Peru. I was all by myself. The others didn't want to go, out of fear. And that's why in Cuba they called me "Lonely Peru." I went all by myself. The rest of the Peruvian delegates didn't want to go.

"They're going to repress me! Travel to Cuba is prohibited," they said.

I was in Cuba for a month. They showed me all the pueblos, how they functioned under socialism. They showed me how there used to be haciendas and how they were now. They showed me all of this. I liked their customs. I liked the form of collective labor. Everyone got involved in collective labor, everyone.

Llamojha shared more memories of Cuba with his CVR interviewers:

They showed me all of the institutions, the factories that now belonged to the pueblo. Then, all the delegates from across the world, we went to cut sugarcane. They call this the *zafra* [sugarcane harvest]. The ministers went to start cutting first. They started to cut the cane and then the rest of us, the delegates, went to cut cane for half a day.

During his time in Cuba Llamojha received the invitation to China.

When I was in Cuba, the invitation from China came, as there were delegates from China in Cuba. The one who contacted me for this was Hilda Gadea, a Peruvian woman who was the ex-wife of Che Guevara. She's from [the Apurímac province of] Andahuaylas. She put me in contact with China.

The Chinese delegates said to me, "On your return, we're going to send you a ticket so that you'll come."

Llamojha told his CVR interviewers that an invitation to the Soviet Union followed shortly thereafter.

Then, Russian delegates invited me. "Let's go to Russia! You'll get political training there. You'll be there for two years."

"Good. Good," I said.

So, then there was a meeting in Santiago de Cuba, in Oriente, a big meeting.

In this big meeting, we were to take turns talking about the political question. So, I spoke about the Russian politicians.

I said, "the Russian political leaders are liars. They deceive the world, saying that Russia is socialist, communist, when it isn't. Russia isn't socialist or communist. Russia, since Stalin's death in '54, has taken another direction. They should not keep deceiving the world!"

I said this in anger. After that, they separated themselves from me, they didn't speak to me anymore.

Llamojha's pointed criticism of the Soviet Union reflected his strong sympathies for the Chinese model of communism in the aftermath of the Sino-Soviet split: a model that prioritized peasants over workers, the countryside over cities, and revolutionary action over statist collaboration. Chinese propaganda circulated quite widely in Peru, and many Peruvians came to share Llamojha's loyalties, with Maoism gaining more traction in Peru than anywhere else in Latin America.[46] Llamojha's stance also reflected his strong political alignment with Maoist CCP legal advisor Saturnino Paredes and the other members of the Partido Comunista del Perú-Bandera Roja. Llamojha's pro-China stance helps explain the rather frosty reception he received in the Soviet Union. His trip to the Soviet Union was only an interim stop on the way to China; his public denunciation of the Soviets while in Cuba had surely foiled any plans for an extended stay in the USSR.

So I went to China. The first flight was to Moscow, and I was in Moscow for five days. But as I had spoken against them while in Cuba, they didn't greet me, they didn't receive me. Only the Chinese embassy received me at the airport.

They took me to a hotel and they left me there, just at the door, nothing more! So I entered the hotel alone. I spoke in Spanish and they didn't understand me. If I had known I was going to go to Russia, I would have prepared, I would have studied. So I asked for a room, but speaking in English.

Here, I interjected with surprise: "You speak English?"

Well, a few words. Enough to get by. They looked for a girl who spoke English, and with her help, I asked for a room. She asked them to give me a room on the second floor. She was always there! They'd named her to serve as my interpreter, and she almost always came to get me for breakfast, lunch, dinner. That's how we were; she accompanied me for three

days. On saying goodbye, she gave me her hand. She had a little ring and I fiddled with it. That really bothered her, and I didn't see her again!

When Llamojha played with that young woman's ring, he was flirting. Young men in Peru's rural Andean communities often teasingly seize pieces of jewelry from the objects of their affection, forcing the women to constantly pester their suitors for the items' return.[47] The young Soviet woman may well have known what he was intimating, or she may have just thought he was trying to steal her ring. He shared many other anecdotes of his time in Moscow.

I arrived in Russia at six in the morning; I thought it was six at night! As it was snowing in Russia, it was really dark and I thought it was time to go to bed. Then, they telephoned me from the Chinese embassy.

"Have you eaten breakfast yet?" they asked me.

"What do you mean, breakfast? It's getting dark out; I'm lying down in bed."

"What? We're getting up now, we're not getting ready for bed! It's getting light outside," they said to me.

"But it's dark out," I said.

"No, that's what it's like here."

I went alone to the dining room to eat. They handed me the menu, but I didn't know the language yet. When they gave me the menu list, I just checked things off. It turned out I'd picked mostly liquors! They brought me a bottle of vodka and a bottle of beer. This is what I had ordered!

Then, I went out by myself to walk around. I walked around the city until I got tired. That's how it was. The whole day, walking around.

They had shops there, really big stores. One was open and I went in. There was nobody there. I knocked on the counter because I wanted to buy a briefcase. It was hanging there with its price. But nobody came out, nobody. And the store's money was on the counter.

I said to myself, "How can they just leave their money here? There's no one here!" After a little while, more people came in. I watched as they looked at the prices, took stuff, and then they put the things in their bags. Then they got out their money, put it on the counter, they took their change and left! That convinced me that socialism still existed in Russia! That's how it was. I grabbed the briefcase, put down my money and took my change! That's how it should be! Because it all belongs to the pueblo, money also belongs to the pueblo. They left their money and took their change!

I asked Llamojha if there had been any meetings or gatherings for him.

There weren't any. I walked alone in the streets, in the avenues. I suffered in that cold! If I had known I was going, I would have taken a coat, something. But I didn't know I was going to go to Moscow!

In Moscow, I was abandoned in the streets. There was a woman selling sweets, and I asked for one. She gave me one and I sat down on the bench. After I ate the candy, I threw the wrapper on the ground, Lima style. Then a lady appeared and she yelled at me in her language, and she made me pick up the wrapper! She showed me that there was a garbage can behind the bench and she made me throw the wrapper in there.

I stayed in Russia for five days. Then, I was contacted by the Chinese embassy to go to China. Moscow, its people, its authorities—I don't know why they hated me. To leave for China, they took me to the checkpoint to endorse my passport. One of them grabbed me, checked me over. They inspected everything. They were bitter, those people. They inspected my pockets, where I had my money. I had 200 dollars; the Cubans had given me 200 dollars and they took all of it from me! They took it! They didn't return it. Right from my pocket.

"What are you taking this money for?" they asked me. They got their revenge against me!

"This stays here!" they said. They didn't return it! After that, they stamped my passport. The delegate from the Chinese embassy said, "It doesn't matter. What can we do? This is how they are."

Then they took me to the airport and I left for China.

I traveled to China and they received me there. A group was waiting for me at the airport and they greeted me with flowers, with Chinese flags and a Peruvian flag. They greeted me because I was representing Peru, because I was a national leader of Peru.

Llamojha shared more details of his arrival with his CVR interviewers:

They greeted me with a fantastic reception. There was a caravan of cars and the minister of agriculture. Here in Peru, they say that this news was published in *El Comercio*, in *La Prensa* [the major national newspapers].[48]

"The top leader from Peru has been received by the Chinese minister," they say the stories said. I haven't read them. So, that's how I arrived in China. I was in China for over a month.

They asked me, "What do you want to see here?"

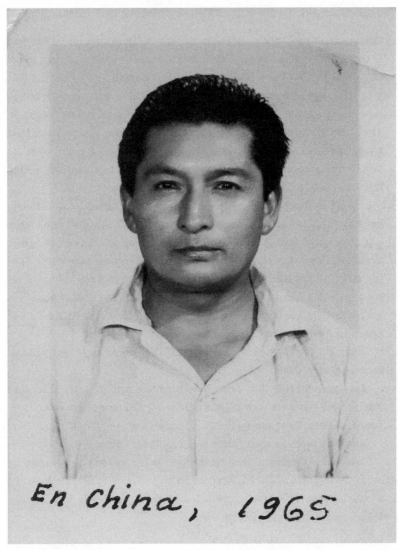

En China, 1965

FIG. 4.1 Llamojha, location unknown, 1965. Photo courtesy of Manuel Llamojha Mitma.

"Above all, I want to learn all about the peasants. How the peasants live, and how the cooperative businesses function."

So, they took me around every day. I didn't have time for anything. From the time I woke up I had to go from one place to the next. They waited for me with a plane, sometimes with a car. I've seen half of China! I've seen where the armed struggle began, where Mao Zedong was.

"He was there in that gorge! That's where he hid like a little animal," they said. There were big holes, and in there were various rooms. That's where the people lived. But it's frightening; there's an echo when you go in. So, when the planes came to bomb the area, they only bombed the ground, not the hillside. They didn't know there were people living there. And that's where Mao Zedong lived. His bed was in there, his shoes, his pencil, his books, his inkwells, it's there. Everywhere that he was, we went.

In our interviews, Llamojha added more details.

I've seen practically the entire country of China. At three in the morning, they'd bring me breakfast at the hotel and at four we had to leave by airplane for another town. That's how it was. Every day, they took me to see places where the community's businesses functioned. They brought me to fields where they were planting grains, showing me how they harvested. In China, they drink a lot of tea. Each place we went, there were a number of teapots on the table, and they always served us tea. Tea instead of wine!

They invited me there as a national leader, and to talk about Peru. They also told me about China, about how it had a revolution. I was there one month and a week, seeing all the country, all of its cities. I had my diary, my notes, but when I came back to Peru, the investigators took everything from me. The Chinese had filled my albums up with stuff throughout my visit. But they took all of that from me. What could they have done with it?

China was a lovely country. The way they worked, they had nice machines, really different ones. For plowing, they had a machine like a wheelbarrow but with a motor. They made me try it.

"Let's see! Try it!" they said. I took hold of it and drove it.

Llamojha visited the communist countries of China and Cuba as leader of Peru's largest peasant organization, but even in this political context that so emphasized class, his hosts paid much attention to his indigeneity, something that he recalled with pride.

University students should be able to speak the Peruvian language, Quechua. I am fluent in the Peruvian language and in other countries they asked me to write and speak in Quechua about my visit. In China and in Cuba, they asked me to write and give my speech in Quechua.

I asked Llamojha what he liked most about China.

The communal works, the exchanges, I liked that. It was socialism. Socialism is really nice.
"You should stay!" they said.
So, I said, "No, I've got my wife. She's going to become *machorra* [barren; also butch or lesbian]."
They didn't understand. "What does *machorra* mean?" they asked me.
"Ahhhhhh . . . *machorra* means that she is going to become an old woman," I said.
Then they looked in a dictionary. In another meeting, they started to criticize me. "You're a liar! That's not what it says in the dictionary!"

After five weeks in China, Llamojha headed home to Peru. As he explained to his CVR interviewers, the return trip took him back to the Soviet Union and through Europe:

From China I came back through Russia. I was in Russia for five days on my return. Then, I went to Poland, and from Poland to Germany, and then to France. The French are really good people. They're not like the Russians, who look at you with hate. But in France, the people are really nice. They invited me to sit down, they talked to me, they offered me coffee, that's how they treated me.
In France, they said to me, "Don't go to Peru! Peru's in danger. The armed struggle of Luis de la Puente, of the MIR [Movimiento de Izquierda Revolucionaria, Movement of the Revolutionary Left] has begun. Don't go! Peru's in danger. Stay here."
But I wanted to know where it would all lead. So I came back in a hurry. I came back here via Portugal, via Spain, then Venezuela, and from Venezuela a direct flight to Peru.
But when I got back to Peru, instead of greeting me with flowers, they greeted me with machine guns! Right when I got off the plane.

In our interviews, Llamojha described the early moments of his capture.

They took me from the airport to the prefecture as a prisoner. Three investigators took me and they made me go up to the third floor. They left me
with just one investigator and he made me sit in the boss's chair.

"Sit down right here!"

"But I'm just fine right here!"

"Sit here!"

What was I supposed to do? The investigator left to go to the bathroom,
and then three officials came up into the room.

They saw me and asked, "Who are you?"

"I'm a prisoner. I'm imprisoned."

"Why is a prisoner sitting in my chair?"

"I was told to sit here!"

"Who made you sit there?"

"The guy who took me prisoner," I said.

"Why did they take you prisoner?"

"I don't know. They detained me in the airport."

"And what were you doing at the airport? You must be a criminal."

"No. I came back from Europe."

"You're coming from Europe?"

"I'm coming from Europe."

After looking at my documents the official said, "How about that!
This Indian wretch has traveled the world, and we haven't even been to
Huancayo!"[49]

Llamojha remained a prisoner in the prefecture for several months. He
described his interrogation, referencing the 1965 guerrilla struggles started
by the MIR and the Ejército de Liberación Nacional (National Liberation
Army).[50]

They asked me, "Why did you go? Who sent you?"

In the prefecture there were various detainees from Cuzco. The armed
struggle of the MIR had begun in Peru. As a consequence, the repression
had begun.

They detained me and they started to talk over the radio, saying that I
had been detained because I had brought weapons from Russia. They had
me for three months in the prefecture, and after that, they sent me to
the barracks.

I asked Llamojha what he thought of the MIR.

The MIR means the Movimiento de Izquierda Revolucionaria. But I had doubts when it [the MIR's guerrilla struggle] began, because they weren't with the masses. They would have had to go across all of Peru and organize the masses for their revolution to triumph. So I wasn't sure they would succeed when they began. And that's how it turned out; they didn't triumph because they weren't united with the Peruvian masses. They were a small group, nothing more. I always had that idea: struggle with the masses.

Llamojha also recalled arguing with other imprisoned leaders while in jail. His reference to Cuzco leaders likely refers to the MIR, as one of their guerrilla fronts was in Cuzco. He commented:

When I was imprisoned in the barracks, I always took part in discussions. There were other leaders there and we had conversations about the peasantry's struggle. We talked, we argued about how to struggle to the very end. Some of the leaders from Cuzco were pretty harsh.

They said, "I don't want to keep fighting. The Indians don't accept us."

I said that this didn't bother me. "I'm just going to continue fighting. There's no problem."

So they said to me, "You're a *kullu* [Quechua: blockhead]."

Llamojha's arrest on his return from China generated some publicity. The Aprista magazine *Presente* reported that Llamojha had been detained after his flight from Paris, asserting that he "acted as a link between Moscow, Havana and Peking communists and Peruvian communists."[51] The magazine's statement was hyperbolic, but it certainly mirrored the Peruvian state's own fears about Llamojha, explaining why authorities kept him in prison for an entire year.[52] His supporters, in turn, used the pages of the newspaper *Bandera Roja* to press for his release.[53] A June 1966 communiqué from the CCP urged "the peasant bases of all the country to demand the immediate liberty of our Secretary General Manuel Llamojha Mitma, imprisoned for the past year even though he had not committed any crime."[54] For the Peruvian state operating in the context of Cold War, however, Llamojha's travels constituted a threat that needed to be punished and contained.

He told his CVR interviewers a great deal about his 1965–1966 imprisonment in the Republican Guard barracks. He explained that thirty political captives were held in a single, small room.

And it had no light, it was dark. So, we carried out a protest so they would open a little window on the door, so that light could come in. And after that, we protested to get visitors. After we had been there for three months, they consented and let us have visits, but visitors could only come for ten minutes. Then we protested so they would give us a half hour. They granted that to us. And so then, one hour, then, two hours. We did this through complaints.

Then I got sick. In China, they were going to operate on me, but I didn't let them. "I have to get back quickly," I had said.

I came back like this, and when I was in prison, I got really sick. I had severe abdominal pain, and I got seriously ill. I couldn't eat, I could only lie down.

To go and get food, we had to walk really far, as much as a block, to get our food. So, everyone went out [from the cell] and outside, the guard counted. And one of us was missing. A lieutenant came in and found me; he was a bad guy. I couldn't stand up, but he dragged me out, hitting me with his sword as we moved toward the dining room.

He forced me into the dining room. I couldn't stand, I had to lie down.

My prison *compañeros* [fellow inmates] declared, "We will not sit down and eat. Make the boss come, the head of the barracks," they said. All of them remained standing.

"Not until the boss comes," they said.

So, the guards immediately called him, General Bedoya, surely by telephone. He lived in Miraflores, he was an Ayacuchano. He arrived after a half hour, and he saw me lying on the floor.

He asked the guard, the lieutenant, "What's going on with this guy? Why is he like that?"

My compañeros said, "He's seriously ill, but they don't want to take him to the clinic."

So Bedoya said to the lieutenant, "If you saw that he was sick, why did you bring him here? You should have taken him to the clinic immediately. Now, you're going to be punished. Tomorrow, you're going to the jungle!"

And he sent the lieutenant to the jungle. Bedoya was a good guy.

Right then they took me to the clinic. The next day, they took me to the Dos de Mayo hospital. In the Dos de Mayo hospital, I was in the hospital's little jail. I was there for three months, waiting for an operation. There, students from San Marcos brought me food.[55] Students from those groups [the leftist political party Patria Roja (Red Fatherland) and the Partido Comunista del Perú-Bandera Roja] brought me food, milk. They helped me. They brought me as much as three liters of milk.

Llamojha also told his CVR interviewers about his interactions with "common prisoners," individuals jailed on apolitical grounds.

> There were others there, common prisoners, and I handed out the food to everyone. There was another prisoner there, an Aprista, from Huancayo. He couldn't stand the common prisoners, and so the common prisoners hated him. But they treated me really well, because I handed out food.
>
> People from Vischongo had sent me money because I needed it for serums, for blood. The money arrived. A commission had brought it to me, they delivered it to me. And after the operation, people from Pomacocha sent me money, from Chacari [a community in the district of Concepción] too, for medicines. So, when they took me to the operating room, the money was on a little table I had. I left it there.
>
> After the operation I said to myself, "Surely those other prisoners have taken the money." But they hadn't! The common prisoners had guarded my money. They guarded it for me, and when I returned, eight days after my operation, they gave it back to me.
>
> "Here's your little bit of money. We guarded it," they said to me.

In our interviews, Llamojha explained that his whole body had swollen before the operation, leaving him incapacitated. The subsequent operation removed tumors from his abdomen, and during our interview he pointed to his stomach, showing where the scars remained. He was very lucky to have had the support of students, peasants, and his fellow prisoners: without their solidarity, it is unlikely that he would have had the funds to buy the blood, medicine, and food he needed to make a full recovery. Such were the dismal realities of the health care system in Peru. Remarkably, after that major health scare, he enjoyed good health for the next four decades.

Back to the Countryside

Llamojha's national political work and international travels consumed much of his energy and attention in the 1960s, but he never stopped worrying about—or fighting for—his home community, Concepción. He resumed active efforts on Concepción's behalf after his release from prison in 1966, helping his community win a major victory against the Ayrabamba hacienda. The resurgence of his local activism coincided with the growing weakness of the CCP: from roughly 1965, many Peruvian leftists began staunchly criticizing the CCP, accusing its leaders of sectarianism and growing isolation from

Peru's peasant masses. Some even claimed that the CCP had essentially ceased to exist.[56]

When Llamojha returned to Ayacucho after his yearlong imprisonment in Lima, he learned a staggering piece of information: when Elodia Vassallo de Parodi's husband purchased the Ayrabamba hacienda in 1914, the transaction had taken place in the city of Ica, and not in Ayacucho as Llamojha and his fellow community members had assumed.[57] Llamojha's earlier searches for Ayrabamba's title had been fruitless simply because he had been looking in the offices of Ayacuchan, rather than Ican, notaries. Llamojha knew that if he could find Ayrabamba's heretofore missing title, then Concepción campesinos would finally have strong legal evidence about their community's borders. That was precisely the evidence they needed to fight the Parodi hacendados' encroachments onto the community's land, so he set out for Ica to look for the document.

> I went to Ica to search for the title. I searched for a week and found nothing, absolutely nothing. I was ready to come home. One night, I went out to a park to sit for a while, and I had a bunch of documents with me. A man sat down beside me on the park bench.
>
> He asked me, "Why are you walking around with so much paper?"
> "I've got problems. That's why I'm here."
> "Where are you from?"
> "Ayacucho," I told him.
> "You've come here from Ayacucho? There are documents from Ayacucho here?"
> "Yes. They should be here, but I haven't found them at any notary."
> "Have you gone to the notary Medina?"
> "No. Where's that? I haven't found that office here. It doesn't exist."
> "This notary's office is located on the outskirts of Ica, just as you are leaving the city. He keeps all the old documents."
>
> I was so lucky to meet this man! The next day, I went to the notary and I found it. The document describing Ayrabamba's sale was there.
>
> I didn't have enough money to get a copy of the document. I had to go to Lima, to our [migrant club] institution, so that they could provide the money. Then I returned to Ica and I got a certified copy of the document. Then I went back to Concepción. It was almost time for the formal border inspection with Ayrabamba, so I got this document just in time!

The land title Llamojha acquired in Ica proved pivotal in a lawsuit initiated by Elodia Vassallo de Parodi's son, César Parodi.[58] As was frequently the case in lawsuits over landownership, the legal battle included a formal inspection of the borders between the hacienda and Llamojha's community.

A lot of people from all the surrounding pueblos had come to Ayrabamba for the border inspection. Court authorities had come from Ayacucho. Parodi was the one who had asked for this inspection; he'd filed a lawsuit against us.

"The hacienda purchased from that plateau onward," Parodi said.

The president of the court asked me, "He says that the land from that plateau on belongs to Ayrabamba. Why are you complaining?"

"This is not how things are, sir," I said to him. "Here is Ayrabamba's title. It shows the borders." I gave him Ayrabamba's title. "Here it is. This is Concepción's land."

I gave the title to the court president and he read it aloud. Then he said to Parodi, "Why have you held the community's land for so many years? You have to return it now."

The people, so many people, started to yell. Parodi started to tremble. "Let them [Concepción community members] have the hacienda's land. We'll give it to them," he said.

The court president replied, "But it's the community's land! How are you going to give them the land if it already belongs to the community?"

So, Parodi said, "Just leave us access to the stream. We use this bit of water for distillation, and to drink."

The president of the court asked me, "Will you allow him use of the water?"

"Yes. This water is free; he can use it."

The court president prepared papers and asked Parodi to sign them, but he didn't want to sign.

The people yelled in Quechua, "Sign it, *taytay* [Quechua: dad]! Sign it!"

Then, the court president said in Quechua, "The land is yours."

This shows that you have to be strong, don't tremble. You can do things with documents. Documents are worth a lot.

Concepción's victory against the Ayrabamba hacienda formed a fitting close to Llamojha's political work in the 1960s—work that was local, national, and international in scope. Although he suffered terrible mistreatment in this decade, imprisoned and tortured by Peruvian governments desperately

FIG. 4.2 Llamojha singing, location unknown, 1967. Photo courtesy of Manuel Llamojha Mitma.

fighting Cold War battles against communism and revolutionary activism, he remembers the 1960s with warm nostalgia. He told his CVR interviewers:

We made agrarian reform in the countryside, as a battle, we took fields. It was lovely. Working with campesinos is a real pleasure.

Sadly for Llamojha, the triumphs of the 1960s did not continue. The remaining decades of the twentieth century brought him and his family a series of troubling hardships, losses, and heartbreaks.

FIVE

"Everything Was Division"

POLITICAL MARGINALIZATION, 1968-1980

Traitor. Sellout. Enemy of the Peasantry. These were just some of the charges Llamojha faced during the 1970s. This time, however, his detractors were not hacendados, abusive district authorities, or even government officials. They were other leftists. Over the course of the 1970s, Llamojha participated in a bitter battle for control over the CCP, a struggle he ultimately lost. His recollections about this period form an account of political marginalization: he was ostracized and attacked by his former allies on the left. His experiences in the 1970s help us understand why his life stories so often celebrated those individuals who—as he phrased it—never abandoned him.

The partisan disputes that plagued Peru's left were intensely heated and hurtful, but they were far from unique. Throughout Latin America's diverse nations—and across much of the world—rival leftist political parties waged acrimonious battles against each other over the twentieth century, hurling insults and invective as they struggled to gain political traction over one another. Leftists angrily disagreed about whether workers should ally with peasants, whether participation in electoral politics was counterrevolutionary, whether or not to pursue armed struggle, and countless other questions. Although leftist political activists still fought important battles for revolutionary transformations, internecine fights often drew activists' energy, attention, and time away from larger social justice struggles and sometimes devolved into startlingly nasty personal attacks.[1] Although leftists in different Latin American contexts made repeated efforts to unite with one another, working hard to transcend both minor and major ideological differences in order to fight more effectively for socioeconomic and political change, unity often proved elusive. Llamojha's particular experiences give us an intensely personal look at how devastating and destructive these conflicts between leftists could be: he was slandered and shunned, and he maintains that his former allies even tried to murder him.

The political battles of the 1970s took place in a period of dramatic change in Peru. Military men under the leadership of General Juan Velasco Alvarado seized power in 1968 and established the Revolutionary Government of the Armed Forces. Unlike other highly conservative military governments that took power in Latin America during the 1970s, Velasco's regime pursued a course of progressive reform. He nationalized several key industries, introduced a major education reform, and tried to fashion a more inclusive nation-state.[2] Crucially, the Velasco government also introduced a comprehensive agrarian reform that effectively dismantled the hacienda system in Peru. The regime seized hacienda land and redistributed it to campesinos, primarily in the form of state-administered cooperatives. Although the course of reform slowed significantly after 1975, when Velasco was ousted in an internal coup, the military government remained in power until 1980.

In issuing the agrarian reform law, Velasco was answering a demand made by many Latin Americans. Across much of the continent, campesinos and leftist activists alike had long been calling for the redistribution of rural land, seeing it as the only solution to the grave social and economic injustices that plagued the countryside.[3] But many Latin American political activists felt deeply unsatisfied with the state-sponsored agrarian reforms that their governments enacted, believing that such programs did not go far enough, fast enough, and fearing that government reforms drained the peasantry's revolutionary potential.[4] That was certainly the case for Llamojha, who angrily opposed the Velasco regime's actions in the countryside. Against this backdrop of dramatic state-sponsored agrarian reform, the CCP fractured into three competing factions in 1973, torn apart by rivalries, ideological differences, and differing attitudes toward the reform. Each of these factions claimed to be the *true* CCP. The invective that passed between the members of these three rival factions was bitter and sharp, but it was far from unusual in the disputes that transpired among leftists in Latin America.

Velasco's Agrarian Reform

When the Revolutionary Government of the Armed Forces seized power in 1968, many Peruvian leftists were thrown into crisis.[5] Long accustomed to denouncing the national government as conservative and beholden to elite interests, left-wing political activists now had to contend with a regime that pledged—and acted—to fulfill many long-standing leftist demands. Many prominent Peruvian leftists responded to the Velasco regime by joining it, taking government jobs and advancing the state's agenda.[6] Some took a more moderate approach, recognizing the regime as reformist and sensing an opportunity to radicalize the course of change in the country. Still others rejected the military government entirely, deriding it as capitalist, imperialist, or even fascist and dismissing its reforms as ruses. Llamojha was in the latter group.

I asked him what he thought about the Velasco government and its agrarian reform.

> The peasantry had fought so much for the agrarian reform. So the Velasco government took power, always talking about agrarian reform, and they issued an agrarian reform law. But they didn't follow through, because the hacendados didn't accept it. I knew the government wasn't going to do it. Agrarian reform was going to be made through struggle, when the pueblo took power.
>
> "While the powerful and the gamonales are in power, it can't be done. To change the situation and the country's system, the pueblo has to take power." I always talked like this. So, some hacendados denounced me, saying I was a communist! That's how it was. How I struggled in those times.

In his interview with the CVR, Llamojha added:

> I printed up communiqués explaining that Velasco's agrarian reform didn't favor the peasantry. I sent out five communiqués along these lines. Others sent out communiqués saying that Velasco's agrarian reform was good. That made for confusion, discrepancies with the peasants. I had the majority of support from the peasantry.

An essay Llamojha wrote in May 1973 was especially forceful in its denunciations of the agrarian reform. He cast the Velasco agrarian reform as "the landlord's path," writing:

The impulse of the landlord's path in the countryside is linked to the objectives of North American imperialism for the development of bureaucratic capitalism in the country. For this, those who adopt the position of the buying and selling of land do it to collaborate with landlords, bureaucratic capitalism, and imperialism.[7]

In this essay he further explained that he staunchly opposed the agrarian reform's stipulations that peasants help the state compensate hacendados for seized lands, something known as the "agrarian debt." He also opposed "the direct intervention of the Government in the execution of the Agrarian Reform" and "the formation of Cooperatives in which the representatives of the landowners and the State outnumber the representatives of the campesinos."[8] To him the proper approach was what he deemed "the peasant's path": the direct confiscation of land by campesinos themselves.[9]

A significant part of his opposition to the Velasco agrarian reform, as his essay suggested, was the distribution of land into state-run cooperatives.[10] He instead wanted land to move directly into peasants' hands. He explained to his CVR interviewers:

> The campesinos realized what a cooperative was, and that cooperatives weren't in the peasantry's favor.
>
> When they formed the cooperative, the hacendados themselves were the managers! With the harvest, the harvest of corn, potatoes, everything, they only gave the peasants one *arroba* [about thirty pounds] per family.
>
> The campesinos turned bitter. They said, "How are we going to live for a full year on just one arroba of corn or wheat? We want our own production from our own land." Saying that, they rejected the cooperatives. In addition, in the countryside, there are fruits like cactus pears and also firewood that campesinos were no longer allowed to collect. But when it was the hacienda, they were free to get firewood, fruit. But not as a cooperative. As a cooperative, they had to pay for one stick of wood, for fruit. They had to pay; they could no longer eat for free. So, the campesinos rejected it.

Llamojha's pointed opposition to the Velasco regime also stemmed from the fact that the military government's Decree Law 19400 tried to do away with independent campesino organizations and replace them with government-sponsored agrarian leagues and federations. That law also created the Confederación Nacional Agraria (National Agrarian Confederation),

FIG. 5.1 Llamojha with his grandson Yuri and daughters Delia, Hilda, and María, Lima, 1972. Photo courtesy of Manuel Llamojha Mitma.

designed to challenge—and ultimately replace—the CCP. In his 1973 essay Llamojha wrote that Decree Law 19400 "represented the vertical, corporatist organization of fascism."[11] He surely feared for the CCP's survival—and for independent peasant political mobilization in general—in a context of active government efforts to champion state-sponsored, state-directed peasant organization.

Political Fractures

By the time the CCP split in 1973, Llamojha had already become deeply enmeshed in heated political disputes among the country's leftists. In the mid-1960s, his sharpest political critiques had been directed against leftists who followed the Soviet political line. In an open letter that he and other leaders of the CCP published in 1964, they accused CCP sub–secretary general Ramón Nuñez Lafore of betrayal.[12] The letter asserted that this "false campesino" was collaborating with the Ministry of Labor and Indian Affairs in efforts that would ultimately divide the CCP. The letter decried Nuñez's "brazen treachery" and stripped him of his role in the CCP.[13] The key to understanding this heated denunciation rests with the fact that Nuñez was sympathetic to the Soviet political line, while Llamojha and the other CCP leaders favored the Chinese Maoist line.[14] Llamojha and his fellow CCP leaders also staunchly opposed cooperation with the Peruvian state, a point that further divided Peru's pro-Soviet leftists from the country's Maoists.

Llamojha had a similarly strong antipathy toward a group that, like him, also rejected the Soviet line: Trotskyists.

> **Trotskyism was not truly the defender of the peasantry. Instead, it distracted peasants with a different way of thinking. It was not truly thinking about the liberation of the peasantry. It wasn't like that.**

Llamojha's opposition to Trotskyism also shaped—and was shaped by—his rivalry with Hugo Blanco, Peru's most famous rural activist and the man who fought alongside Cuzco's La Convención peasants in the renowned land struggles of the early 1960s.[15] When the CVR interviewers asked Llamojha about Blanco, Llamojha's reply made reference to the armed campesino militias Blanco had formed to defend seized hacienda lands:

> **Hugo Blanco wrecked things because he's a Trotskyist, nothing more than a provocateur. There was an organization, it had nine hundred armed men.**

> But he formed this group without consulting with the pueblo and then started attacking police posts. They confronted the police and the ensuing repression was against the campesinos. There was a massacre in the valley. They totally razed it, the dead campesinos were thrown into the river.

But while Llamojha was quick to denounce Trotskyists, communists of the Soviet line, and members of many other leftist political parties during our interviews, he was always extremely reluctant to specify his own particular ideological sympathies. Not once in our interviews did he self-define as a Maoist, a communist, a socialist, or even a Marxist. Instead, whenever I asked him about his political sympathies, loyalties, and ideas, he spoke about his commitment to campesinos and social justice. In his interview with the CVR, he labeled his political vision "the philosophy of the peasantry."

> The philosophy of the peasantry is to liberate oneself from the clutches of the dominant classes, uniting the peasants and fighting until the total liberation of the peasantry. We the peasantry are suffering. It's the countryside that suffers in everything! So, I always shared this idea, or rather, this explanation with the peasantry, that we have to work united and fight to free ourselves from everything that is feudal slavery, from capitalism. Capitalism is now in its last phase, which is imperialism. And from there, it's going to tumble down because of its own weight. So, we have to take our own path.

Llamojha also told his CVR interviewers that he taught Karl Marx's ideas about the stages of economic development to Peruvian campesinos.

> I also had to orient on my part. I explained to them that the time is going to come, because we are living in the fourth stage. Like it or not, the fifth stage has to come. It's not because someone wants it, but because this is the law of the world. This is what the struggle for liberation is like.
>
> In the world, there are only five stages. We are now living in the fourth stage, in capitalism. Every stage ends with a struggle, with blood. Now, too, we have to pass to the fifth stage with blood, with struggle.
>
> This is what I explained to the masses, in congresses, too. I gave guidance in this sense, this was my orientation, philosophically. In the world, there are only five stages in the development of humanity.
>
> So, the campesinos asked, "What is the first stage?"
>
> I explained about the primitive community, here in Peru.

> **"So, what is the second?" The campesinos asked me. They would ask me this in Quechua.**
>
> **I explained to them, "the second is slavery and the third is feudalism and the fourth is capitalism."**

Llamojha did not explicitly attribute these ideas to Marx. When his CVR interviewers asked if these ideas reflected a party orientation, he answered simply:

> **They were from my own judgments, according to my studies of books.**

In our interviews, I noted that the five stages of history were Marx's idea and asked Llamojha if he had ever read Marx. He replied:

> **As it happens, that's what I used to educate myself. I really liked his writings about how peasants used to live, about how they should defend themselves, about how they suffered, all of that. I read that and I based my thinking about how to continue fighting on that. And the campesinos really respected me for it.**

But when I asked Llamojha if he characterized himself as a Marxist, noting that many Peruvians of the era did so even if they did not belong to a political party, he was more reserved. He laughingly responded:

> **Well, I more or less sympathized. But I didn't give it all of my heart.**

Llamojha took a similar stance on communism and socialism. Despite his express political sympathies for the communist regimes in Cuba and China and his repeated assertions about the merits of socialism, he never labeled himself a communist or a socialist.

His reticence to self-identify as a Marxist is far from surprising. Accusations of communist affiliations had landed him in jail from the late 1940s forward. More pressing still, twenty-first-century Peru is still reeling from the violence and devastation of the 1980–2000 war that began when militants of the Peruvian Communist Party-Shining Path launched an armed struggle, and many Peruvians continue to equate Marxism, socialism, and communism with terrorism. That context can also help us understand Llamojha's insistence that he never belonged to a political party, despite his close work with members of the Partido Comunista del Perú-Bandera Roja.

I asked Llamojha if he, like so many other members of the CCP, belonged to Bandera Roja.

No. Sure, we talked, but I never formally joined the party.

When I pressed the point, asking why he didn't become more involved, he replied:

I said to them, "I can't. I don't have enough knowledge of the issue." I went to their meetings, but I didn't have any formal role at that time.

I asked him if he had ever belonged to any political party at all.

No, not a single one. I just went to their meetings, nothing more, but I never joined a party. I went to their meetings, but I just wanted to be an independent, nothing more! Besides, they gave you jobs to do, and I wouldn't do them!

They wanted me to go to the pueblos, to make propaganda for the party. That's why I didn't want to join! I was with the peasantry, with the Confederación Campesina del Perú, and that was enough. The Confederation called on me to go everywhere, and I didn't have time for anything else. They called me to Cuzco, Piura, Chiclayo; they called me everywhere.[16]

It is entirely possible that Llamojha never joined or even actively sympathized with any political party. A person could certainly be a leftist without belonging to a political party. But it is nonetheless clear that in the 1960s, Llamojha took sides with Saturnino Paredes, the CCP's legal advisor and head of the Maoist Partido Comunista del Perú-Bandera Roja, sharing Paredes's opposition to the Soviet line and praising China. But in the 1970s Llamojha's alliance with Paredes came to a disastrous end. I asked Llamojha what had happened with Paredes.

It's because Paredes cheated us badly. He always went to China and got money, saying he was making revolution, armed struggle, in Peru. Saying that there were already two liberated pueblos, Pomacocha and Eccash.

"They are liberated!" he said.

He was bringing a mountain of money from China, millions, claiming he was carrying out armed struggle in all of Peru. But he wasn't.

In China they asked me, "How's the revolution going?"

"There's no revolution at all there."

"But Paredes is taking money and arms from here, to make revolution. He says there are already two liberated pueblos."

And I said, "There is nothing. It's a lie."

Paredes was cheating China. So China sent investigators, delegates from

China, to investigate. And they discovered the truth. So when Paredes returned to China, China didn't want to receive him. And they cut this aid to Paredes.[17] So he went over to another country that was socialist, a small country. Albania. He started to go there, and he started getting money from there because China had rejected him on discovering the truth. I clarified all of this. After that, Saturnino Paredes didn't want to even see me. His supporters denounced me, saying that I was earning 60,000 [soles] working for the government, working for SINAMOS [Sistema Nacional de Apoyo a la Movilización Social (National System to Support Social Mobilization), a Velasco government agency]. They said this. They distributed flyers throughout all of Peru.

Here, there was one pueblo, Chacari [a community in the district of Concepción]. Paredes sent his people there to kill me. Chacari invited me to go to their fiesta and I went to lead the community's anniversary procession. A group that Paredes had appointed was there to kill me. They surrounded me and grabbed me around the chest.

"You're a traitor to Paredes!" they said.

The people who were there, they defended me. Always. The people who were holding the fiesta came to free me. They grabbed Paredes's supporters, they threw punches and freed me. The people defended me. Because they all knew me. That's how it was with Paredes, the division.[18]

Llamojha was not the only activist who split from Paredes. The Maoist university professor Abimael Guzmán broke ties with Paredes in 1969 and went on to found the Peruvian Communist Party-Shining Path in 1970.[19] Members of the political party Vanguardia Revolucionaria likewise opposed Paredes, believing that his politics had taken an unduly radical turn when he switched his allegiance from China to Albania. As prominent Vanguardia Revolucionaria activist Andrés Luna Vargas laughingly phrased it, "Enver Hoxha's Albania! Imagine that! What esoterism! Imagine that! Here? No way."[20] Ricardo Letts Colmenares, one of Vanguardia Revolucionaria's founders, offered a similar perspective. He commented, "Saturnino separated himself from the Chinese line and went to the Albanian line of Enver Hoxha. What craziness!" Letts also expressed sadness that Paredes had taken such a "dogmatic and sectarian" turn.[21]

Vanguardia Revolucionaria's leaders were also deeply unsatisfied with the CCP's direction, feeling that Paredes's extremist politics had led the CCP astray and that it had fallen into a period of inactivity and decay after 1966.[22] One

Vanguardia activist wrote that by 1970 "the participation of the bases was insignificant, the proceedings were bureaucratic," and the CCP did not "play the role of coordinator, organizer, centralizer, nor effective leader."[23] Letts similarly recalled: "Our sense was that it was a shame that it [the CCP] was running down a dead-end street, a narrow pass of dogmatic, sectarian deviation," and that if the CCP continued along that path, it "was going to have immense difficulties in transforming itself into a great organization of the masses."[24]

These tensions came to a head in May 1973 at the CCP's Fourth National Congress in Eccash, Ancash. At that congress, members of Vanguardia Revolucionaria and their sympathizers broke from Paredes, noisily withdrawing from the Eccash congress and making plans to hold their own CCP congress.[25] I asked Llamojha about the events in Eccash.

> **Yes, they carried out a campesino congress in Eccash. But because we were already divided, I didn't go. There, too, they agreed to kill me! This is what Paredes did. Everything was division. He divided the Peasant Confederation.**

Llamojha initially allied himself with the Vanguardia Revolucionaria activists who broke from Paredes at Eccash.[26] But when Vanguardia supporters chose party activist Andrés Luna Vargas rather than Llamojha as the leader of their newly established rival faction of the CCP, Llamojha split from it and established his own faction of the CCP, supported primarily by peasants from the department of Cuzco.[27] Suddenly, there were three competing factions of the CCP, each claiming to be the only legitimate Confederación Campesina del Perú.

Llamojha described this division, making reference to Letts:

> **Letts Colmenares started organizing another Peasant Confederation. The Peasant Confederation started to split, it started to weaken. That's why the Confederation divided into three. One was the Confederation I led, another was led by Saturnino Paredes. And then came Letts Colmenares with another Peasant Confederation. That lowered the peasants' morale, and the struggle had already been losing force. Because there was an agrarian reform, this had confused the peasants, because many of them were not perfectly oriented. That's what happened. Letts Colmenares started to go around, dividing the people, and that led to the weakening of the Peasant Confederation.**
>
> **Only Cuzco stood firm. When I was working in Ayacucho, a number of people came from Cuzco to talk with me. Cuzco didn't want the Peasant**

Confederation to disappear, so they came to Ayacucho to look for me, so that we could be resolute and not allow the Confederation to divide.

Paredes had dismissed me; he wanted nothing more to do with me. But Cuzco, they never left me. [Peasants from the department of] Piura, they didn't leave me. They always followed me.[28]

The three-way split of the CCP generated terrible animosities and much bitter invective, quickly marginalizing Llamojha, whose faction was easily the smallest and the weakest of the three. A 1973 story in the pro-Paredes newspaper *Bandera Roja* proclaimed that Llamojha "has fallen into the dirtiest political and social degeneration, turning into a dummy of Trotskyist and officialist puppets. He doesn't represent any campesinos from Ayacucho, nor those of his Community of Concepción, which he abandoned long ago."[29] Although that story's claims about Concepción were unfair, it is true that some individuals with whom Llamojha had once worked closely turned against him. At the second provincial convention of Cangallo campesinos, held in October 1974 in Pomacocha, delegates "declared Manuel Llamoja [*sic*] M. a traitor and campesino sellout for participating in the game plotted by the military regime in its efforts to divide the peasant movement and the PERUVIAN PEASANT CONFEDERATION."[30] These words came as a direct consequence of the fact that the convention's organizers were Paredes's allies. The insults continued in subsequent years. In a 1978 publication, Paredes's faction of the CCP declared Llamojha and several other leaders "enemy agents . . . enemies of the peasantry and agents of exploiters."[31]

While the sharpest denunciations against Llamojha came from Paredes's camp, members of Vanguardia Revolucionaria also criticized him. A 1974 publication produced by Vanguardia Revolucionaria referred to "Manuel Llamojha's insignificant clique," commenting that he had "in previous years helped liquidate the campesino movement with his mistaken line and now tries to pass as the maximum leader of a false CCP."[32] Llamojha was equally critical of Vanguardia Revolucionaria. When his CVR interviewers asked him about the party, he accused it of working on behalf of the Velasco regime and its agency SINAMOS:

They aided Velasco. They were always on the side of the bourgeoisie, and for that reason, I didn't agree with them. I explained this to the campesinos. Our clear position was to make agrarian reform with our own hands. And that's what we have done.

When one of the CVR interviewers pointed out that Vanguardia Revolucionaria had taken a similar position, leading peasant land seizures of haciendas in the province of Andahuaylas, Llamojha responded:

> They took lands to deliver them to SINAMOS. Vanguardia organized to seize land, but with the end of delivering it to SINAMOS, because SINAMOS had started to fail in the sierra. So, in came Vanguardia Revolucionaria, surely they were in agreement with SINAMOS. They seized the lands and delivered them to SINAMOS to form a cooperative.

Llamojha's characterizations of the 1974 Andahuaylas land seizures stem from Vanguardia Revolucionaria's controversial negotiations with the Velasco government following the invasions. Representatives of Vanguardia Revolucionaria and the Andahuaylas peasant federation struck an agreement with the military government whereby the regime recognized Andahuaylas campesinos' legitimate claim to the invaded lands. In exchange, campesinos had to accept the "agrarian debt," paying for the seized lands over a period of time to help compensate the aggrieved hacendados. To many Peruvian leftists and even some members of Vanguardia Revolucionaria, this agreement represented an unacceptable capitulation and a deplorable alliance with the military government.[33]

Beyond Vanguardia Revolucionaria's acceptance of the agrarian debt in Andahuaylas, there is an additional reason why Llamojha cast Vanguardia's land invasions as serving the government: accusing one's rivals of affiliation with the military government was a quick and effective way to deride them. Paredes made precisely this sort of accusation against Llamojha, asserting that Llamojha was on the Velasco regime's payroll. Llamojha's opposition to Vanguardia Revolucionaria's land seizures was also owing to the fact that state authorities blamed him for the invasions. He told his CVR interviewers:

> That's how it was in Andahuaylas. They seized sixty haciendas in the name of the Confederación Campesina del Perú.
>
> As it was done in the name of the Confederación Campesina del Perú, and as I was better known—because Vanguardia just formed that year, and that same year they seized the lands in the name of the Confederation—I was blamed.[34] The authorities and the hacendados themselves believed that I was leading the seizure of the haciendas. I didn't even know they were seizing the haciendas, and they started to pursue me, to look for me everywhere, but they didn't manage to find me.

When I was in Vischongo, twenty civil guards came to my pueblo to capture me, but they didn't find me in my pueblo. In Concepción, there were just three opponents [the abusive district authorities Grimaldo Castillo, Raúl Agüero, and Joaquín Chávez], the rest of the community was with me.

So, these three people said to the guards, "he must be in some *anexo* [small district community or annex]. You guys, divide yourselves into three groups and go and look for him."

They divided up into groups and they went to all the anexos, while five of them remained in the pueblo, waiting. That is, there was an order that they guard my house, but just at night.

These three people had said, "He's going to come back at night. You should wait at his home."

They watched over my house the whole night. I was returning from Vischongo, and when I was close to my pueblo, at the river, the lieutenant governor warned me.

"Don't go into the pueblo, because they are waiting for your return. They're going to come at night and watch over your house. Better if you go back from here," he said to me.

"But if they are only going to go at night, nothing is going to happen." Saying that, I went to my house, I dropped off my packages, and then I left. I went to another place, up into the hills. From there, I sent a message to the pueblo. So, the campesinos, a large number of campesinos, came up into the hills, to find me and to hold an assembly. We held an assembly there. I was there for fifteen days, because the guards would not leave the pueblo. The campesinos, poor things, they were always with me. They never abandoned me. They always came up into the hills, they brought me food.

I continued my questions about Vanguardia Revolucionaria by asking if Llamojha knew Lino Quintanilla, one of the party's most prominent activists. Llamojha replied with a story about the 1974 seizure of the Rurunmarca hacienda.

I met Lino Quintanilla when he came to this side [the Ayacucho side of the border between the departments of Ayacucho and Apurímac], to the Rurunmarca hacienda. There had been a land invasion there. Various communities invaded the Rurunmarca hacienda. It was a sugar-growing estate, and they invaded.

One community was called Pujas, and Lino Quintanilla, I don't know why, didn't want Pujas to enter the hacienda. So, three Pujas delegates came here by night to inform me and to ask me to speak with Lino to allow Pujas to take part.

"Why shouldn't we participate in this hacienda seizure?" they asked.

We arrived at the hacienda. They [Lino Quintanilla's supporters] had put guards in various spots, and we couldn't pass. So we arrived there and they stopped us.

"Who are you? Where are you going?" they asked. I showed my document.

"Ah! You can pass. You are a national delegate, you are a representative of Peru. You have to enter!"

So, I entered the other sector. Lino Quintanilla was there. He was in control of this part of the territory, with various communities. I arrived there, and sent a note to Quintanilla.

"I want to talk with you guys," I said.

He replied, "You have to come with five delegates!"

I went the next day. They let me pass and I spoke with Lino Quintanilla.

"You! What are you doing here?" he asked me.

"I came, they called on me, they informed me about what's happening, so that's why I've come."

"But what are you going to do here?" he asked me.

"Well, I have to talk with the masses. That's why I've come."

"You don't have to do anything!" he said to me. "I'm here. I'm in charge."

"That's fine, but I'm with the masses," I said to him.

"How can you be with the masses? I'm with the masses!"

"But here I am," I said to him.

He said to me, "You have to be with me! You can't be with the others, with those dirty leaders from Pujas!"

"But why?" I asked.

"This is how it is. They don't want us to take the haciendas."

"But they are not opposed. They have actually already taken the other side. The other part of the hacienda," I said.

"Be very careful! You shouldn't be leading badly," he said.

"How can I be leading badly?"

This was how we argued.[35]

Llamojha's recollections connect the aftermath of his encounter with Quintanilla to the start of his new job at the teachers' cooperative—the central office of the teachers' union—in the city of Ayacucho.[36] That job quickly led to more criticism from his former allies and, later, to misguided accusations of his involvement in the Shining Path. He explained:

> I was there [in Rurunmarca] for five days. After that, I returned to Concepción and three delegates came from the University of Huamanga. The students' union of Ayacucho had sent delegates to bring me to Ayacucho.
>
> "Something might happen to you here! Let's go!" they said.
>
> So, the three delegates brought me to Ayacucho to inform the university [about the events at Rurunmarca]. When I arrived in Ayacucho, the teachers gathered so I could speak to them.
>
> I spoke and they asked me, "When are you going to go to Lima?"
>
> "I want to go now, but I don't have money for the trip," I said.
>
> I didn't have the means. So the teachers said to me, "Well, in the teachers' cooperative, they need a custodian."
>
> They took me on for a month. But as they saw my work, how I acted, they asked me to stay. I was there until '81. I was working in the cooperative, but I had full permission to leave when there were peasant meetings in other places. And I went. The teachers themselves sent me.
>
> "Go to such and such a place, meetings, congresses. Go!" they said. I had full permission to leave, and my salary continued.

Nelson Pereyra was head of the teachers' cooperative at the time. He recalled: "The cooperative was run by people of a leftist tendency. And we knew very well that Mr. Llamojha Mitma was jobless and in a critical economic situation."[37] At the teachers' cooperative, Llamojha soon began working in the document reception office. He gathered together all of the cooperative's documents, sorting them and putting them into files. He also took responsibility for responding to the queries the cooperative received.

> Every kind of document, every kind of letter that came to the cooperative, I'd answer them, all of them, writing memos.

Llamojha quickly developed a warm relationship with many of the teachers working at the cooperative. He described it during his interview with the CVR:

> The teachers helped me. We spent a lot of time with the teachers who were clearly revolutionaries. Sure, some had petit bourgeois ideas. But there were others whose thinking was proletarian.
>
> When I was working in the teachers' cooperative, too, anything that

happened, they [regional authorities] would blame me. Students went out on a march in protest or workers went out on demonstrations and strikes, they'd come to get me. They'd take me prisoner, pulling me out of my workplace. One time, ten civil guards came to take me away, and my work compañeros defended me. They defended me, and so they took all of us away! The cooperative was closed a week, because every last one of the employees was imprisoned, to defend me! That's how it was.

Many of these "work compañeros" were members of the Peruvian Communist Party-Shining Path. Although Nelson Pereyra was not affiliated in any way with the Shining Path, he recalled that members of the Shining Path dominated the Ayacucho teachers' cooperative.[38] Some of Saturnino Paredes's allies thus took Llamojha's new job as proof that he was working with Abimael Guzmán, the Ayacucho university professor who had broken from Paredes in late 1969 and subsequently formed the Shining Path. A publication by the pro-Paredes faction of the CCP charged: "the traitor Llamojha, oriented by the sinister enemy agent Manuel Abimaíl [sic] Guzmán Reynoso who formed the group named 'Shining,' proclaimed himself 'secretary general' of the CCP, and acts at the service of groups outside the campesino movement, only to keep himself employed in a teaching cooperative controlled by said traitor group."[39]

Another pro-Paredes document claimed that Llamojha "finds himself manipulated by the so-called 'Shining Path' group led by the professor Guzmán," and the same document denounced "the 'Shining' divisionists who manipulate the traitor Llamohja [sic] and make him sign divisionist documents."[40] These comments were biting and malicious, but back in the 1970s these statements did not carry the same kind of weight they do today. In the 1970s, the Shining Path was widely regarded as little more than a fringe political group with little influence outside Ayacucho and had yet to acquire its reputation as a violent, extremist organization.[41]

A few other activists from the 1970s told me that Guzmán participated in Llamojha's faction of the CCP, so I asked Llamojha about his relationship with Guzmán. Mindful of the sensitive nature of the issue—today, many Peruvians quickly cast any association with the Shining Path as involvement in terrorism—I simply asked Llamojha if Abimael Guzmán sought his advice in the 1970s.

Advice? No. Sure, he asked about the struggle of the campesinos. And I started to meet with him in Ayacucho, when he was a professor. He looked

for me with other people, to talk. So we talked during meetings. He always attended meetings of the campesinos. But at that time, he didn't say anything about taking up arms. Only about the peasantry's struggle. That's all he talked about. We always saw each other in the peasant meetings.

In Lima, I went to his house. I went twice. But what I didn't like is that he wouldn't talk the way we are talking now.

I'd say to him, "This problem in the sierra, how are we going to solve it?"

"Well, the peasants will take care of this," he'd say to me. "Go and talk with the students from the university," he'd say to me. That's all he'd say to me. He didn't talk much.

I also asked Llamojha if Guzmán participated in the CCP.

No, he barely participated. He appeared at the last minute, but he never went to the CCP.

Members of the Shining Path did, however, take part in the national congress that Llamojha convened in 1975 for his faction of the CCP. This congress was held at the Guamán Poma de Ayala school in the city of Ayacucho, a school run by the San Cristóbal de Huamanga University's education faculty. Guzmán was a professor in that faculty, and many of the teachers at Guamán Poma were members of the Shining Path.[42] Llamojha described this congress:

In this congress that we held in Ayacucho, a national congress, delegates from Cuzco came, they also came from Piura. And there, I stepped down. I had served so many years as secretary general.

Cuzco didn't want to let me leave the secretariat. Piura didn't want it either. They said to me, "You aren't going to resign!"

The people from Piura, from the department of Tumbes, they didn't want to let me go. "How can we allow that?" they asked.

This 1975 congress was a terrible disappointment. Because Llamojha's faction of the CCP was small in size and limited in influence, very few delegates came to the gathering.[43] Weak from the start, Llamojha's ties with Guzmán and members of the Shining Path fizzled shortly afterward. Guzmán came to the conclusion that unions were nothing more than deviations from the true course of revolution and that they threatened to delay the onset of armed struggle and popular war. Guzmán thus ended all Shining Path work in the peasant union movement.[44] Llamojha remembered this attitude and discussed it with his CVR interviewers. He explained that when Shining Path members went out into the countryside,

> they told the communities that unions were no longer worth anything. I asked about this in various meetings that I was invited to, I asked them why. And so they attacked me.
>
> "Why? Because is there really any chance that a union is going to make a revolution?" they said to me.
>
> "But then who is going to help the armed struggle? Campesinos have to help, because they have organized. And if they don't, there's not going to be any armed struggle. That's how it is!" I said. We argued hard about this.
>
> So, when they invited me to meetings, I said, "If the group, or better said the peasants, aren't going to help the armed struggle, then how are you going to make armed struggle? Because the fight, the armed group, needs the support of the peasantry. And if the unions die? Then how are you going to make a revolution?"
>
> But they didn't pay attention to me. So, from there, they marginalized me because of this. When I talked this way, they marginalized me.
>
> "You're a reactionary," they said to me. That's how they talked to me.

Another component of the Shining Path's rejection of Llamojha involved his constant discussions of campesinos' Inka heritage and the injustices of colonialism. In his 1970 address to the CCP, Llamojha argued:

> Since the fall of the Inkaic State of Tawantin Suyo [the Quechua term for the Inka Empire], we have been subjected to the most opprobrious and cruel exploitation and servitude by the Spanish colonists . . . who imposed a feudal colonial government, converting all of Peru into feudal domains and staining the immense fields of the Fatherland's ground with blood. From that instant, millions of us campesinos have been fighting for the recuperation of the lands that were seized from us through the force of arms.[45]

The Shining Path's leadership had no patience for Llamojha's anticolonial vision, insisting on a rigidly classist understanding of Peru's problems as rooted firmly in the workings of international capitalism. The Shining Path also proved brutally disrespectful of Andean cultural practices and beliefs.[46] It is no surprise, then, that a Shining Path militant dismissed Llamojha's revolutionary potential, disparaging his respect for indigenous rights and history with the comment that he "has Incanist ideas."[47] Years before the Shining Path launched its armed struggle, its collaboration with Llamojha had come to a decisive end.

A Last Chance for Unity

With his own faction of the CCP languishing, Llamojha found one final opportunity to resume a prominent role in national peasant struggles. In August 1978, campesinos from the department of Cuzco convened the Special National Congress for the Unification of the Peruvian Peasantry, held in Quillabamba.[48] Congress organizers invited delegates from all three competing factions of the CCP, hoping to consolidate these rivals into one organization. I asked Llamojha about this meeting.

> That was when things were bad between Paredes and me. When I arrived in Quillabamba, Paredes's people did too. They went to this congress in Cuzco on Paredes's behalf and they started to accuse me.
> "He doesn't represent anybody! He is a traitor!" they said.
> But the delegations in attendance didn't pay attention. Instead, they asked that I speak. Paredes's people didn't want me to speak, but the masses ruled there. The masses ruled.[49]

Delegates at the Quillabamba congress elected Llamojha president of a "National Commission of Unification of the Peruvian Peasantry."[50] Although Llamojha's faction of the CCP was far smaller and weaker than the other two, his election as president is not surprising. Certainly, he stood to gain the most from reunification and was probably much more enthusiastic than either Vanguardia Revolucionaria or Paredes's representatives about the prospect. Even more important, peasants from Cuzco made up eighty-eight of the ninety-eight delegates in attendance, and Cuzco campesinos had formed Llamojha's key base of support since the CCP's fracture in 1973.

Reunification did not happen. At Vanguardia Revolucionaria's subsequent Fifth National Congress of its faction of the CCP in Equeco-Chacán, Cuzco, delegates voted on several proposals for expanding their faction, including one proposal to attempt reunification with the other two factions. But they ultimately chose instead to unite with the remnants of the recently disbanded National Agrarian Confederation, rejecting the opportunity to resume working with Llamojha and Paredes.[51] Llamojha was present when that vote happened, attending the congress in the hope of reuniting the CCP.[52] After watching the chance for reunification crumble, he returned to Ayacucho and his job at the teachers' cooperative. His leadership of the CCP had come to a definitive end. By 1979, Paredes's faction of the CCP had also weakened significantly.[53]

Vanguardia Revolucionaria's hold on the CCP was now solid, and there was no place for Llamojha in that body. His relationship with Paredes and his sympathizers was likewise beyond repair. By this point, Llamojha had also been shunned by Shining Path party members, who rejected his enduring commitment to peasant unions and his indigenist views. At the close of the 1970s, then, his political marginalization was complete. Tragically for him, the 1980s proved even more devastating than the difficult years of the 1970s.

SIX

A Wound That Won't Heal

POLITICAL VIOLENCE, DISPLACEMENT, AND LOSS, 1980–2000

"The bullets were flying," Llamojha told his CVR interviewers. "I was sure they were going to kill me." He was describing his daring escape from police who sought to arrest him on charges of terrorism, charges that arose shortly after members of the Partido Comunista del Perú-Sendero Luminoso (Peruvian Communist Party-Shining Path) launched an armed struggle in May 1980. Party militants began their so-called People's War in rural Ayacucho, hoping to capture the countryside and then conquer Peru's cities, ultimately aiming to liberate Peru's impoverished masses by destroying the Peruvian state.[1] The conflict quickly spiraled into a brutal insurgency and state counterinsurgency. The overwhelming majority of the over 69,000 Peruvians killed in this twenty-year war were rural indigenous men, women, and children. Llamojha's adversaries were quick to accuse him of involvement in several Shining Path attacks, alleging that he was a member of the militant party. These charges were the most serious accusations Llamojha had ever faced. Because of the extremity of the Shining Path's violence and the intensity of the Peruvian state's counterinsurgency, those accused of participation in Shining Path actions usually found themselves labeled terrorists by the Peruvian government and military. Such accusations carried the very real risk of decades in prison or, worse, extrajudicial murder.

These accusations had a devastating impact on Llamojha's life. He and Esther were forced to flee their home in Concepción, escaping Ayacucho for Lima, where they had to scrape together a life as impoverished internal political refugees. They were among 600,000 Peruvian men, women, and children who were displaced because of the violence. With Peru's economy in shambles and a long record of imprisonments, it was almost impossible for Llamojha to find work and support his family. He had to remain away from his beloved community and his home region of Ayacucho for two full decades because it was simply too dangerous to return.

Tragically, these accusations of terrorism also touched Llamojha's children. Walter, Hilda, and Herbert Llamojha were all arrested on spurious charges during the years of violence. Walter very nearly lost his life in one of the war's most notorious state-sponsored atrocities, a deadly government assault on the El Frontón jail. Llamojha's youngest son, Herbert, suffered an even sadder fate. Denounced by Llamojha's brother in a striking act of familial betrayal, Herbert was arrested on charges of participating in the Shining Path's first armed assault, and he vanished after Shining Path militants attacked the jail where he was imprisoned. No one knows what happened to him. Herbert's permanent disappearance marks the central sorrow in Llamojha's life.

The 1980s formed the most painful period in his history, and his rich supply of stories nearly dried up when his narrative reached the onset of the internal war in 1980.[2] He had far less to say about the 1980s and 1990s than the earlier decades of his life, but his experiences were echoed throughout much of Latin America's late twentieth-century history. In El Salvador, Nicaragua, and Guatemala, revolutionary efforts for change were met with deadly counterinsurgencies that cost the lives of hundreds of thousands of men, women, and children. The horrors of political violence forced many to flee their homes and communities as refugees, deeply traumatized by all they had seen and lost. In South America, military dictatorships took hold in Uruguay, Brazil, Chile, and Argentina, and individuals suspected of leftist activities—or even just sympathies—were routinely arrested and tortured. Tens of thousands were also permanently "disappeared," killed extrajudicially by soldiers and police who claimed no knowledge of their whereabouts.[3] Political violence left Llamojha, his family, and countless other Latin Americans with wounds that won't heal.

Losing Herbert

Two hours after midnight on July 15, 1980, civil guards stormed into Llamojha's home in Concepción and seized his youngest son, Herbert. The guards took Herbert to the provincial capital, Cangallo, and locked him in jail, accusing him of having helped lead an assault on the Ayrabamba hacienda five days earlier.[4] The attack on Ayrabamba was the Shining Path's first major armed action following the launch of its armed struggle in May 1980. To this day the Shining Path celebrates the Ayrabamba assault as a major, heroic action and praises the leadership role that Augusta La Torre, Shining Path's second-in-command and the wife of Abimael Guzmán, played in the assault.[5]

The Ayrabamba attack began early on the morning of July 10, 1980. Sixty-seven-year-old César Parodi Vassallo—son of the hacendada Elodia Vassallo de Parodi—awoke to a loud explosion. He first thought that the noise came from a radio, but the smell made him realize it was dynamite. Then came a banging on the door. "Open the door!" someone called. "Who are you, damn it?" César asked.[6] When he didn't get a response, he went out onto the terrace and called out to his nephew Carlos. Carlos didn't answer, and when César saw his bedroom door start to give way, broken by a pick, he decided to run. Sliding down a broken ladder, dressed only in his pajamas, the elderly man ran through his fields and across the Pampas River toward the police post in the neighboring community of Ocros.[7]

Down the hall from his uncle, Carlos Parodi Donayri had lain sleeping in his room, alongside his wife, Flora Gutiérrez Zea, and their four young children. At the same moment the intruders banged on César's door, eight armed individuals burst into Carlos's bedroom and grabbed him by his arms and legs. The assailants fired two gunshots at the ceiling and then tied up Carlos and his wife by their hands and feet. In the darkness, Carlos was unable to recognize any of his attackers.[8] The assailants verbally and physically assaulted him and his wife and seized a number of goods and a hefty amount of cash from the bedroom. After several hours, they led Carlos outside to the hacienda's *bagacera*, the area where processed sugarcane stalks and fibers are left to dry. Carlos saw an estimated 50 campesinos standing in the bagacera; others testified that as many as 150 were present.[9] Herbert Llamojha was among those peasants.

Born in 1956, Herbert had grown up in Lima, arriving in Peru's capital when he was just seven years old and remaining there until 1978. He had come back to Concepción because of necessity. His family had been informed

FIG. 6.1 Herbert Llamojha, Lima, 1969 or 1970. Photo courtesy
of Manuel Llamojha Mitma.

that their lands in Concepción were subject to seizure if they remained un-
worked, and as Llamojha was employed in the teachers' cooperative in the
city of Ayacucho, responsibility for maintaining the family's terrain fell to
doña Esther, who had been living in Lima with her children since the mid-
1960s. She decided to move back to Concepción, and Herbert chose to go
with her. Coming back to Concepción was a sacrifice for him. The family's
dire economic situation had delayed his graduation from secondary school,
as he had needed to work while studying; moving back to Concepción ended
his studies altogether.[10] But his sister María recalled that Herbert would not
even consider staying in Lima. She explained that he was very attached to
their mother, so he decided to come back with her to Concepción. As María
explained it, Herbert's concern about his mother's welfare meant that "he
couldn't leave my mother on her own."[11]

In Concepción, Herbert labored on his parents' plots of land, but he also
assumed an active role in the community's affairs. Much like his father, he

became someone to whom local campesinos turned for help: peasant workers from the Ayrabamba hacienda asked him to write a formal complaint on their behalf, denouncing the lack of social security and payment problems on the estate. Herbert also began serving as secretary of both Concepción's community council and its health committee, and he wanted to play an even more active role in Concepción's affairs.[12] But he found himself stymied by the same men who had long harassed his father: the abusive district authorities Grimaldo Castillo, Joaquín Chávez, and Raúl Agüero. In a March 1981 letter, Herbert wrote that Grimaldo Castillo and his allies "believe themselves owners and gentleman of the community. For that, they have the posts of political and communal authority in their power, without giving young people the opportunity to be authorities."[13]

The day before the assault on the Ayrabamba hacienda, Herbert was in the nearby community of Chacari, harvesting corn and wheat. That afternoon, he and around forty other campesinos went to a meeting where a young man from Lima told everyone that they would soon be called to carry out a "popular harvest" on Ayrabamba's lands to recover all that the hacendados had failed to pay to their workers. That call for the popular harvest came early the next morning, and a few hours later Herbert arrived in Ayrabamba alongside a number of other campesinos.[14]

When Herbert got to Ayrabamba, he saw a man and a blond woman paying the hacienda's workers. The woman asked individual hacienda workers how much they were owed for unpaid work on the hacienda, and then she gave them money from a leather bag hanging around her neck—cash that she and fellow assailants had seized from Carlos Parodi's bedroom.[15] We now know that the woman distributing the money was Augusta La Torre, whose nom de guerre was Comrade Norah.[16]

Soon thereafter, several people brought Carlos Parodi outside, his hands bound with twine, and placed him in the center of a group of campesinos. The leading assailants started to berate Carlos for the abuses he had committed against campesinos, denouncing all of his wrongs. After each of these denunciations the crowd applauded. One of the leaders held a knife against him; another kicked him, forcing him to kneel. Many in the group were armed, some with guns, others with slingshots and sticks, and some called for his execution. The leaders then warned him that this was his last chance to leave the hacienda. If he didn't leave, they would come back and evict him by force. After these denunciations, the assailants gave him a few more kicks and then took him to a storage room and locked him in.[17]

Augusta La Torre then opened the hacienda's store to the assembled campesinos, who quickly began taking all they could. Some seized blouses and shoes, others took sandals, locks, medicines, and even towels, quickly emptying the store. But before any further action could ensue, a lookout announced that the police were on their way, so the assault's leaders called on everyone to retreat to Concepción. Once the participants had gathered in Concepción's central plaza, a Shining Path activist announced that the campesinos "had now opened the breach or the path of the poor" and that they should all be ready for the distribution of lands. The campesinos applauded. Another militant then warned "the servants of the government, Víctor Llamojha [Herbert's uncle] and Grimaldo Castillo Gutiérrez" to avoid any further engagement with the Parodi hacendados. If they failed to do so, they would be executed by the pueblo. After one more speech, everyone went back to their home communities. It was about one o'clock in the afternoon. By the time César Parodi finally made it back to Ayrabamba with civil guards, the attackers had long since fled the hacienda.[18]

By Herbert's telling, he was little more than a bystander at the events at Ayrabamba. After his arrest, he told court authorities that he had done nothing more criminal than take a handful of oranges from the hacienda's orchard. He hadn't taken anything else from the hacienda or its store "for fear that the police would discover it."[19] The initial police reports did not name Herbert as one of the leaders of the attack, but Carlos Parodi and his wife, Flora Gutiérrez, subsequently accused Herbert of playing a much more active role in the assault. Carlos claimed that he had heard Herbert's voice among those denouncing him outside on the bagacera, and Flora claimed that she saw him walking around with a weapon.[20] Five days after the attack on the hacienda, civil guards pulled Herbert from his home and placed him under arrest, charging that he was one of several "intellectual and material authors" of the assault.[21]

Herbert maintained that the accusations against him stemmed from personal enmities rather than his actual involvement in the events at Ayrabamba. He rejected Flora Gutiérrez's accusations as slander motivated by a desire for vengeance. As he phrased it, "she says this because I spoke the truth about the abuses the hacendado commits."[22] Herbert similarly charged that Carlos Parodi had accused him in retaliation for his public denunciation of Parodi's financial misdeeds. In addition, Herbert testified that his other accusers— including his father's long-standing enemy Grimaldo Castillo—"accused him of being the ringleader because of personal quarrels" and because of hostility against him.[23]

There was an especially troubling element to Herbert's arrest: he had been betrayed by members of his own family. In one of our interviews, Llamojha explained:

> **They seized my son from here. My brother Víctor and my sister Donatilda brought the police here. They broke down the door and entered the house, and they captured him here in the house.**

Herbert himself made a detailed accusation against his uncle Víctor. In court documents, Herbert charged that Víctor had no knowledge whatsoever about who actually participated in the Ayrabamba assault and had denounced him solely because he had "ill will" against him.[24] Herbert was not the only one to accuse Víctor. The indigenous peasants Félix Gómez Salvatierra, Rufina Rosa Martínez, and Marina Loayza Palomino likewise blamed Víctor for their arrests. These individuals explained that they had previously denounced him for a variety of wrongdoings, including embezzlement of Concepción's community funds, misappropriation of local church funds, and spreading misinformation about Concepción's school.[25] Marina Loayza also charged that Víctor was closely allied with her other accuser, the district authority Grimaldo Castillo, and that the two men "constantly go to Ayrabamba and are very good friends with the Parodi family. This family even gave a series of gifts to these two people."[26]

In our interviews, Llamojha offered similarly staunch criticisms of his brother. Llamojha explained:

> **Víctor was always in favor of the hacendados, he was always with the hacendados and he was never with the pueblo. He spoke in defense of the hacendados, saying that they were the pueblo's means of support. He never agreed that the fight should be against the hacendados. Here, in the pueblo itself, there were three persons in favor of the hacendados. He was with that group, and he didn't agree with what I was fighting for: for the pueblo and for the liberation of Peru. He didn't agree with this.**
>
> **He was always on the hacendados' side and he always contradicted me and the others who fought against the hacendados. He always protested, and he always accused me, saying that I was inciting the pueblo, the Indians, to rebel.**

Because I always fought against the hacendados, he couldn't stand to see me. That's how it was with us.[27]

While Herbert sat in jail, accused of orchestrating the attack on Ayrabamba, two more charges were levied against him. In November 1980, he and six others were accused of having downed telegraph poles and stolen telegraph wire in the nearby community of Puccka in the closing days of June. This accusation came from Grimaldo Castillo, who reported to civil guards that Herbert and the other six men all "belong to the faction of Shining Path, the same ones who continuously carry out meetings in the main plaza of the district of Concepción, carrying a red flag and threatening the authorities for the simple fact that the authorities don't belong to this political organization."[28] Herbert staunchly denied the charges against him. He asserted that "he does not belong to any political party, much less is he an agitator with the Shining Path political faction." He also denied carrying out political meetings in Concepción, though he noted that he did "attend the assemblies of the peasant community of Concepción in which truths about the pueblo's problems are spoken."[29] The judge ultimately ruled in Herbert's favor, noting that while it was clear the telegraph poles and wire had been vandalized, there was insufficient evidence to establish responsibility for the act.[30]

The second additional charge against Herbert was levied for a crime that was actually committed while he sat in jail. Someone detonated sticks of dynamite in the doorway of Grimaldo Castillo's home in the early morning hours of October 14, 1980. The door was nearly destroyed, but no one was hurt. A civil guard reported that "the presumed authors of the terrorist attack on the home of the Governor of the district of Concepción Grimaldo Castillo Gutiérrez were the ringleading agitators of the Shining Path faction." The guard then listed eight people, including Herbert.[31] A subsequent civil guard report repeated these charges, asserting that all of the accused "continuously commit a series of offenses" against the public peace, holding meetings in the district's main plaza under a red flag.[32] Grimaldo Castillo blamed Herbert and four others, accusing them of being ringleaders who "carry out acts that go against the public peace." Grimaldo Castillo added that the accused men were "trying to generate psychosis in the residents so that . . . they would become convinced and would join the Shining Path faction."[33]

Herbert denied his involvement in the bombing and insisted that he did not belong to the Shining Path. His main defense was timing: he was in jail when Grimaldo Castillo's home was bombed. As Herbert phrased it, his involvement was "an impossible crime, because I simply could not have been in two different places at the same time."[34] Again, the court agreed, ruling that it could not determine the guilt of the accused. But Herbert did not have the same fortune in the trial for the July 1980 attack on the Ayrabamba hacienda. He was convicted of the charges against him—assault and armed robbery—and sentenced to seven years in prison.[35]

Because of his "extremely bad economic situation," Herbert could not afford a lawyer and had to represent himself.[36] But even without the aid of an attorney, he made several impassioned calls for his release from jail, writing numerous letters in his own defense.[37] Like the documents Llamojha had penned in earlier decades, Herbert's letters often stressed the Parodis' abuses, invoking the image of the gamonal, the extremely abusive local strongman. In a September 1980 letter, Herbert charged that his imprisonment was owing only to the "depraved maneuvers" of Ayrabamba's hacendados, who were "scheming against the community of Concepción, as they are accustomed to doing when those whom they exploit resist their gamonalist impositions."[38] Another letter described Ayrabamba as a "stronghold of the blackest feudal gamonalist exploitation." The same letter asserted that the Parodis "submerge our peasant community in gamonalist terror and perpetuate the exploitation to which they have tied us for more than a half century of pain and tears."[39] Herbert also made many appeals for his conditional release, stressing his good behavior in the Cangallo jail and in the community of Concepción. None of these strategies worked, and he remained in jail.[40]

After several months in the Cangallo jail, Herbert and his coaccused were transferred to the prison in the department capital, Ayacucho. From that prison, he and eleven others wrote of the abuses and mistreatment they were suffering there. Their troubling letter explained:

> We twelve people find ourselves detained in the Ayacucho jail for nearly one year, without reaching the justice that belongs to us by right because of the bias of the Cangallo trial judge, Dr. Juan Flores Rojas, imputing our participation in the incident that took place on the tenth of July of last year, when in reality we had nothing to do with the action. . . . Some of us were taken by guards in our homes, even without arrest orders, only because of false, anonymous claims. Others of us were taken by *sinchis* [shock troops] on the path from our fields where we were working. . . . We have been inhumanely tortured by civil guards, sinchis, justices of the peace, lackeys of the hacienda, using ground chilis, hot water thrown on the most vul-

nerable parts of our body, using cactus spines and other things to batter us while naked; using tanks of water . . . to choke us until we faint.[41]

The letter closed by asking for a swift trial. I have found one additional letter from Herbert. In September 1981 he wrote to the Ayacucho courts requesting copies of old documents pertaining to Concepción's 1965 legal conflict with Ayrabamba. He was probably planning to use those documents to support his legal defense, invoking history much as his father always did.[42] But then he vanishes from the archival record. Just a few months later, Herbert himself disappeared.

Into Hiding

Llamojha could do very little to help his imprisoned son—he could visit, he could offer his advice, and he could bring him food, but he could not get Herbert out of jail. And it was not long before Llamojha was unable even to visit Herbert, as the mounting number of accusations against Llamojha himself forced him to go into hiding. Although Llamojha was in the city of Ayacucho at the time of the assault on Ayrabamba and had absolutely no involvement in the events there, various people nonetheless accused him of a role in the attack. Civil guards labeled Llamojha the leader of the assault, asking one Concepción resident to explain his involvement "in the recent terrorist attacks in company with other elements under the direction of known agitator Manuel Llamocca Mitma."[43] The guards also described an envelope supposedly sent by "the so-titled lieutenant colonel Manuel Llamocca Mitma, commander general of the armed forces of the liberation of Peru."[44] Llamojha recalled the accusations against him.

> They blamed me. I don't know how this group [Shining Path militants] entered the hacienda. I didn't know.

These groundless accusations of involvement in the Ayrabamba assault were not the only spurious claims Llamojha faced. He was also accused of leading armed attacks on two military barracks. He told his CVR interviewers about these charges, explaining that his accusers were his longtime local enemies, the three abusive district authorities Grimaldo Castillo, Joaquín Chávez, and Raúl Agüero:

> They were servants of the hacendados, until the end. They couldn't stand the sight of me. So when the armed struggle began, they presented a docu-

ment to the prefecture. This person Castillo got eleven people to sign, and they sent it to the prefect saying that I had taken the barracks in Huanta, and in San Miguel. I hadn't even gone there! So, there came a really strong order for my capture.

When I asked Llamojha about this order for his arrest, he noted the role played by his brother Víctor and explained:

They accused me of belonging to the Communist Party that was organizing the armed struggle. Here, in Concepción, those two or three people who were against me, they tricked people into signing a document against me. My own brother got them to do all of this. The denunciation said that I was a terrorist with the community under my sway. So, six police officers came to the teaching cooperative.

They entered the cooperative. I was working upstairs on the second floor, in the secretary's office; that's where I worked. I don't know what I was thinking, but I had closed the door. The police came up to the secretary's office, but as it was closed, they didn't knock on the door. If they had knocked on the door, I would have come out and they would have arrested me. The six police officers remained seated down below, on the first floor, because my compañeros had said to them, "He isn't here. He has left the commission." They were down there, waiting.

My compañeros came upstairs to advise me. "How are you going to get down? How are you going to leave? Where can you escape from?" they said.

So I said, "I will leave through the door, because they don't know me."

I came down from above, and the six police officers were sitting there. Because they didn't know me, I greeted them—I shook their hands, and I left. I went to my house. You have to be serene; if you act nervous, they'll get suspicious. I wasn't nervous, I greeted them, I shook the police officers' hands, and I left. After that, I didn't return to my workplace, because the police came every day to wait for me.

Llamojha hid in the hills surrounding the city of Ayacucho for an entire month, sleeping amid cactuses. He told his CVR interviewers:

Happily, a teacher protected me. He was from the north, from Huachao, his last name was Regalado. As he lived down the hill, I went to his house and he gave me food. I was sleeping in the hills, and the bullets were flying, day and night. The soldiers walked around, shooting. The bullets passed right over me, whistling. The bullets made holes in the cactus pears, in the *paqpas* [maguey leaves], everything. I was there, the bullets were flying, I was sure they were going to kill me.

Knowing that his life was in jeopardy, Llamojha made the difficult decision to flee to Lima. Because of the urgent orders for his arrest, he knew that if he presented his national identity documents at the checkpoints, guards would arrest him immediately. He thus forged a birth certificate to attempt to escape. In our interview he explained:

I was hidden for a month. After that, my wife and I escaped to Lima.

It was in '81, in December. There was a checkpoint leaving Ayacucho. I had made up a birth certificate to be able to get through, but they wouldn't let you pass with just a birth certificate. You had to have your national identity document. But I couldn't present that, because of my name. So I didn't have any documents to present.

"If you don't have documents, you can't pass," they said.

They took me inside the checkpoint. Then, because the police were busy stopping all the cars, I immediately left the checkpoint and got back on the bus. We rode to Pisco and then to Chincha. From Chincha, we had to take a car because people said they wouldn't stop cars at the checkpoints; they'd just let them through.

Once we got to Lima, I looked for my son Walter at his workplace, because we didn't have the money to get all the way to his house. But I couldn't find him. We took a taxi to his house, but he wasn't there either, so a neighbor paid the taxi driver.

That daring escape was not the end of Llamojha's travails, for he was still a wanted man. He told his CVR interviewers:

When I arrived, my enemies had already communicated with Lima. So, they looked for me, going to the homes of all of my *paisanos* [fellow Concepción community members living in Lima].

My paisanos said, "No, he's not here. He hasn't been here in a really long time. He must be dead by now."

The masses helped me. They never left me alone. That's how the masses are. That's why I like being with the masses, they protect me. They help me in everything.

Llamojha's youngest daughter, María, followed her parents to Lima shortly thereafter. Knowing that soldiers would likely detain her because of the arrest orders for her father, the teenager employed her father's own strategies: she forged identity documents using a fake name and crafted a letter that supposedly granted her official permission to travel without parental accompaniment.[45]

Llamojha was in hiding in Lima when his son Herbert disappeared. On March 2, 1982, Shining Path militants attacked the Ayacucho prison where Herbert and his co-accused were jailed in an attempt to liberate imprisoned members of their party. Witnesses later reported hearing explosions of dynamite and seeing large columns of smoke in the air. The well-coordinated assault managed to free 304 prisoners, of whom approximately 70 had been accused of being members of the Shining Path.[46] We know that Herbert Llamojha escaped that night, but that is all we know. Police may have killed him right outside the jail, or they may have arrested him and killed him later. Or perhaps he fled the scene and then died elsewhere. His fate is unknown.

The first time Llamojha spoke to me about Herbert's disappearance came toward the end of our first interview together, when I asked him how many children he had.

> I have five, two men, three women. But the boy died. As it happens, they detained him over Ayrabamba. After that, there was the seizure of the Ayacucho jail. All the prisoners left, they escaped. My son, too, escaped from there. The Ayrabamba hacienda did this to my son. From there, my son, I don't remember the date, my wife remembers, a group went to liberate all the prisoners. In this, many prisoners escaped and some who didn't want to leave, stayed. My son escaped, and after that, we don't know anything.

Llamojha broke down crying when he told me this, and I rushed to comfort him. All that mattered at that point in the interview was to give comfort to an elderly man in terrible emotional pain, and out of compassion, neither Alicia nor I broached the subject of Herbert's disappearance with Llamojha again. Llamojha himself mentioned Herbert in another interview, after Alicia commented that it must have been difficult for Llamojha to be apart from his children during all his years of activism.

> Yes, it was hard to leave them. As I was being pursued, it made me sad. My kids got used to being without me, to being on their own. That's why, when my sons grew up, they helped me in the struggle, in representing the pueblo. That's why they killed the one son. He was the bravest. They took my son from here [Concepción] and killed him.

Llamojha also wrote about the Ayrabamba assault in one of his personal notebooks but carefully avoided any mention of Herbert's name. The passage reads as follows:

THE SEIZURE OF AYRABAMBA

The seizure of Ayrabamba occurred on the tenth (10) of July 1980. Days later, thirty-eight campesinos were detained by the instruments of exploitation, the Civil Guard, under the command of César Parodi, a murderous gamonal [gamonal de horca y cuchillo]. Eleven of the detained were kept in the Cangallo jail. A while later, they were transferred to Ayacucho, where an oral hearing took place in the months of September and October 1981 in the Ayacucho Court of Justice. When the oral hearing concluded, nine campesinos were sentenced, some to three years and others to seven years in jail.

The assault on Ayacucho's dungeon jail took place in the month of March 1982, and in the massive escape that resulted, five of the nine prisoners sentenced, born in Concepción, fled. There only remained four who did not want to leave. They were:

1. Alfredo Hinostroza Palomino

2. Marina Loayza Palomino

3. Rosa Martínez Sulca

4. Teodocia Gómez Ochoa

Months later, they were transferred to Lima.[47]

Llamojha kept Herbert's name out of this essay, his son's constant absence surely too painful to even write about. Llamojha is not the only one who suffers; Herbert's disappearance remains a searing hurt for the Llamojha family. Llamojha's eldest daughter, Hilda, began crying when asked about Herbert. Through heavy tears she explained, "I lost my brother . . . when I think of him, I ask 'where could he be?' If he had just died, we could have recovered his body."[48] Walter Llamojha commented that Herbert's disappearance "was very painful, for my mom, my dad, for us. We still miss him, to this day. What happened? What could have happened to him? It's very worrisome and we always miss him."[49] María Llamojha explained, "I think it's something that only people who have experienced can understand. It's not . . . I mean you don't have a person who has died and whom you can bury, and that's very

FIG. 6.2
Herbert
Llamojha,
location
unknown,
late 1970s.
Photo courtesy
of Manuel
Llamojha Mitma.

important. It's not the same to have someone disappeared. That's so terrible, and it was terrible for my mother, too, to not be able to find my brother's body. Even today, it's like a hole, like a wound that won't heal." She added, "You have no place to mourn, if he's dead. And you always wonder. When I'm traveling, I always look at other people, wondering if maybe it's him, thinking that maybe he had a nervous breakdown and doesn't recognize us."[50]

Herbert's disappearance was soon followed by other nightmares for Llamojha and his family. The 1982 killing of district authority Grimaldo Castillo brought a renewed surge of state suspicion against Llamojha. Because of Castillo's decades' worth of abuses, Shining Path militants placed him on one of their notorious "black lists"—documents that recorded the names of particularly abusive individuals whom Shining Path activists would then target for assassination. Shining Path militants publicly executed Grimaldo Castillo in Concepción's central plaza in late March 1982. They cut his tongue from his mouth, cut off his testicles, and hung him from a post, where he bled to death.

As a warning to others, they placed a sign on his body that read: "This is how snitches and enemies of the pueblo die. Long live the armed struggle!"[51] Tragically, this kind of absolutist violence became the Shining Path's hallmark over the long course of the war. Worse still, as the first wave of black list executions came to an end and the state's counterinsurgency gained strength, Shining Path militants turned their extreme violence against humble indigenous peasants whom they deemed insufficiently cooperative.

Llamojha made reference to this kind of violence when I asked his opinion about the Shining Path.

I thought it was bad. He [Guzmán] said, "we have to kill the pueblos' authorities." I didn't agree with that. How could we kill authorities who are campesinos? It was a really bad idea to kill low-level authorities. They killed the governor who was here, and I didn't agree with that. How could they kill the pueblo's authorities? The authorities were from the pueblo itself, from the indigenous masses. I didn't agree with that.

The Shining Path always had different kinds of ideas, ideas that went against the peasantry. They thought it was easy to lead, and when the campesinos didn't easily submit themselves to Shining Path's leadership, they [Shining Path militants] spoke against them and contemplated killing them. No way. That's not how you lead. I didn't agree with that.

In hiding in Lima at the time of Grimaldo Castillo's assassination, Llamojha had nothing to do with this longtime authority's death. Nonetheless, because Llamojha had denounced Castillo's abuses for so many years, Castillo's children blamed him for their father's murder.

In the time that the armed struggle started, a group came here. They pulled Castillo out of the office—he worked in the post office—they pulled him out and they shot him in the plaza.[52] So, his kids rebelled against me, saying that I had sent them [Shining Path militants] to kill him!

With so many accusations against him, life in Lima proved extremely difficult. At the most basic level, Llamojha had serious trouble finding employment, a major problem given his family's perilous economic situation. At times the family worried simply that they would not have enough to eat. I asked him what kind of work he did in the 1980s.

Sometimes in construction, when I could find it. I couldn't find work, because all the hacendados had put up all sorts of red tape against me.

FIG. 6.3 Llamojha (lower right), construction work, Lima, 1984. Photo courtesy of Manuel Llamojha Mitma.

I couldn't get work without my papers. I had to get statements of good conduct, and the police wouldn't give them to me. Finally, I went to the prefecture in Lima and solicited this.

"You have a record! How are you going to work? Businesses want someone clean, and you are fighting with the hacendados," the prefect said to me. Then he gave me my document.

"Here it is, then. Your record. It's so long, and for all of Peru. You have committed offenses against all the hacendados you've been around. How can we give you a letter of good conduct, when you haven't had good conduct?"

That's how it was. My son [Walter] housed us. We were there until 2000.

Llamojha's difficulties finding work were compounded by the severe economic crisis of the mid-1980s. The ravages of internal war and the populist economic policies of Aprista president Alan García—in power from 1985 to 1990—plunged Peru into financial crisis.[53] The economic catastrophe was particularly acute in Lima, as many of the country's 600,000 internal refugees had fled there trying to escape the violence and devastation wrought by the Shining Path militants and counterinsurgent military forces in the Andean countryside. These internal refugees struggled to find adequate food, lodging, and employment, often arriving in Lima with minimal, if any, resources.[54] Many of Lima's poorest women responded to the crisis by participating in the Comedor Popular (Common Kitchen) movement, pooling resources to jointly acquire, prepare, and serve food to their impoverished families. Doña Esther was one such woman; she joined the Comedor Popular Santa Rosa de Lima, in Lima's San Juan de Lurigancho neighborhood.

She started to work in the Comedor Popular, and we got our rations there. She was a leader and directed the Comedor. The other women considered her their leader and they named her to be the boss. Life got better for us with the Comedor. I started to work there, too, as a security guard, and so we had food. Our kids got to eat that food.

Adding to his difficulties, Llamojha became even more politically marginalized during the 1980s. A fellow activist from Ayacucho recalled seeing Llamojha in Lima during these years and commented: "It seemed really strange to me that a leader of his importance, because of all he had contributed to the peasant movement, wasn't given his due. It's really too bad."[55] Llamojha was also constantly harassed by police. His daughter María recalled that police always came to their house looking for Llamojha. And when she said he wasn't home, they would force open the door and barge in. They would look through all of Llamojha's papers, all of his things, searching the house "from corner to corner." She explained: "That's why my dad didn't stay with us much. He was always in different places, fleeing from capture."[56]

The police soon looked beyond Llamojha, targeting his two eldest children for arrest. Police interrogated Walter about one of his acquaintances, and when they grew dissatisfied with his answers, they simply arrested Walter and placed him in the notorious El Frontón prison, holding him on groundless charges. This was the same island prison where Llamojha had been held in the early 1940s, accused of being an Aprista revolutionary. Walter recalled how his mother traveled to see him. "Don't cry. I'm going to get out," he said to her, knowing that he had been wrongfully imprisoned. Doña Esther worked with lawyers to get her son out of jail. Just fifteen days after Walter was finally released, the El Frontón jail became the scene of one of the civil war's worst atrocities. In June 1986, soldiers responded to a protest by imprisoned Shining Path militants in the jail's "blue pavilion" by killing an estimated 119 prisoners, about 80 percent of the prisoners in that section.[57]

Llamojha later described this massacre, an atrocity his son Walter only barely escaped. In the pages of his personal notebook, Llamojha wrote:

GENOCIDE IN THE PRISONS
June 1986

In 1986, President Alan García Pérez ordered the killing of 286 prisoners of the dungeon prisons of El Frontón and Lurigancho.

In May of 2001, the *ingeniero* [general title of respect for educated persons, literally *engineer*] Ricardo Letts Colmenares formulated a criminal denunciation against Alan García, ex-president of Peru, before the Public Prosecutor's Office, but this enemy of the Peruvian people archived it, with the argument that there was no such massacre of prisoners. That would mean that the prisoners died unnoticed; but the pueblo hasn't forgotten this nor will it ever forget. There will quickly arrive a new prohibited dawn for the poor, where the pueblo will present itself before its enemy assassins, presenting them the corresponding bills so that they will pay dearly, that is to say with high interest.

The millionaires and their assassin governments will pay very (very) dearly, for the thousands and millions of campesinos, workers, and students assassinated throughout the country. The pueblo is the Supreme Authority. The millionaires know this very well.

I state and authorize this, signing and marking it in honor of the truth.[58]

Just as police arrested Manuel's son Walter, they seized his daughter Hilda. Police stormed into her home in 1984 and arrested her, despite the fact that she was pregnant. When they questioned her about her father's whereabouts, she answered that he was dead. The police then replied, "You're a terrorist!" and took her to jail.[59] Walter and Hilda's only "crime" was their name: the arrests surely reflected the Peruvian government's desire to intimidate Llamojha by persecuting his children.

Although the worst years of political violence wound down in 1992, after Guzmán was captured in Lima, life remained precarious for Llamojha and his family. It was still too dangerous, too risky, to return to Ayacucho. The 1990s were indeed difficult years for many Peruvians, as the regime of President Alberto Fujimori imposed harsh austerity measures and continued committing major human rights violations. That regime was also exceptionally corrupt, as Fujimori and his spy chief, Vladimiro Montesinos, engaged in systematic bribery. Worse still, Fujimori strangled Peruvian democracy: he shut down congress in 1992, staging a self-coup that allowed him to operate without the restraints of democratic procedure, and made numerous efforts to silence media outlets that opposed him.[60]

Llamojha offered angry opinions about Fujimori in the pages of his personal notebooks. In a May 2002 passage he wrote:

In the government of the dictatorial regime presided over by the disastrous foreigner Alberto Fujimori, 211 businesses were sold; but it is not known where the money from this sale is to be found.

This fact will be judged by the pueblo, for the pueblo is the Supreme Authority that will never forgive.[61]

In a subsequent passage Llamojha wrote: "Fujimori passed more than 120 laws that he felt like dictating. This is how it is, damn it!"[62] Llamojha also denounced the damage Fujimori and his government were doing in the countryside, writing,

The current regime of "Cambio 90," acting under dictatorial military authority, has promulgated its sinister laws with the aim of destroying the Campesino Communities' ancestral social structure and system of collective property, and of selling their lands to the highest bidders to convert them into feudal estates. The campesino community members will be subjected to humiliation, treated like servants and slaves.[63]

It was not until the year 2000, when Fujimori's regime collapsed in scandal and Peru transitioned back to democracy, that Llamojha and doña Esther felt safe enough to move back to Concepción. Many of Peru's thousands of internal refugees similarly began returning home to their rural communities in this period.[64] Even then, memories of the internal war's violence and the power of old accusations continued to haunt Llamojha.

> **In 2000, I came back to this pueblo. At the very moment that I got out of the car, two people saw me and ran to the police post. "The terrorist has arrived!" they said.**
>
> **The police post immediately communicated with Ayacucho, asking if there was an arrest warrant or not. There wasn't. "There's nothing," they answered, and for that reason they didn't detain me. But to this day, those two people can't look at me.**
>
> **After that, the mayor denounced me to Lima, presenting a document that said I had come to Concepción with twenty men and had attacked and seized the police post.**

Nothing came of these frivolous charges, but they carried a sting that still hurts Llamojha today.[65] He was being blamed for the very political violence that had upended his life. The terrors of the internal war had forced Llamojha to flee from the community he so loved and to remain away for nearly twenty years, struggling to survive as a displaced person. The revolutionary and counterrevolutionary violence had brought an abrupt end to his political activities and left him falsely branded a terrorist. Worse still, he had seen his children subjected to political persecution, including the permanent disappearance of his youngest son. These tragedies made the 1980s the most devastating period of Llamojha's complex life and left him and his family with—as his daughter María put it—a wound that wouldn't heal.

FIG. A.1 Llamojha, Concepción, 2013. Author photo.

"You Have to Stand Firm"
THE ELDERLY ACTIVIST, 2000–2015

Using the bright glare of an exposed light bulb to help him see, Llamojha sat at his desk, looking through his many papers about past and present struggles. We had celebrated his ninety-second birthday earlier that day in May 2013, but that evening he had stubbornly resisted our calls for him to rest, relax, and go to bed early. He simply had too much work to do. Despite his failing eyesight and limited mobility, he remains determined to continue his activist work as an elderly man. This afterword reflects on Llamojha's commitment to activism across the twentieth century and into the twenty-first. He pushes on, maneuvering through the terrible difficulties of aging, illness, and loss.

Although Llamojha has lived into the twenty-first century, he built his life as an activist in Latin America's "century of revolution."[1] He fought for change in the heady years of the 1940s, 1950s, and 1960s, when fundamental social, economic, and political transformation seemed not only possible but imminent, a time of incredible revolutionary excitement and exhilaration throughout Latin America and much of the world. He continued these struggles in the 1970s, when Peruvian activists fell into the kind of bitter infighting that hobbled much of the Latin American left, and he pressed forward through the 1980s and 1990s, when the militants of the Shining Path used extremist violence in their pursuit of revolutionary transformation. Llamojha's political struggles took place on multiple fronts—local, regional, national, and international—and he fought his battles simultaneously as an indigenous man, a peasant, a father, and a leftist.

But Latin America's century of revolution was also a century of counter-revolution.[2] Llamojha was routinely jailed for his political efforts, harassed and sometimes tortured by police whose superiors had instructed them to detain this supposedly dangerous communist activist. These arrests sometimes took place during periods of authoritarian rule—under the military dictatorships that ruled Peru intermittently between 1948 and 1980—but many of the arrests took place when Peru had democratic governments. As in much of Latin America, repression of political activists in Peru was never confined to times of military rule. Just as crucially, Llamojha suffered the painful realities of local authoritarianism. Many of the figures who were most determined to stop Llamojha and see him imprisoned were district political authorities who were themselves of rural and indigenous backgrounds. Throughout Latin America, some of the most energetic counterrevolutionary efforts came from individuals of relatively humble origins who mobilized ideologies of anticommunism to further their own claims to economic, political, and social power.[3] Llamojha also lived through two devastating decades of counterinsurgent violence that forced him to flee from his home and beloved community, that pushed him into a difficult existence as an internal refugee. That terror led to the arrests of three of his children and the permanent disappearance of his youngest son, Herbert. For countless Latin Americans caught in the horrors of twentieth-century dirty wars, Llamojha's terrible experiences are all too familiar.

Latin America's century of revolution and counterrevolution brought stunning changes that we find echoed across Llamojha's life. His determined efforts to learn to read and write foreshadowed the astonishing expansion of education and literacy in twentieth-century Latin America. When he moved to Lima as a teenager, he was part of a wave of rural-to-urban migration that ultimately transformed most Latin American countries into places where more people lived in cities than in the countryside. His energetic fights for campesinos' land rights were also part of broader efforts that eventually resulted in the effective dismantling of the hacienda system. Llamojha saw political connections forged across national borders, with new global solidarities forming around shared dreams of justice and change. He also witnessed the enfranchisement of indigenous peasants, long denied the right to vote because of their race, their class, and—for women—their gender. And in the first years of the twenty-first century, two men of Quechua heritage were elected into Peru's presidency, something that would have seemed impossible just a few decades earlier.[4] Llamojha has also lived to see the dramatic resurgence of explicitly socialist political projects in several Latin American countries, with left-wing governments coming to power in Bolivia, Chile, Venezuela, Brazil, and Ecuador.[5]

Sadly, many things also remained stubbornly unchanged across the twentieth century, even into the present day, despite the concerted efforts of activists like Llamojha. The divide between Latin America's rich and poor remains stark, and anti-indigenous racism, though perhaps more muted in its everyday expression than in previous decades, still carries oppressive force. Injustices still pervade the countryside, leaving campesinos to fight difficult battles against powerful—often foreign—mining, oil, and agricultural corporations.[6] Many Latin Americans continue to feel excluded and ignored by their governments, as democratic rule has not always created inclusionary political systems based on the meaningful, engaged participation of ordinary citizens.[7] The forces of political reaction also remain strong. When Llamojha was a teenager, he boldly proclaimed, "Now Peru is mine," certain that revolutionary triumph was at hand. But Peru has yet to become the kind of just and equal society he had envisioned.

With the disappointments and tragedies of twentieth-century upheavals, many activists turned away from social justice struggles. Some did so for their very survival, distancing themselves from political activism in an attempt to save themselves and their loved ones from the cruel nightmares of violent political repression. For many, it came down to a literal choice of life over death. Others moved away from activism in despair, their hearts broken by the betrayals of former allies, the tenacious persistence of inequalities and injustices, and the seemingly relentless crush of neoliberal economic policies. For many activists it seemed that one person would never be able to make a lasting difference and that thoroughgoing change would remain forever unattainable. Such activists' dejection is easy to understand and easy to share. But Llamojha remains unwilling to give up, resolute in his commitment to keep fighting for change even as an elderly man. His continuing determination is one of the most remarkable characteristics of this very remarkable man.

Ongoing Struggles for Justice

On his return to Concepción in 2000, Llamojha immediately resumed his political work on behalf of his community, launching an effort for postwar justice even though he was almost eighty.

> During the time of danger, they installed a barracks up in the area called Joyllor Jocha and they started to sack all of the pueblos. Thirteen homes were destroyed, right down to their foundations, but first they were looted. Soldiers would come into a home and loot everything. They took everything, even campesinos' sandals, every little thing. Nothing at all was left in the houses.
>
> Twenty-three little children were dismembered in the barracks. They grabbed the children by their feet and chopped them up.
>
> When I arrived, the barracks was still here; the killings were still going on. So I started to write letters to send to Lima, to the ministry and to the government, to put a stop to this. I couldn't let this be; I had to denounce it all. And that's why the barracks pulled out of here. They came from Lima to see, to investigate, and then they immediately withdrew the barracks.

This sort of military violence typified counterinsurgency efforts in Peru's Andean regions, as soldiers, particularly in the early years of the internal war, automatically associated indigeneity with support for the Shining Path. Driven by racist stereotypes of indigenous peoples as inherently violent and easily manipulated by political radicals, Peru's military and political leaders incorrectly assumed that Shining Path militants effectively controlled indigenous peasants and responded by razing the countryside.[8] Llamojha's denunciations of military violence included an impassioned letter to the CVR decrying the abuses committed by soldiers stationed in his community. Llamojha wrote:

> The cruel tragedy of the pueblos of the district of Concepción started that fateful day, Monday the 27th of September 1982, when by order of the then Peruvian president, the terrible figure Fernando Belaúnde Terry, more than 300 soldiers . . . took the pueblo of Concepción in an assault of blood and fire, and looted humble homes, proceeding with savagery and cruelty. They mistreated men, women, the elderly and children. They raped women and youth, doing so in the presence of their parents. Without showing even a minimum of respect for human rights, they sav-

agely sacked homes as true enemies of humanity, taking everything from them. . . . The so-called "members of the Armed Forces of Peru" burned and destroyed homes, acting with cruelty and malice, like true enemies of the Peruvian people.[9]

Llamojha also prepared a detailed pamphlet about the abuses, condemning the military's misdeeds and demanding the immediate withdrawal of the barracks. He made photocopies of the pamphlet and distributed them in Concepción's central plaza, pasting the remaining copies on electrical poles throughout the community.

His postwar political battles were also intensely personal. Being back in Concepción brought hard, tangible reminders of all his family had lost. Herbert was gone, his still-unexplained disappearance an ongoing sorrow for his family. Even Llamojha's home was destroyed: twenty years of political violence and harsh Ayacucho weather had left the family's adobe brick house in ruins. He explained:

The soldiers knocked it down. They demolished the door in order to enter and then they seized all of my documents. The soldiers took all of this. And then they abandoned the house and the rain destroyed it all.[10]

Llamojha also lost his treasured document archive and personal library to the violence. He still speaks with much sadness about the fact that soldiers seized his archive when the violence began to escalate in 1982.

Because I traveled to all the pueblos of Peru, I recorded the situation of all the pueblos, in written form. I wrote and I gave each pueblo the original while I kept a copy; I kept the copies here. But because there was the danger of the armed struggle, soldiers came into my home and took away everything. What could they have done with it all? They took all the documents, from all of Peru. I don't know what they took them for.

I also had all my books, I had a huge number of books in my pueblo. But when the armed struggle started in 1982, the army entered my house and they took all of my books. For what? What could they have done with so many books? A huge number of books. I had a big suitcase full of them, and the soldiers took them all.

In the three decades that have passed since the Shining Path launched its armed struggle, Llamojha has rebuilt some of his library and document collection. When I emailed him—via his daughter María—a photograph of a letter he wrote in 1958, María told me, "I read him the letter you sent. He remembered it and got really excited. He was astonished that you have these documents! He asked me to see if you have others. He hopes you can send all that you have so that he can conserve them in his personal archive. . . . He was so happy with the letter that I printed it off and once he had it in his hands, he didn't want to let me have it back, and he packed it away carefully among his things. He's so loving, like a kid with a new toy."[11]

He eventually managed to reestablish part of his document collection, storing his papers in a large bureau in his Concepción home. He commented:

> **I have documents about all the struggles I went through. I have everything here. People can come here and read, study everything that happened in Concepción. I've got documents about Concepción since its foundation. I investigated and searched for all the documents in Lima.**

These documents and books are important to Llamojha in and of themselves; he treasures them as a historian and intellectual.[12] But these archives also matter greatly to him because as he has advanced in age, writing and teaching have been two of the key ways he has managed to continue pressing for change.[13]

During the first years after his return to Concepción in 2000, he found an effective method for sharing his political ideas: the radio. For a few years, he hosted a daily radio program on which he told local listeners about the history of Concepción and its surrounding communities. He also used his radio program to denounce continuing injustice. He told his CVR interviewers:

> **The police used to be good, but not anymore. Now they're against the pueblo. For example, in Concepción we have a police post, and it's good for nothing. When we go to make a complaint, they don't attend to us. They demand money, beer; they're good for nothing. As we now have a radio in Concepción, I talk daily for an hour, and I attack the police there. I tell them to go to hell. For the poor, there is no justice.**

After returning to Concepción, Llamojha also began educating individuals directly. University students writing their senior theses often traveled to Concepción in the first years of the twenty-first century to interview him about Ayacucho's past. His daughter María recalled how he requested a Peruvian history monograph shortly after his ninetieth birthday; he wanted to study it so that he could better answer questions from the university students who came to visit him.[14] These visits from students were deeply important to him. After the sudden death of Esther from an aneurysm in May 2011, his Lima-based children brought him to the capital and urged him to move there permanently. He refused: he wanted to be in Concepción, where students and campesinos would be able to find him and seek his advice. When he was in Lima for a subsequent medical appointment, Llamojha commented:

> In recent years, students have been coming to Concepción from the university in Ayacucho. They always come to ask me about the peasantry, about what Peru was like, about what the arrival of the Spaniards was like. All of that. Because of that, I always have to study! Happily, the students never leave me alone. I'm always happy there [in Concepción]. Here [in Lima] I'm sad!

These connections with university students are not new. I have found documents showing that Llamojha's ties with university students stretch back all the way to the 1950s, and he recalled how during the 1960s and 1970s he often gave talks to students at Ayacucho's San Cristóbal de Huamanga University and at Lima universities, including San Marcos and the Pontifical Catholic University of Peru.[15]

> The universities of Lima always called me. San Marcos, the Catholic University, they always invited me to talk about the peasantry, about the struggle with the hacendados and the problems in the countryside. San Marcos was like my home! They'd feed me there, and I'd even stay and sleep there. Many students wanted to know about these things, so they'd gather at night. They'd ask about Peru, about how it has been since the arrival of the Spanish, about how campesinos live in the sierra, about how the hacendados behaved. This is what the students asked.

These memories, though, are tinged with nostalgic sadness. In one interview Llamojha commented:

> Back then, we were really strongly united with them [university students]. I was really well treated, they respected me. That's how we used to be. Now, I'm poor and no one comes to see me. What is my fate?

As an elderly man, the main way Llamojha has been able to share his ideas and experiences is through writing, a task he has always loved.

> I always wrote. I liked to write histories. I also wrote poems, but it's hard to think them up. I wrote about the question of the struggle, that's what

I wrote about. Now, too, a book is going to be published. I have writings, loose sheets about the struggle, and I'm going to publish a book. The campesinos are demanding I do this.

A few years after his return to Concepción, Llamojha self-published a 158-page book titled *History and Tradition of the Pueblo of Concepción*. It describes Concepción's precolonial history under the Inka and the community's experience under Spanish colonial rule. Llamojha's anticolonial perspective is clear: he describes the "genocide perpetrated by the voracious and bloodthirsty Spaniards who invaded the territory of Tawantin Suyo [the Quechua term for the Inca Empire]."[16] He offers a detailed description of the envarados (indigenous authorities), discussions of Concepción's geography and topography, and a history of the community's migrant club in Lima. The book then documents Concepción's annual celebrations of Carnaval and Easter and goes on to detail the community's struggles against the Ayrabamba hacienda.

When he entered his eighties, Llamojha began spending much of his time filling the pages of his personal notebooks, recording as much of his diverse historical knowledge as he could. He generously shared some of his notebooks with me, and they revealed an exceptional range of historical interests and knowledge. He notes, for example, that celebrations of Christ's birth have been commemorated on December 25 since the fourth century, that Peru has manufactured noodles since 1860, and that the first modern Olympic games were held in Athens in 1896. His notebooks are also packed with richly detailed information about Ayacucho's precolonial, colonial, and republican history. Importantly, he has used these notebooks to voice his continuing dedication to social justice struggles. Two passages from the early twenty-first century are particularly instructive. In the first, from January 2004, he writes about those who had to flee their rural communities during the years of the internal war, just as he and Esther did.

DISPLACED PERSONS

During the years of political violence in Peru, more than 300,000 were displaced from the pueblos of Peru's whole interior. Their lands were left abandoned. When they wanted to return to their pueblos, they were impeded by the secret agents of the dominating high society, and the soldiers and police did not permit them to enter their pueblos. This is how it is, damn it!

A second passage—written when Llamojha was ninety-one—likewise shows his enduring activist commitment:

Sunday, the first of January 2012.

Today, Sunday, the first of January begins the year two thousand twelve, another year of pain, blood, and tears that we the poor will continue suffering. We continue to suffer the tragedy of our fate but the damned dominant class of Peru and the Planet will disappear when their day arrives. This is how things are. Viewed from the dialectical point of view, everything has a beginning and end.

    Chainam chay majtakúna. [Quechua: This is how those people are.]

Beyond writing and teaching, Llamojha worked to remain active in local politics, attending meetings of Concepción's village council. In one interview he also relayed that he was helping campesinos who had recently occupied some vacant lands near Concepción.

Down below, in the valley, some campesinos have seized land. They've occupied unused land, and they're going to form a new pueblo called Puka Orjo Pampa. I've now got to write about how this land was—it was empty in distant times, and it wasn't even a hacienda in the Spanish era. It was empty land, and the campesinos lived there with their cattle. Now, the campesinos have taken the land. And now I have to act. I'm going to write about the land's borders.

Llamojha's continuing commitment to social justice struggles is not surprising: he dedicated his life to the fight for change and for justice. Although he accomplished much during his years as an activist, he also faced enormous personal hardships, including repeated imprisonments, political marginalization, and the loss of his son. Yet as he looked back on his life during our interviews, he expressed no regrets about his activist past.

Regrets about the struggle? No. I don't regret anything, I have no regrets. Nothing turned out badly, it was always good. There was triumph in all the activities. I'd like to go back to that time! Because I was with the masses, because the masses respected me.

But while he may not regret the past, he does fear for the future. One of his sharpest concerns as an elderly activist is that younger people have forgotten his generation's past political efforts and grown apathetic about social justice struggles.

> The new generation doesn't take much of an interest. They're barely interested. So only us older ones are continuing the struggle.

In another interview, he reflected:

> How we struggled for Concepción! Now the new generation doesn't know how to struggle. They don't know much about what the struggle was like back then, because they're youngsters.

Llamojha's concerns about the younger generation eased somewhat when he earned some long overdue public recognition of his life of activism. In September 2010, the scholars Ricardo Caro and Valérie Robin published a feature story on Llamojha's life in the national newspaper *La República*.[17] The following year, he was formally honored by his community. At a November 2011 ceremony commemorating the fifty-seventh anniversary of Concepción's recognition as a district, local authorities presented Llamojha with a trophy and a large golden medal, honoring the work he had done for Concepción. That evening, he danced in a celebration with members of his family, moving to the music with a crutch under his arm. Alicia asked him how he felt about this special recognition.

> I felt really happy when they congratulated me. They have recognized my struggles from those times, and that's why the mayor told me I had to be there, so they could record my statements.

He has also witnessed some political vindication of his generation's activist work. With the collapse of the Soviet Union and the end of the Cold War, countless observers spoke about the global triumphs of capitalism and liberal democracy. For many, it seemed that utopian political projects and socialist experiments—the "dreamworld" of Marxism—had come to a definitive end.[18] But in the first years of the twenty-first century, popular protests and democratic elections have brought leftist governments to power in several Latin American countries. Socialism has proved very much alive, as have trenchant national and international opposition to that political turn. The inspiring dreams and bitter debates that so shaped Llamojha as a younger man continue today, just as they surely will tomorrow. The legacies of twentieth-century political struggles and counterstruggles endure.

FIG. A.2 Llamojha with Hilda, Walter, and María Llamojha Puklla, Concepción, 2011. Photo by Alicia Carrasco Gutiérrez.

The Difficulties of Aging

As an elderly activist, Llamojha has also had to confront the hardships of aging. Those hardships include a creeping feeling of loneliness, greatly exacerbated following his wife's sudden death. Although his eldest daughter, Hilda, her husband, and her son moved to Concepción from Lima following doña Esther's death, Llamojha has often felt alone, cheered mainly by calls from his children. In a passage from May 23, 2012, he wrote:

> This morning, my daughter María called. She's now back in Lima. She told me she's well and that she'll come back [to Concepción] soon. Talking with her left me happy. She worries about me, and I'll be waiting for her return.[19]

A passage from the following day:

> In the morning, my daughter Delia called me . . . she works in a hospital, as she is an obstetrics nurse. When I got this call from my daughter, I was really happy. Delia lives with her husband in Arequipa. She studied at Ayacucho's San Cristóbal University.[20]

These calls helped him greatly, but he still felt quite lonely. Many mornings, he would walk out to Concepción's central plaza and sit on one of the benches, hoping that someone would join him for a conversation. Hilda has noted that her father loved visits and the chance to talk about the past but became sad and depressed when he did not have visitors.[21] In one of our interviews he recalled some French scholars' visit to Concepción.

> On their first trip, we spent four days together. We talked all about the struggle. It was lovely. My life is really happy when [such visits] happen. When it doesn't, I'm sad. I feel like crying.

Advancing age has also brought serious physical hardships. In a passage from January 2012, Llamojha describes his day's activities. The quality of his once beautiful handwriting has deteriorated, and the page is dotted with blotches of white correction fluid. At the bottom of the page, he has written: "I don't know why I can't write well. I'm like a donkey."[22] In his interview with the CVR, he lamented the fact that he was no longer able to craft the intricate stamps he had once made to adorn his political documents:

> Now they don't turn out well. I don't know why. I think someone has done witchcraft against me.[23]

Part of the problem is that Llamojha is losing his eyesight. A stroke in 2001 left him with partial facial paralysis and weakened vision. Over the next few years, additional retinal damage occurred and left him completely blind in his left eye. Sadly, the vision of his right eye also began deteriorating rapidly. The loss of his vision is particularly upsetting for him, as his failing eyesight means that it is harder and harder for him to do what he most loves: read and write. In a May 2012 notebook passage he laments, "I can't write well because my vision is failing. My fate is sad."[24]

His notebooks also describe his ailing health. In a passage from 2004, he wrote about the day's emergency trip to the city of Ayacucho. His blood pressure had been dangerously high for three days, and after a worried phone call from his daughter María, he agreed that he needed to go to the department capital for medical treatment.[25] That health emergency had no lasting consequences, but in 2008, on a short walk to a local store in Concepción, he fell and broke his hip. Most doctors were unwilling to operate, given his advanced age. The family finally found a doctor prepared to do so, and Llamojha's children and other relatives pooled together money for the expensive surgery and medicines. Always energetic, always determined, he then stubbornly refused the doctor's orders to rest and recuperate. A week after the surgery he insisted on getting up and going for a walk. The ensuing damage to his hip required another surgery. After the second surgery, his mobility remained hampered, and he had to walk with the aid of a crutch. He commented on his reduced capabilities in a January 2012 notebook passage:

Today is the birthday of my deceased wife, Esther Honorata Puklla Fernández. If she were alive, she would be 79 years old this year. Today, my daughter Hilda, accompanied by her son Manuel and her husband Eulogio, went to the cemetery to visit her mother's grave. I could not go because of my disability [invalidez] as I cannot go on foot. That's why they went to the cemetery alone. It's more than two kilometers out of town. In addition, a torrential rain fell and got them wet.[26]

Failing health is not Llamojha's only concern as an elderly man. In our interviews, he sometimes grew frustrated at himself, upset at his inability to recall names or events, and asserted that he couldn't remember anything anymore.

I'm losing my memory. Someone has done witchcraft against me. I even forget my name. I used to get mad when people talked like that.

"I'm even forgetting my name," they'd say.

And I'd say, "How can you forget your own name?" But sure enough, in the questions I'm asked, I can't even remember my own name easily. It's strange, but it's true!

Llamojha's health problems suddenly turned acute in April 2014, when he suffered a massive stroke while at home in Concepción. His family rushed him to the nearby hospital in Vilcashuamán, and he was quickly transferred to a hospital in the city of Ayacucho because of the severity of his condition. He regained consciousness after two days in the hospital, but he was largely paralyzed and could speak only with great difficulty. After he had spent several days in the hospital, a doctor informed the family that he would have to leave by the end of the day: there was nothing more the hospital could do for him. His family managed to bring him to Lima, where he remained bedridden in his son Walter's home.

Notified of Llamojha's illness by the historian Ricardo Caro Cárdenas, Llamojha's longtime political rival Andrés Luna Vargas—of the Vanguardia Revolucionaria faction of the CCP—visited Llamojha in Lima. The men had not seen each other in decades. Llamojha asked Luna Vargas what the CCP was doing these days, and Luna Vargas generously replied, "Nothing . . . you didn't leave us even a single hacienda to demolish. You demolished every last one!"[27]

That moment of laughter and joy, though, was surrounded by much sadness. Llamojha was deeply upset by the fact that he was mostly unable to move, that speaking was so difficult, and that he was so far away from his beloved Concepción. His family worked hard to comfort him, staying by him constantly. It seemed unlikely that he would live much beyond his ninety-third birthday, but with his astonishing will to continue fighting, he made remarkable improvements. He poured his energy into physical therapy, and by August 2014 he was able to stand for brief periods and had regained much of his speech. By September he was once again walking, if only for a few short meters. Today, in August 2015, he is eager to return to Concepción and resume his activist work. His determination is both moving and inspiring.

Confronting the devastation of unrealized political dreams, the nightmares of counterinsurgent terror, and the ruthless advances of age, many would have understandably retreated from the fight for social justice. But Llamojha remains compelled to continue working for change. During our interviews he reflected on the responsibilities of an activist. His ideas seem a fitting close for this book.

You have to struggle. You have to organize the masses well and not abandon them. You have to continue the struggle until you attain all the peasantry's goals, until you attain the goals of the pueblo, which needs to liberate itself from the clutches of tyranny.

I like struggling with the masses when they stand firm. It gives you strength, you see, it gives you worth and courage. The struggle is really lovely when the masses are united.

In the peasant struggle, you have to stand firm. You can't waver and lead the masses. The masses recognize their leader. When their leader stands firm and doesn't get frightened, the masses support him. You have to struggle without getting demoralized, because if you lose heart, everyone gets demoralized. You have to fight until the ultimate triumph.

Manuel Llamojha Mitma died in Lima on May 31, 2016. Following his death, his family returned him to Concepción for burial.

NOTES

INTRODUCTION

1. Florencia Mallon offers useful definitions of colonialism and decolonization in relation to indigenous peoples in Mallon, "Introduction: Decolonizing Knowledge, Language and Narrative," 1.

2. See Drinot, *Che's Travels*.

3. See Mallon, "*Barbudos*, Warriors, and *Rotos*," 179–215.

4. Heilman, *Before the Shining Path*, 198–200.

5. It is impossible to quantify Peru's contemporary indigenous population. The last time the Peruvian census classified people by race was 1940, and today, many people who are identified by others as indigenous do not self-identify that way. The reverse is also true. Scholar David Sulmont has shown that estimates of the percentage of Peru's indigenous population thus vary widely, from as low as 19 percent to as high as 75 percent. The best estimates seem to fall in the 35–39 percent range. See Sulmont, "Race, Ethnicity and Politics in Three Peruvian Localities," 47–78.

6. Handelman, *Struggle in the Andes*, 25.

7. For the Peruvian case, see Contreras, *El aprendizaje del capitalismo*; Jacobsen, *Mirages of Transition*; Mallon, *The Defense of Community*; Manrique, *Yawar Mayu*.

8. One of the most famous discussions of this process is Matos Mar, *Desborde Popular y Crisis del Estado*.

9. For excellent new research on Latin America's experience of the Cold War, see Grandin and Joseph, *A Century of Revolution*; Joseph and Spenser, *In from the Cold*.

10. Comisión de la Verdad y Reconciliación (CVR), *Informe Final*.

11. Heilman, *Before the Shining Path*.

12. Gorriti, *Shining Path*, 47. The book was originally published in Spanish as *Sendero: Historia de la guerra milenaria en el Perú* (Lima: Editorial Apoyo, 1990).

13. CVR, *Informe Final*, vol. 2, chap. 1.1, subsection 2: Partido Comunista del Perú-Sendero Luminoso (Peruvian Communist Party-Shining Path, PCP-SL) 1980–82, 36.

14. Like most early twentieth-century Marxists, Gramsci believed that peasants were incapable of generating independent political thought and thus were unable to become "organic intellectuals." See Forgacs, *An Antonio Gramsci Reader*, 302, 309.

Steven Feierman built on—and wrote a powerful corrective to—Gramsci's ideas in his book *Peasant Intellectuals*.

15. Oficina Nacional de Estadística y Censos, *Censos Nacionales de Población, Vivienda y Agropecuario 1961*, vol. 5, *Departamento de Ayacucho*, 61.

16. Mallon, *Peasant and Nation*, 275.

17. Llamojha Mitma, *Historia y tradición del Pueblo de Concepción* (self-published manuscript in Llamojha's personal collection). In addition, Llamojha's 1970 address to the CCP—published in the Confederation's newspaper and republished in the journal *Campesino*—was twenty-four pages of single-spaced historical analysis of Peruvian campesino struggles across the twentieth century. Llamojha Mitma, "Las luchas campesinas y la Confederación Campesina del Perú," 43–67.

18. Interview with Adolfo Urbina (pseudonym), November 3, 2003.

19. Cangallo subprefect to Ayacucho prefect, March 10, 1962, Archivo Regional de Ayacucho (ARA), Subprefectura Cangallo (SC), Ministerios 1962 dossier.

20. Interview with María Llamojha, November 9, 2011.

21. Interview with Nelson Pereyra, June 26, 2011.

22. Informal conversations with several leaders of the CCP during visit to the CCP central office in Lima, June 23, 2011.

23. Manuel Llamojha Mitma: Candidato Campesino a una Diputación, handbill, February 1962, ARA, SC, Institutos Armados 1962 dossier.

24. These labor practices changed over time and should not be read as part of a static and timeless "Andean identity." Anthropologist Orin Starn offered a trenchant critique of anthropologists' tendency to essentialize rural Andean peoples. His arguments triggered a vigorous and healthy debate among scholars of the Andes. See Starn, "Missing the Revolution," 63–91; Starn, "Rethinking the Politics of Anthropology," 13–38.

25. The term "unethnic" borrows from an insightful article by anthropologist Frank Salomon. Salomon, "Unethnic Ethnohistory," 475–506.

26. This complexity has caused much hand-wringing among academics, both in and outside of Peru. Because most people in rural Andean communities self-define as campesinos, the question of what—if any—qualifier to place before the term *campesino* is a particularly vexing one. Is it appropriate to call these individuals indigenous, Quechua, or even Andean when they themselves largely resist using such labels? The question becomes especially difficult as one moves out of Peru's southern Andes, where Aymara and Quechua remain dominant languages in the countryside, and into the central and northern Andes, where people mostly speak Spanish. Many scholars working in these areas have chosen to speak of such persons simply as *campesinos*, implying the absence of any ethnic or racial identity. That casting seems fitting to a degree, given regional residents' broad rejection of the label *indigenous*, but fails to account for the strength of recognizably Andean economic and cultural practices among the area's rural men and women. See Salomon, "Unethnic Ethnohistory," 476.

27. This shift toward self-labeling as *campesinos* was well under way by the 1940s, partly as a consequence of the devastating 1927 military repression of a series of indig-

enous uprisings and the legal prohibition of a major indigenous rights organization: the Comité Pro-Derecho Indígena Tawantinsuyo (Tawantinsuyo Pro-Indigenous Rights Committee). Mobilizing under the rubric of *indigenous* became politically dangerous in the aftermath of the Tawantinsuyo Committee's repression, so it is hardly surprising that rural Andean leaders, in their next major effort to form a national organization to press for their rights, shied away from the term *indigenous*: they formed the Confederación Campesina del Perú (Peruvian Peasant Confederation; CCP) in 1947.

Another factor in the shift away from the label *indigenous* was urban migration. The 1930s and 1940s marked the start of a massive migration of people out of rural Andean communities to the coastal capital city of Lima. Economic, social, and political power had been overwhelmingly concentrated in Lima since colonial times, with the city and the larger coastal region racialized as a nonindigenous, European zone. The Andean people who came to Lima encountered terrible discrimination and exclusion, with many opportunities closed to people deemed Indians. For these people, the label *campesino* offered a chance for social mobility that the label *Indian* did not. The shift toward the identifier *campesino* was further cemented by the rise of parties like APRA and the Communist Party, as these organizations advocated along class lines and presented primarily class-based socioeconomic analyses of Peruvian society.

Peru also has a second major divide that is just as ideologically charged as the split between the coast and the Andean sierra: the divide between the highland Andes and the lowland Amazon. Since the Spanish conquest—and perhaps even before—a pointed distinction has existed between indigenous peoples who live in the Andes and those who live in the Amazon. The linguistic, religious, agricultural, and political differences between these two groups were and are profound, and many Andean people see Amazonian peoples rather than themselves as Peru's true Indians, thus making the label *campesino* all the more appealing as a self-identifier. For extensive discussions of Peruvian indigenous identity, see García, *Making Indigenous Citizens*; García and Lucero, "Exceptional Others," 253–270; García and Lucero, "Authenticating Indians and Movements," 278–298; Gelles, "Andean Culture, Indigenous Identity and the State in Peru," 239–266; Greene, "Getting Over the Andes," 327–354; Greene, *Customizing Indigeneity*; Orlove, "Putting Race in Its Place," 207–222; Remy, "The Indigenous Population and the Construction of Democracy in Peru," 107–130.

28. In 1969, Peruvian president General Juan Velasco Alvarado officially renamed Peru's Andean "indigenous communities" as "campesino communities" and changed the "Day of the Indian" to the "Day of the Campesino," aiming to transcend racism in a country where the word *indio* was a brutalizing racial insult. The historical reality, though, is that Velasco's move only made official a process that Andean people had begun much earlier.

29. Llamojha's ideas reflect what anthropologist Marisol de la Cadena observed among grassroots urban intellectuals in Cuzco. She found that these men and women embraced a "de-Indianized" mestizo identity that rejected the racialized connotations of indigeneity that cast indigenous peoples as uneducated, impoverished, and strictly

rural. Yet these same individuals simultaneously cherished and celebrated their Andean cultural heritage. De la Cadena, *Indigenous Mestizos*.

30. Albó, "El retorno del Indio," 309.

31. Quoted in García and Lucero, "Un País Sin Indígenas?," 159.

32. "Comunicado a los pueblos de Cangallo," February 1962, ARA, SC, Oficios de los Institutos Armados 1962 dossier.

33. Joanne Rappaport and Abelardo Ramos discuss how different motivations and institutional interests shape the collaboration process between academics and activists and between indigenous and nonindigenous researchers. See "Collaboration and Historical Writing," 132–133. For further reflections on collaborations between indigenous and nonindigenous intellectuals, see Rappaport, *Intercultural Utopias*, 83–114; Warren, *Indigenous Movements and Their Critics*, 69–85.

34. Beasley-Murray, Cameron and Hershberg, "Latin America's Left Turns," 319–330; Blanco and Grier, "Explaining the Rise of the Left in Latin America," 68–90.

35. I drew my inspiration from the extensive methodological reflections in Reuque Paillalef, *When a Flower Is Reborn*; Tula, *Hear My Testimony*; and James, *Doña María's Story*.

36. A key work on the testimonio genre is Beverley, *Testimonio*.

37. Jan Rus and Diane L. Rus discuss the advantages and disadvantages of adding introductions, explanatory footnotes, and historical context in publications produced by native intellectuals. "Taller Tzotzil of Chiapas, Mexico," 152, 169. See also Rappaport and Ramos, "Collaboration and Historical Writing," 140.

38. This book forms part of an extensive Peruvian literature consisting of biographies, autobiographies, memoirs, and testimonies written by and about campesinos, workers, and non-elite political activists. The most famous of these works include Pévez and Oré, *Memorias de un viejo luchador campesino*; Larico Yujra and Ayala, *Yo fui canillita de José Carlos Mariátegui*; Valderrama and Escalante, *Gregorio Condori Mamani*; Burenius and Torres, *Testimonio de un fracaso Huando*; Muñoz, Matos Mar, and Carbajal, *Erasmo Muñoz, yanacón del Valle de Chancay*; Béjar, *Perú 1965*; Blanco, *Land or Death*; and Gavilán, *Memorias de un soldado desconocido*.

39. I wrote an initial draft of the book and translated it into Spanish, and then I brought copies of my Spanish translation to Llamojha in May 2013. When I presented the draft to him, I ceded editorial control, stressing that I would make any deletions, corrections, and additions that he desired. I also made the draft available to his adult children and explained that I was open to discussing and working through any concerns they might have. Llamojha, his daughter María Llamojha Puklla, and I decided on necessary changes together. Jan Rus and Diane L. Rus offer a thoughtful discussion of editing practices—both for reasons of style and contentious content—with a native publishing project, "The Taller Tzotzil of Chiapas, Mexico," 162–163.

40. For thoughtful discussions on the strengths, limitations, and academic reputation of biography, see Banner, "Biography as History," 579–586; Nasaw, "Historians and Biography," 573–578; Kessler-Harris, "Why Biography?," 625–630.

41. Mallon, "Introduction: Decolonizing Knowledge, Language and Narrative," 3.

42. Mallon describes this practice of document sharing in *Courage Tastes of Blood*, 9.

43. Myerhoff, "Life History among the Elderly," 105.

44. I generated these follow-up questions in response to what I had learned from previous interviews and from archival documents.

45. A social worker by training, Alicia was born in Ayacucho and is fluent in both Quechua and Spanish. She and I jointly transcribed all of the interviews. All translations of Llamojha's Spanish stories and archival documents are my own. Alicia also translated brief Quechua segments of the interviews into Spanish.

46. The original recordings and a transcript of the interview are available at the CVR's archive in Lima, the Defensoría del Pueblo Centro de Información para la Memoria Colectiva y los Derechos Humanos (CIMCDH). I encourage interested researchers to listen to the recordings, as the transcript is incomplete. For ease of reading, I have edited out pauses, interruptions, and repetitions in Llamojha's CVR testimony.

47. Oral history scholar Alessandro Portelli reflects on this phenomenon in *Death of Luigi Trastulli*, 55. For theoretical considerations of life stories, see Linde, *Life Stories*.

48. This formulation of memory is shaped by the voluminous scholarship on the subject, much of which has been informed by Maurice Halbwachs's work on collective memory and Pierre Nora's discussions of sites of memory. See Halbwachs, *On Collective Memory*; Nora, *Realms of Memory*. For the Latin American context, key works on memory include James, *Doña María's Story*; Jelín, *State Repression and the Labors of Memory*; Stern, *Remembering Pinochet's Chile*. There are, of course, many other ways that we could interpret Llamojha's life stories. We could read them as auto-ethnography, which Mary Louise Pratt defines as a colonized person's discussion of self, using the language of the colonizers. See Pratt, *Imperial Eyes*. We could also read these stories as examples of what Stephen Greenblatt considers "self-fashioning," whereby individuals craft and express their identities in relation to their contexts. Greenblatt, *Renaissance Self-Fashioning*.

49. Portelli, *Death of Luigi Trastulli*, 50.

50. Much has been written about the power differentials in anthropological and oral history research. See Starn, *Nightwatch*, 16; Scheper-Hughes, *Death without Weeping*, 28.

51. Joanne Rappaport and Abelardo Ramos discuss how the tensions in a collaborative research project they worked on stemmed less from the differences between Western academic research culture and the indigenous researcher than from the differences between academics and activists. "Collaboration and Historical Writing," 140.

CHAPTER 1: "I'M GOING TO BE PRESIDENT OF THE REPUBLIC"

1. Orlove, "Down to Earth," 209; Drinot, *Allure of Labor*.

2. De Oliviera and Roberts, "Urban Growth and Urban Social Structure in Latin America," 255.

3. Llamojha was born on a plot of land named Marka Marka, at the base of a Chachas tree.

4. Concepción now belongs to the province of Vilcashuamán, created in 1984.

5. Llamojha's mother was born in Tantar, a small community neighboring Concepción.

6. Salomon and Niño-Murcia, *Lettered Mountain*, 128.

7. Davies, *Indian Integration in Peru*, 131–134.

8. Salomon and Niño-Murcia, *Lettered Mountain*, 139.

9. Davies, *Indian Integration in Peru*, 94; Hazen, "Awakening of Puno," 124.

10. Mantilla, *Libro de lectura*.

11. Bastinos, *Mosaico literario epistolar para ejercitarse los niños en la lectura de manuscritos*. This is the fifty-eighth edition of the book. Salomon and Niño-Murcia note that *Mosaico* was tremendously influential in Spain and Latin America. It was a collection of manuscripts that demonstrated how to produce different genres of documents. Salomon and Niño-Murcia, *Lettered Mountain*, 131.

12. Indeed, Peruvians routinely connected literacy with both race and class identity, automatically associating illiteracy with indigeneity and peasant life and regarding education as central to what anthropologist Marisol de la Cadena calls "de-Indianization." See de la Cadena, *Indigenous Mestizos*; García, *Making Indigenous Citizens*, 87–88; Heilman, *Before the Shining Path*, 13.

13. Salomon and Niño-Murcia, *Lettered Mountain*, 25; Heilman, *Before the Shining Path*, 13.

14. For more on hacienda-campesino relations in Peru, see Diez Hurtado, *Comunes y haciendas*; Mallon, *Defense of Community*; Manrique, *Yawar Mayu*; Rénique, *La batalla por Puno*; Taylor, *Bandits and Politics in Peru*.

15. María Elodia Vassallo de Parodi.

16. Sources on the 1920s and the Tawantinsuyo Committee include Heilman, *Before the Shining Path*, 42–70; de la Cadena, *Indigenous Mestizos*, 86–130; Arroyo, "La Experiencia Del Comité Central Pro-Derecho Indígena Tahuantinsuyo," 1–24; Leibner, "Radicalism and Integration," 1–23; Kapsoli Escudero, *Ayllus del sol*. The Tawantinsuyo Committee also pressed for indigenous peasants' citizenship rights, respect for indigenous peoples, and educational opportunities.

17. Memorial presentado por los vecinos indígenas del pueblo de Concepción, September 20, 1929, Proyecto Especial de Titulación de Tierras Ayacucho (PETT), Concepción de Chakamarka dossier, fol. 1.

18. Memorial presentado por los vecinos indígenas del pueblo de Concepción, September 20, 1929, PETT, Concepción de Chakamarka dossier, fol. 13.

19. Martín Sulca, Nicolás Zea, Alejandro Salvatierra, and Mariano Quispe to Ayacucho prefect, March 29, 1930, PETT, Concepción de Chakamarka dossier, fol. 16.

20. On campesinos' frustrations with Peru's political and court systems, see Heilman, *Before the Shining Path*; La Serna, *Corner of the Living*.

21. Klaiber, *Religion and Revolution in Peru*; Klaiber, *Catholic Church in Peru*, 172–206.

22. Stein, *Populism in Peru*, 56–57, 65. See also Lund Skar, *Lives Together, Worlds Apart*.

23. Klaiber, *Catholic Church in Peru*, 185, 190.

24. Salomon and Niño-Murcia, *Lettered Mountain*, 2; de la Cadena, *Indigenous Mestizos*.

25. Masterson, *Militarism and Politics*, 29. For the ties between Andean peasants and the Peruvian military, see Méndez, "Tradiciones liberales en los Andes," 125–153. For a famous fictional account of cadet life in one of Lima's military barracks, see Vargas Llosa, *La ciudad y los perros*.

26. González-Cueva, "Conscription and Violence in Peru," 89.

27. Heilman, *Before the Shining Path*, 20–21; Diez Hurtado, *Comunes y haciendas*, 158; Davies, *Indian Integration in Peru*, 49.

28. Stein, *Populism in Peru*, 200; García Bryce, "A Revolution Remembered, a Revolution Forgotten," 277–322. On the tense relations between the military and APRA, see Masterson, *Militarism and Politics*, 50.

29. Aguirre, *The Criminals of Lima and Their Worlds*, 132–136.

30. Davies, *Indian Integration in Peru*, 103; Klarén, *Modernization, Dislocation, and Aprismo*, 129. On the significant regional variations of APRA, see Nugent, *Modernity at the Edge of Empire*; Heilman, "We Will No Longer Be Servile," 491–518; Taylor, "The Origins of Apra in Cajamarca," 437–459.

31. See Klarén, *Peru*, 277.

32. The committee later changed its name to the Indian Community of Concepción Chacamarca Pro-Defense Committee and finally to the Concepción Social Central.

33. Handelman, *Struggle in the Andes*, 30–31.

34. Lund Skar, *Lives Together, Worlds Apart*, 107–112.

35. Comité Pro-Comunidad Indígena de Concepción Chacamarca to director of Indian affairs, July 23, 1946, PETT, Concepción de Chakamarka dossier, doc. 2034939, fol. 815.

36. Members of the Comunidad de Concepción de Chacamarca to director of Indian affairs, February 15, 1947, PETT, Concepción de Chakamarka dossier, fol. 2.

37. Paulino Guerrero, M. J. Llamojha Mitman, and Rosendo Mendoza Villagaray to Cangallo subprefect, February 22, 1947, Archivo Regional de Ayacucho, Subprefectura Cangallo, Vischongo 1947 dossier. Llamojha occasionally added an *n* to his surname in the 1940s.

38. The central government in Lima appointed the prefect, the leading authority in a department, who in turn appointed provincial subprefects as well as district authorities.

39. I discuss the issue of abusive authorities throughout *Before the Shining Path*. Nineteenth-century Peruvian writer Manuel González Prada described such abusive authorities, commenting that indigenous communities suffered "the tyranny of the justice of the peace, the governor, and the priest, that unholy trinity responsible for brutalizing the Indian." González Prada, *Páginas libres*, 343.

1. The importance of the Jhajhamarka (officially spelled Ccaccamarca) struggle is shown by the fact that it became the subject of a book by the Peruvian scholar and activist Aracelio Castillo. See Castillo, *Reforma agraria por la vía campesina.*

2. Hobsbawm, "Peasant Land Occupations," 138. For a periodization of Peru's twentieth-century land struggles, see Neira, *Los Andes,* 73, 199. A key source on Peruvian peasant struggles over land and resources in the period immediately preceding the 1940s is Mallon, *Defense of Community.*

3. Gilbert Joseph calls for deeper consideration of the "*grassroots* dynamics and meanings of the Latin American Cold War," in "What We Now Know and Should Know," 19.

4. Manuel Llamojha Mitma, *Memoria descriptiva del distrito de Concepción* (2011), unpublished manuscript in Llamojha's personal collection, 16.

5. See Burns, *Colonial Habits.*

6. For a discussion of the term *gamonal,* see Flores Galindo, *Buscando un Inca,* 102. For a consideration of gamonal violence, see Poole, "Performance, Domination, and Identity in the *Tierras Bravas* of Chumbivilcas (Cusco)," 97–131.

7. This probably happened in the 1920s.

8. Neira, *Los Andes,* 200; Handelman, *Struggle in the Andes,* 124–154.

9. Both the Parodi and Martinelli families owned haciendas around Concepción and played prominent roles in Ayacucho politics.

10. Unfortunately, Llamojha was unable to recall whether or not he had written this particular document.

11. Cupertino de la Cruz to director of Indian affairs, March 4, 1948, Proyecto Especial de Titulación de Tierras Ayacucho (PETT), Ccaccamarca dossier, fol. 1116.

12. Cupertino de la Cruz to director of Indian affairs, March 4, 1948, PETT, Ccaccamarca dossier, fol. 1116.

13. Subinspector Humberto Abad Ramírez to head of the IV Police Region, May 29, 1948, PETT, Ccaccamarca dossier, fol. 206.

14. Salomon and Niño-Murcia, *Lettered Mountain,* 137.

15. Subinspector Humberto Abad Ramírez to head of the IV Police Region, May 29, 1948, PETT, Ccaccamarca dossier, fol. 208.

16. Salomon and Niño-Murcia, *Lettered Mountain,* 147. See the next chapter for a discussion of *tinterillos,* shyster scribes who used their literacy to manipulate and abuse their neighbors.

17. Seventeen Ccaccamarca campesinos to minister of justice and work, June 22, 1948, PETT, Ccaccamarca dossier, fol. 56. The letter also noted that Llamojha had relatives in Jhajhamarka, and in fact one of his sisters did reside there.

18. "Acta de la fundación del Sindicato de Yanaconas de Ccaccamarca (Jhajhamarca)," February 14, 1948, PETT, Ccaccamarca dossier, fol. 198. Although Llamojha uses the spelling "Jhajhamarca" in this document, he subsequently began using a *k* in the final syllable.

19. See Klarén, *Peru,* 293; Peloso, *Peasants on Plantations,* 109–153.

20. Subinspector Humberto Abad Ramírez to head of the IV Police Region, May 29, 1948, PETT, Ccaccamarca dossier, fol. 206.

21. See Klarén, *Peru*, 293.

22. Subinspector Humberto Abad Ramírez to head of the IV Police Region, May 29, 1948, PETT, Ccaccamarca dossier, fol. 206.

23. Subinspector Humberto Abad Ramírez to head of the IV Police Region, May 29, 1948, PETT, Ccaccamarca dossier, fol. 206.

24. Subinspector Humberto Abad Ramírez to head of the IV Police Region, May 29, 1948, PETT, Ccaccamarca dossier, fol. 207.

25. Vicente Condori Condori to civil guard sergeant commander, August 13, 1948, Archivo Regional de Ayacucho (ARA), Subprefectura Cangallo (SC), Institutos Armados 1948 dossier.

26. Luis Alfredo Gutiérrez to director of Indian affairs, July 8, 1948, PETT, Ccaccamarca dossier, fol. 54.

27. Subinspector Humberto Abad Ramírez to head of the IV Police Region, May 29, 1948, PETT, Ccaccamarca dossier, fol. 206.

28. Baptismal certificate prepared by Manuel J. Llamojha Mitman, November 21, 1947, PETT, Ccaccamarca dossier, fol. 201.

29. Drinot, "Creole Anti-communism," 703–736; Heilman, "To Fight Soviet Agents in the Fatherland," 94–120.

30. Subinspector Humberto Abad Ramírez to head of the IV Police Region, May 29, 1948, PETT, Ccaccamarca dossier, fol. 206.

31. Subinspector Humberto Abad Ramírez to head of the IV Police Region, May 29, 1948, PETT, Ccaccamarca dossier, fol. 207.

32. Vicente Condori Condori to civil guard sergeant commander, August 13, 1948, ARA, SC, Institutos Armados 1948 dossier.

33. Vicente Condori Condori to head of the IV Police Region, May 18, 1948, PETT, Ccaccamarca dossier, fol. 46.

34. Luis Alfredo Gutiérrez to director of Indian affairs, July 8, 1948, PETT, Ccaccamarca dossier, fol. 54.

35. It is equally doubtful that Llamojha had any lingering sympathies for APRA by 1948, as the hacendados Carlos and Ernesto Cárdenas were themselves prominent Apristas. Their affiliation would likely have ended any remaining interest Llamojha had in the party. See Heilman, "To Fight Soviet Agents in the Fatherland," 112. For a discussion of politics among Ayacucho's hacendados, see Glave and Urrutia, "Radicalismo político en élites regionales," 1–37.

36. Subinspector Humberto Abad Ramírez to head of the IV Police Region, May 29, 1948, PETT, Ccaccamarca dossier, fol. 207.

37. "M. J. Llamocca Mitma" to "Mr. Cupertino de la Cruz," May 1, 1948, ARA, SC, Institutos Armados 1948 dossier, fol. 8.

38. I made this point in "To Fight Soviet Agents in the Fatherland," 114.

39. "Junta Directiva," n.d., PETT, Ccaccamarca dossier, fol. 199.

40. "Resolución Apoyo Externo," December 20, 1977, PETT, Ccaccamarca dossier,

fol. 23; Casimiro Yupanqui, Miguel Quispe, and Mariano Joya to Ayacucho prefect, March 30, 1964, ARA, Ex-Prefectura. Unfortunately, prefectural documents dating from the 1960s forward were not yet organized into dossiers at the time of research. These documents were simply labelled "ex-prefectura" documents in the Ayacucho Regional Archive. As noted in the introduction, the Velasco government recategorized "indigenous communities" as "campesino communities" in 1969.

CHAPTER 3: "JAIL WAS LIKE MY HOME"

1. Comité Interamericano de Desarrollo Agrícola (CIDA), *Tenencia de la Tierra y Desarrollo Socio-Económico del Sector Agrícola Perú*, 394; Handelman, *Struggle in the Andes*, 62–81; Klarén, *Peru*, 281, 307, 315.

2. Paulo Drinot, introduction to *Che's Travels*, 3, notes the dearth of attention to Latin America's 1950s.

3. It was a hacienda in the district of Cocharcas.

4. Handelman, *Struggle in the Andes*, 30.

5. Handelman, *Struggle in the Andes*, 30.

6. Huanta is a province in northern Ayacucho, Andahuaylas is a province in the neighboring department of Apurímac, and Huamanga is a central Ayacucho province, where the city of Ayacucho is located. Llamojha noted that Grimaldo Castillo's father, Alejandro Castillo, was also very abusive.

7. Heilman, *Before the Shining Path*, 139.

8. Heilman, *Before the Shining Path*, 199–200.

9. For a detailed study of envarados, see Rasnake, *Domination and Cultural Resistance*. See also La Serna, *Corner of the Living*, 46–51.

10. Heilman, *Before the Shining Path*, 24–26.

11. The exact date of the foregoing events is difficult to pinpoint; I found no record of this incarceration in Ayacucho's archives. That archival absence means little: many documents—even entire court cases—are missing or misfiled.

12. Representatives of Concepción de Chakamarca to director of Indian affairs, June 22, 1959, Proyecto Especial de Titulación de Tierras Ayacucho (PETT), Concepción de Chakamarka dossier, fols. 106–107.

13. Manuel J. Llamojha Mitma, Samuel Cárdenas Zea, and Emilio Llamojha Mitma to Dr. Alberto Arca Parró, June 25, 1959, PETT, Concepción de Chakamarka dossier, fols. 104–105.

14. Manuel J. Llamojha Mitma, Samuel Cárdenas Zea, and Emilio Llamojha Mitma to Dr. Alberto Arca Parró, June 25, 1959, PETT, Concepción de Chakamarka dossier, fols. 104–105.

15. Interview with Emilio Llamojha, August 21, 2012.

16. This canceled convention is discussed in the next chapter.

17. Sarah Radcliffe discusses Peruvian women's mid- to late-twentieth-century activism in "'People Have to Rise Up—Like the Great Women Fighters,'" 197–218.

18. The contradictory attitudes about women in Llamojha's stories are not unusual. A similar contradiction emerges in much of the literature about gender relations

in Peru's rural Andean communities. Some scholars have highlighted structures of gender complementarity in these communities, noting how Andean women's and men's roles balance and complete one another. Yet other scholars have stressed the prevalence of domestic violence and women's local political subordination. See Silverblatt, *Moon, Sun and Witches*; Bourque and Warren, *Women of the Andes*; Harris, "Complementarity and Conflict," 21–40; Harvey, "Domestic Violence in the Peruvian Andes"; Boesten, "State and Violence against Women in Peru." I thank Frank Salomon for pointing out this contradiction to me.

19. Abel Alfaro to Ayacucho prefect, April 22, 1959, Archivo Regional de Ayacucho (ARA), Ex-Prefectura.

20. One such document is Subprefect Alberto Flores Leyva to Ayacucho prefect, October 15, 1959, PETT, Concepción de Chakamarka dossier II, fol. 61.

21. "Está Preso Por Defender su Pueblo," *Sierra* 19:486, 1st and 2nd fortnights, January 1960, 4. *Sierra* is available in the Biblioteca Nacional del Perú in San Borja, Peru.

22. On the conditions in Peruvian prisons, see Aguirre, *Criminals of Lima*, 164–184.

23. The actual court case appears to be missing, but reference to Llamojha's imprisonment and the charges appears in Cangallo subprefect to Ayacucho prefect, official letter no. 46, October 22, 1957, ARA, Subprefectura Cangallo (SC), Oficios Remitidos a la Prefectura 1957 dossier.

24. Manuel J. Llamojha Mitma and others to president of the Ayacucho Supreme Court, March 6, 1957, ARA, Corte Superior de Justicia (CSJ) criminal case, dossier (*legajo*) 1189, fol. 1.

25. Manuel J. Llamojha Mitma and others to president of the Ayacucho Supreme Court, March 6, 1957, ARA, CSJ criminal case, dossier 1189, fol. 1. Nothing came of Llamojha's complaint. The judge in question accused Llamojha of utilizing the services of an immoral scribe (*tinterillo*) to write the letter and of tricking his fellow prisoners into signing it.

26. On the history of corruption in Peru, see Quiroz, *Corrupt Circles*.

27. These lawyers included individuals named Cavero, García Blásquez, and Gutiérrez.

28. Interview with Hilda Llamojha, November 19, 2011.

29. Interview with Walter Llamojha, November 19, 2011.

30. Interview with Hilda Llamojha, November 19, 2011.

31. Interview with Walter Llamojha, November 19, 2011.

32. Interviews with Emilio and Víctor Llamojha, August 21, 2012.

33. Interview with Walter Llamojha, November 19, 2011.

34. "Movimiento Democrático Peruano," November 24, 1961, ARA, SC, Oficios recibidos y remitidos de la Prefectura 1961 dossier. For Emilio Llamojha's service as Concepción's district mayor, see Emilio Llamojha Mitma to presiding judge, April 28, 1966, ARA, Juzgado de tierras: Fuero Comun Agrario, dossier 49, file (*expediente*) 1, fol. 10.

35. Interview with Víctor Llamojha, August 21, 2012.

36. Interview with Walter Llamojha, November 19, 2011.

37. Interview with Hilda Llamojha, November 19, 2011.

38. "Vda. de" stands for "viuda de," or "widow of."

39. Manuel J. Llamojha Mitma to Dr. Manuel Prado, May 2, 1958, PETT, Concepción de Chakamarka dossier, fols. 125–126.

40. Representatives of the community Concepción de Chakamarca to director of Indian affairs, June 22, 1959, PETT, Concepción de Chakamarka dossier II, fol. 106.

41. Salomon and Niño-Murcia, *Lettered Mountain*, 137.

42. Heilman, *Before the Shining Path*, 107–115; Becker, "In Search of Tinterillos," 95–114.

43. Subprefect Guillermo Tutaya to Ayacucho prefect, June 26, 1958, PETT, Concepción de Chakamarka dossier, fol. 131.

44. Ayacucho prefect to director general of government, July 3, 1958, PETT, Concepción de Chakamarka dossier II, fol. 19.

45. Criminal trial against Manuel Llamojha Mitma for crimes against the public good in the counterfeit production of money, initiated April 5, 1961, ARA, CSJ Cangallo Province criminal case, dossier 1212, file 10. *Sierra* published a story decrying Llamojha's imprisonment for the counterfeit case. "¿Un error o un abuso de autoridad?" *Sierra* 25:514, 1st and 2nd fortnights of July 1961, 8.

46. Court certificate prepared by the head of the Cangallo public jail, October 14, 1958, fol. 30; Court certificate prepared by secretary of the Supreme Court of Justice, April 24, 1958, fol. 944. Both documents from PETT, Concepción de Chakamarka dossier.

47. Statement to police by Abel Alfaro, August 19, 1959, PETT, Concepción de Chakamarka dossier, fol. 154.

48. Alfonso Martinelli and Abel Alfaro to minister of labor and Indian affairs, June 13, 1958, PETT, Concepción de Chakamarka dossier, fol. 953. Martinelli owned the La Colpa hacienda.

49. Alfonso Martinelli and Abel Alfaro to minister of labor and Indian affairs, June 13, 1958, PETT, Concepción de Chakamarka dossier, fol. 953.

50. Virgilio Landazuri to director of Indian affairs, July 4, 1958, PETT, Concepción de Chakamarka dossier, fol. 955.

51. Resolución Ministerial no. 251, July 22, 1958, PETT, Concepción de Chakamarka dossier, fol. 957.

52. Concepción campesinos to Dr. Ricardo Elías y Aparicio, September 21, 1958, PETT, Concepción de Chakamarka dossier, fol. 965.

53. Junta Directiva of the Centro Social Hijos del Distrito de Concepción to director general of Indian affairs, October 6, 1958, PETT, Concepción de Chakamarka dossier, fol. 969.

54. Whenever the text indicates that someone said something in Quechua, that means that Llamojha used Quechua during the original interview.

55. Subprefect Alberto Flores Leyva to Ayacucho prefect, October 15, 1959, fol. 61; Primitivo Mayhua to Cangallo subprefect, April 20, 1959, fol. 60. Both documents from PETT, Concepción de Chakamarka dossier.

56. "Acta: Elección del Personero o Mandatario Legal," June 19, 1960, PETT, Concepción de Chakamarka dossier, fol. 1025.

57. "La Comunidad de Concepción Eligió su Personero Legal," *Sierra* 24:503, 1st and 2nd fortnights of December 1960, 4.

58. Concepción campesinos to secretary general of the Peruvian Peasant Confederation, August 4, 1960, PETT, Concepción de Chakamarka dossier, fol. 1043.

59. Vidal Alcántara Cárdenas to head of the organizational division of Indigenous communities, August 5, 1960, PETT, Concepción de Chakamarka dossier, fol. 1042.

60. Concepción campesinos to secretary general of the Peruvian Peasant Confederation, August 4, 1960, PETT, Concepción de Chakamarka dossier, fol. 1043.

61. Juan H. Pévez, Alberto Izarra, and Francisco Huamán to minister of labor and Indian affairs, n.d., PETT, Concepción de Chakamarka dossier, fol. 1045.

CHAPTER 4: FOR JUSTICE, LAND, AND LIBERTY

1. Zolov, "Expanding Our Conceptual Horizons," 47–73; Gould, "Solidarity under Siege," 367–368; Gott, *Rural Guerrillas in Latin America*. For international travels, see Rothwell, *Transpacific Revolutionaries*, 1, 26. For the broader Latin American experience of the Cold War, see Sorensen, *Turbulent Decade Remembered*; Grandin and Joseph, *Century of Revolution*; Joseph and Spenser, *In from the Cold*.

2. There were also long-standing tensions between the military and APRA that stretched back to the 1930s. See Masterson, *Militarism and Politics*, 17, 46–47. For the 1962–1963 military government under Ricardo Pérez Godoy, see Villanueva, *Un año bajo el sable*.

3. Masterson, *Militarism and Politics*, 187.

4. Handelman, *Struggle in the Andes*, 86, 111, 121; Comité Interamericano de Desarrollo Agrícola (CIDA), *Tenencia de la tierra*, 395–398; Flores Galindo, "Apuntes sobre las ocupaciones de tierras y el sindicalismo agrario."

5. Handelman, *Struggle in the Andes*, 119–121. For a discussion of the Belaúnde regime, see Kuczynski, *Peruvian Democracy under Economic Stress*.

6. Masterson, *Militarism and Politics*, 216, notes that this often-quoted number comes from Rogger Mercado. See Mercado, *Las guerrillas del Perú*.

7. For a detailed discussion of the Pomacocha land seizure, see Heilman, "Yellows against Reds."

8. The department of Ayacucho was not home to as many land seizures or as much peasant mobilization as took place in departments like Cuzco, Junín, and Pasco. Some scholars go so far as to say that Ayacucho lacked major peasant mobilizations in the 1960s. See Rubio Giesecke, "Las guerrillas peruanas de 1965," 140; Poole and Rénique, *Peru*, 36; Degregori, *Qué Difícil es ser Díos*, 185. The cases noted in this chapter show that Ayacucho's countryside was not as quiescent as these scholars suggest.

9. Civil guard report, April 19, 1962, Archivo Regional de Ayacucho (ARA), Subprefectura Cangallo (SC), Institutos Armados 1962 dossier.

10. Germán Rivera Medina to Ayacucho prefect, November 28, 1963, ARA, Ex-Prefectura.

11. Report by Subprefect Aquilino Cornejo, official document no. 109, August 20, 1965, ARA, SC, Ministerios 1965 dossier.

12. Stories on the planned convention appeared in the migrant newspaper *Sierra* in "Los campesinos de Cangallo Tendrán Convención Provincial," *Sierra* 26:522, 1st and 2nd fortnights of February 1962, 4; "Se realizará la Convención de Campesinos," *Sierra* 26:524, 1st and 2nd fortnights of April 1962, 4; "No se realizó la proyectada Convención," *Sierra* 26:525, 1st and 2nd fortnights of May 1962, 1. *Sierra* is available in the Biblioteca Nacional del Perú, in San Borja.

13. Federación Provincial de Campesinos de Cangallo circular, March 9, 1962, copy, ARA, SC, Vilcashuamán 1962 dossier. The periodical *Unidad* ran a story outlining the congress's objectives. "Convención de Campesinos de Cangallo," *Unidad*, April 2, 1962, 3. *Unidad* is available in the Biblioteca Nacional del Perú, in San Borja.

14. It was not until the 1970s and 1980s, with the rise of liberation theology, that activist priests and Catholic political activists began talking about the compatibility of Christianity and leftist social justice struggles.

15. Cangallo subprefect to Ayacucho prefect, Of. No. 19, March 10, 1962, ARA, SC, Ministerios 1962 dossier.

16. Ayacucho prefect to director of Indian affairs, March 21, 1962, ARA, SC, Institutos Armados 1962 dossier. The prefect also justified his decision on the grounds that congress organizers did not have authorization from the Bureau of Indian Affairs. "Convención campesina contra formas esclavistas de labor," *Expreso*, March 27, 1962, 9. *Expreso* is available in the Biblioteca Nacional del Perú, in San Borja, Peru.

17. Civil guard Huber Mendiolaza to Cangallo subprefect, document no. 53, March 28, 1962, ARA, SC, Institutos Armados 1962 dossier. The original accusation about graffiti appears in Statement by Ruperto Delgado, February 20, 1962, ARA, Ex-Prefectura.

18. Statement by Manuel Llamocca Mitma, May 5, 1962, ARA, SC, Institutos Armados 1962 dossier.

19. "Convención campesina contra formas esclavistas de labor," *Expreso*, March 27, 1962, 9.

20. Officials from the Ministry of Labor and Indian Affairs telegrammed the prefect shortly after the story appeared, reminding him that unfree labor systems had been outlawed in the 1920s and instructing him to investigate the abuses outlined in the *Expreso* article. See Ministerio de Trabajo y Asuntos Indígenas Telegrama no. 229, March 30, 1962, Proyecto Especial de Titulación de Tierras Ayacucho (PETT), Pomacocha dossier.

21. Ranque, "Les origines et les divisions des partis maoistes peruviens dans les annees 1960," 31.

22. Manuel Llamojha Mitma: Candidato Campesino a una Diputación, handbill, February 1962, ARA, SC, Institutos Armados 1962 dossier.

23. Chapter 5 provides a detailed consideration of Llamojha's political and ideological sympathies.

24. Report no. 55, prepared by Jorge E. Bendezú, November 14, 1962, ARA, Ex-Prefectura.

25. "Cerca de un millón de campesinos estarán representados en su III Congreso Nacional," *Unidad*, November 15, 1962, 8.

26. Surprisingly little has been written about this key figure in the Peruvian left. His supporters have produced an informative web page about his life and political work, available at the blog of Frente Democrático Popular: http://fedep-peru.blogspot .ca/2011/03/dr-saturnino-paredes-macedo.html [accessed March 4, 2016].

27. Rothwell, *Transpacific Revolutionaries*, 54. An outstanding source for the global impact of the Sino-Soviet split is Lüthi, *Sino-Soviet Split*.

28. The new parties took the names Unidad and Bandera Roja from the titles of their respective periodicals. For divergent attitudes toward peasants, see Rothwell, *Transpacific Revolutionaries*, 52.

29. Axel Ranque, one of the only scholars to mention Llamojha, states that Paredes selected Llamojha to head the CCP because of their personal ties and Paredes's view that he could trust Llamojha. Ranque, "Les origines et les divisions des partis mao-istes," 20.

30. "Segundo Congreso Nacional Campesino," *Unidad*, June 16, 1962, 8.

31. Confederación Campesina del Perú, *Estatutos y declaración de principios de la Confederación Campesina del Perú*, 3. At a subsequent meeting of the CCP in November 1963, Llamojha and other members of the CCP approved a proposal for an agrarian reform law. See *Reforma Agraria Peruana*, 158.

32. The size of the CCP at this point is almost impossible to measure. The sympathetic Communist Party periodical *Unidad* claimed in 1962 that the CCP represented nearly one million campesinos via its delegates. A CCP publication, in turn, reported that more than 150 delegations attended the 1962 congress. See "Cerca de un millón de campesinos estarán representados en su III Congreso Nacional," *Unidad*, November 15, 1962, 8; "Acuerdos tomados por el II congreso nacional campesino," *La Voz del Campesino* 11, July 1967, 23. That said, several scholars have asserted that the CCP was neither particularly well known nor especially strong during the 1960s and early 1970s. See Handelman, *Struggle in the Andes*, 150; Rénique, *La batalla por Puno*, 192. The CCP likely had several hundred individuals who considered themselves members during the early 1960s, based on the fact that about two hundred delegates attended the 1963 special congress. See "El Congreso Nacional Extraordinario de la Confederación Campesina del Perú," *Bandera Roja* 1:3, December 2, 1963, 2. *Bandera Roja* is available in the Biblioteca Nacional del Perú, in San Borja. Ricardo Caro Cárdenas provided me with a copy of this issue of *La Voz del Campesino* from his personal collection.

33. Fioravanti, *Latifundio y sindicalismo agrario en el Perú*, 125–126; Blanco, *Land or Death*.

34. "¿Qué pasa en La Convención?" *Unidad*, December 31, 1962, 7.

35. "Hermanos Campesinos," *Boletín Informativo de la Confederación Campesina del Perú*, May 1965, 3. This bulletin is available in the Hoover Institution Archives at Stanford University.

36. These efforts are reported in "Convención Regional de Comunidades del Centro," *Bandera Roja* 2:2, March 20, 1964, 8; "La tierra a quien la trabaja," *Bandera Roja*

4:14, 2nd fortnight of May 1966, 6; "Confederación Campesina del Perú Comunicado," *Bandera Roja* 2:8, July 24, 1964, 7.

37. Masterson, *Militarism and Politics*, 191, 200 n. 50; Sulmont, *El movimiento obrero peruano*, 91.

38. On the election campaign, see Handelman, *Struggle in the Andes*, 85. It is possible that Llamojha's encounter with Belaúnde happened well before 1963, as Belaúnde traveled across Peru during and between the 1956, 1962, and 1963 presidential campaigns. For Belaúnde's perspective on his travels across Peru, see Belaúnde Terry, *Pueblo por pueblo*.

39. Masterson, *Militarism and Politics*, 209.

40. "Primer Congreso Provincial Campesino de Huamanga," *Bandera Roja* 2:8, October 2, 1964, 5.

41. *Sierra* reported that Llamojha's arrival in China was the culmination of his "trajectory of struggle." "De Concepción," *Sierra* 24:565, 1st fortnight of July 1965, 4.

42. Interview with Pelayo Oré Chávez, December 24, 2011.

43. Central Intelligence Agency, Intelligence Information Cable: Plans of the MIR for Revolutionary Action, Distributed February 12, 1964, p. 3, reel 5, Peru; Central Intelligence Agency, OCI no. 0515/63, March 27, 1963, Memorandum: Cuban Training of Latin American Subversives, pp. 2, 35, reel 1, Cuba; both in United States Central Intelligence Agency, CIA *Research Reports: Latin America, 1946–1976* [5 microfilm reels] (Bethesda, MD: University Publications of America, 1982).

44. "Jovenes peruanos becados a Moscú," *Unidad*, December 8, 1966, 5.

45. The Peruvian ban on travel is noted in *Hispanic American Report* 15:4, April 1962, 348.

46. Rothwell, *Transpacific Revolutionaries*, 61–62; Hinojosa, "On Poor Relations and the Nouveau Riche," 60.

47. My thanks to Alicia Carrasco for helping me understand the implications of this story.

48. The news was also reported in the Chinese press: "Manuel Juvenal Llamojha Mitma, National Secretary of the Federation of Peruvian Peasants, arrived here today as the guest of the National Committee of the Agricultural and Forestry Workers' Trade Union of China. He was met at the airport by Sung Chuan, Vice Chairman of the host organization, and Lu Tsung-ying, Deputy Director of the International Liaison Department of the All-China Federation of Trade Unions." "Peruvian Peasant Leader Arrives in Peking," NCNA-English [Xinhua News Agency], Peking, June 6, 1965, U.S. Consulate General, *Survey of China Mainland Press*, no. 3475, June 11, 1965, 23. For a discussion of foreigners' political tours of China, see Rothwell, *Transpacific Revolutionaries*, 26.

49. Huancayo is the capital city of the department of Junín. As was often the case, Llamojha shared a slightly different version of this anecdote with his Truth and Reconciliation Commission interviewers.

50. See Ministerio de Guerra, *Las guerrillas en el Perú y su represión*; Mercado, *Las guerrillas del Perú*; Rubio Giesecke, "Las guerrillas peruanas de 1965"; Brown and

Fernández, *War of Shadows*; Béjar, *Perú 1965*; Campbell, "Historiography of the Peruvian Guerrilla Movement"; Gott, *Rural Guerrillas in Latin America*; Koc-Menard, "Social Mediation and Social Analysis," 114–125.

51. "Universidades: foco de subversiones comunistas," *Presente* 102, September-October 1965, 36. *Presente* is available in the Nettie Lee Benson Collection at the University of Texas-Austin library.

52. Unfortunately, I was unable to find any court record of Llamojha's imprisonment between 1965 and 1966.

53. "Libertad para Manuel Llamojha Mitma," *Bandera Roja* 4:20, May 1966, 7.

54. "Llaman justicia comuneros de Pomacocha," *Bandera Roja* 4:22, July 1966, 6.

55. For a discussion of student political radicalism at San Marcos University, see Lynch, *Los jóvenes rojos de San Marcos*.

56. Neira, *Los Andes*, 226. Similar charges appear in Montoya's *Lucha por la tierra*. It is difficult to assess assertions about the CCP's weakness in this period. Although Llamojha kept a detailed archive of all his work with the CCP, that archive was confiscated, and almost surely destroyed, by soldiers in 1982. Few documents held by the present-day CCP reach back past the 1973 fracture of the CCP, and Peru's National Library holds only CCP publications produced after 1973. The historian can only hope that copies of 1960s-era CCP publications, especially the CCP periodical *Voz Campesina* (Peasant Voice), survive in personal archives in Peru. So far, only a scattered few issues are known to exist.

57. In our interviews, Llamojha said that Ayacucho's congressional deputy Pedro C. Cárdenas was the one who told him the Ayrabamba title would be in Ica.

58. This lawsuit was likely initiated in 1965, based on a comment in Herbert Rolando Llamojha Puklla to president of correctional tribunal, September 21, 1981, ARA, Corte Superior de Justicia, Cangallo Province criminal cases, dossier 188, file 28480, fol. 944. I have not been able to locate the court record of the actual lawsuit.

CHAPTER 5: "EVERYTHING WAS DIVISION"

1. Angell, "The Left in Latin America since c. 1920," 163.

2. There is an enormous literature on the Revolutionary Government of the Armed Forces and its reforms. Key works include Cleaves and Scurrah, *Agriculture, Bureaucracy, and Military Government in Peru*; Caballero, *Agricultura, reforma agraria y pobreza campesina*; Matos Mar and Mejía, *La reforma agraria en el Perú*; McClintock, *Peasant Cooperatives and Political Change in Peru*; Lowenthal, *Peruvian Experiment*; Seligmann, *Between Reform and Revolution*; Mayer, *Ugly Stories of the Peruvian Agrarian Reform*; Cant, "Land for Those Who Work It."

3. Of course, many campesinos were themselves leftist activists. The two groups were not mutually exclusive.

4. Mallon, *Courage Tastes of Blood*, 107–111.

5. Hinojosa, "On Poor Relations and the Nouveau Riche," 68–69.

6. Prominent examples include the 1965 guerrilla leader Héctor Béjar and the Ayacucho Trotskyist peasant leader Antonio Cartolín.

7. Manuel Llamojha Mitma, "La lucha entre dos lineas y la reconstitución de la Confederación Campesina del Perú (May 1973)," *Informativo Agrario: Circulo de estudios Artemio Zavala* 3 (August 1973), n.p. I am very grateful to Ricardo Caro Cárdenas for providing me with a copy of this publication.

8. Llamojha Mitma, "La lucha entre dos lineas y la reconstitución de la Confederación Campesina del Perú (May 1973)," n.p.

9. Llamojha Mitma, "La lucha entre dos lineas y la reconstitución de la Confederación Campesina del Perú (May 1973)," n.p.

10. For discussion of the cooperatives, see McClintock, *Peasant Cooperatives and Political Change in Peru*; Horton, *Haciendas and Cooperatives*; Montoya, *La Sais Cahuide y sus contradicciones*; Mayer, *Ugly Stories of the Peruvian Agrarian Reform*, 111–182.

11. Llamojha Mitma, "La lucha entre dos lineas y la reconstitución de la Confederación Campesina del Perú (May 1973)," n.p.

12. "Confederación Campesina del Perú," *Bandera Roja* 2:2, March 20, 1964, 8. Not coincidentally, this letter was published in *Bandera Roja*, the paper that represented the views of Peruvian Maoists.

13. "Confederación Campesina del Perú," *Bandera Roja* 2:2, March 20, 1964, 8.

14. Neira, *Los Andes*, 224.

15. See Blanco, *Land or Death*.

16. Cuzco and Piura are Peruvian departments. Chiclayo is a province in the department of Lambayeque.

17. Rothwell discusses China's decision to cut funding to the Peruvian Communist Party in 1967, explaining that China generally stopped funding other communist parties at this time. Rothwell, *Transpacific Revolutionaries*, 57, 106 n. 35.

18. It is difficult to determine the exact year when Llamojha's relationship with Paredes collapsed. Llamojha asserts that the break occurred around 1965 or 1966, and—in keeping with the story Llamojha narrates—other scholars have noted that Paredes faced serious criticism in 1965 at the Fifth Conference of the Peruvian Communist Party; he was accused of embezzling funds and failing to build the military resources needed for armed struggle. See Poole and Rénique, *Peru*, 31. But Llamojha and Paredes were still working together at the CCP's Third National Congress in 1970. I suspect that the complete split happened shortly after this congress. The fact that Llamojha's story mentions the Velasco government agency SINAMOS (Sistema Nacional de Apoyo a la Movilización Social [National System to Support Social Mobilization]) supports such a periodization, as this body was not created until 1971.

19. Comisión de la Verdad y Reconciliación, *Informe Final*, vol. 2, chap. 1.1, subsection 1: PCP-SL (Partido Comunista del Perú-Sendero Luminoso) Origen. For a detailed discussion of the fractures in the Peruvian left during the 1970s, see Hinojosa, "On Poor Relations and the Nouveau Riche."

20. Interview with Andrés Luna Vargas, June 23, 2011.

21. Interview with Ricardo Letts Colmenares, October 22, 2012.

22. Confederación Campesina del Perú, *IV Congreso Nacional Campesino*, 8–9.

23. Confederación Campesina del Perú, *iv Congreso Nacional Campesino*, 10.

24. Interview with Ricardo Letts Colmenares, October 22, 2012.

25. Interview with Andrés Luna Vargas, June 23, 2011; Rénique, *La batalla por Puno*, 192–193. Rénique's discussion of the events at Eccash is one of the few academic treatments of the ccp's fracture.

26. Llamojha attended Vanguardia Revolucionaria's National Campesino Assembly—held from August 31 to September 1, 1973—where Vanguardia Revolucionaria established its own faction of the ccp and made plans to convene a national congress the following year. At that National Campesino Assembly, Llamojha ran in the election to choose a president for the assembly but lost that election to Vanguardia Revolucionaria activist Andrés Luna Vargas. Valderrama, "Movimiento campesino y la reforma agraria en el Perú," 103–113; interview with Andrés Luna Vargas, June 23, 2011.

27. A number of sources note Cuzco peasants as Llamojha's key base. See "¿Quién es quién en el campo?," *Marka*, July 12, 1979, 26, 29. *Marka* is available in the Nettie Lee Benson Collection at the University of Texas-Austin library. sinamos, *Vanguardia Revolucionaria*, 36.

28. Discussion of Piura campesinos' support for Llamojha appears in Arce Espinoza, *Perú 1969–1976*, 56.

29. "Alerta contra el divisionismo," *Bandera Roja* 11:52, September 1973, 18.

30. "II convención provincial de campesinos de Cangallo," *Tierra y liberación: Órgano de la Federación Departamental de Comunidades y Campesinos de Ayacucho (FEDCCA)* 1:1, January 1975, 11. This issue of *Tierra y liberación* is contained in Scholarly Resources Inc., *Documenting the Peruvian Insurrection* [microfilm] (Woodbridge: Primary Source Microfilm, 2005), reel 1, folder 1.

31. Confederación Campesina del Perú "Justiniano Minaya Sosa," *Conclusiones y resoluciones del V Congreso Nacional*, 14.

32. Confederación Campesina del Perú, *Manifiesto: Por la Unificación de las luchas populares!* (n.p., 1974), 2. This publication is contained in Scholarly Resources Inc., *Documenting the Peruvian Insurrection* [microfilm] (Woodbridge: Primary Source Microfilm, 2005), reel 1, folder 1.

33. Mallon, "Chronicle of a Path Foretold?," 108–111. For Vanguardia Revolucionaria's criticisms of the Velasco regime, see Confederación Campesina del Perú, *iv Congreso Nacional Campesino*, 11. Llamojha was not the only activist to assert that peasant land seizures benefited the military government. Saturnino Paredes voiced similar claims, as did Shining Path founder Abimael Guzmán. See Arce Espinosa, *Perú 1969–1976*, 80–81. Guzmán disliked land invasions, as he felt that they would diminish campesinos' enthusiasm for a later armed struggle. See Mayer, *Ugly Stories of the Peruvian Agrarian Reform*, 223.

34. Vanguardia Revolucionaria actually formed much earlier; it was founded in 1965.

35. Lino Quintanilla himself reflected on the seizure of Rurunmarca, speaking about it in a November 1974 speech at the Pontificia Universidad Católica del Perú in Lima. Not surprisingly, his perspectives differed sharply from Llamojha's; he insisted

that Llamojha simply refused to assume a leadership role in the land seizures and lied to the peasantry about his motives. The speech was transcribed and published as Quintanilla, *Testimonio de Andahuaylas*. That book is distinct from Quintanilla's well-known memoir, *Andahuaylas: La lucha por la tierra (Testimonio de un militante)*.

36. The Velasco government created the teachers' cooperatives, with one cooperative per department. Like agrarian cooperatives, the teachers' cooperatives were supposed to promote teachers' interests and connect them to the state. Drysdale and Myers, "Continuity and Change," 300.

37. Interview with Nelson Pereyra, June 26, 2011. I am grateful to Pereyra's son, Nelson Pereyra Chávez, for organizing this interview.

38. Interview with Nelson Pereyra, June 26, 2011. For further discussion of teachers and their complex political roles in Peru, see Angell, "Classroom Maoists"; Contreras, *El aprendizaje del capitalismo*, 214–253; Degregori, "Harvesting Storms," 128–130; Heilman, *Before the Shining Path*, 172–175, 179–184; Isbell, *To Defend Ourselves*, 226–228, 233; Seligmann, *Between Reform and Revolution*, 181–185; Taylor, *Shining Path*, 91–95; Portocarrero and Oliart, *El Perú desde la escuela*; Wilson, "Transcending Race?"

39. Confederación Campesina del Perú "Justiniano Minaya Sosa," *Conclusiones y resoluciones del V Congreso Nacional de la Confederación Campesina del Perú "Justiniano Minaya Sosa,"* 14.

40. Confederación Campesina del Perú, *Cuarto Congreso Nacional*, 51–52.

41. Hinojosa, "On Poor Relations," 62–63.

42. Interview with Franco Silva (pseudonym), February 14, 2012; Degregori, *Qué difícil es ser Dios*, 141–143.

43. Degregori characterized the congress as a "resounding failure." Degregori, *Qué difícil es ser Dios*, 141; interview with Franco Silva (pseudonym), February 14, 2012.

44. Degregori, *Qué difícil es ser Dios*, 141.

45. Llamojha Mitma, "Las luchas campesinas y la Confederación Campesina del Perú," 64–65.

46. Mallon, "Chronicle of a Path Foretold?," 115–116.

47. Ricardo Caro Cárdenas discovered this document in the Truth and Reconciliation Commission collection, Centro de Información para la Memoria Colectiva y los Derechos Humanos in Lima and generously shared a copy with me.

48. "Congreso Campesino en Quillabamba," *Sur* 7, October 1978, 1.

49. After the congress, Paredes's supporters claimed that peasants at the congress had criticized both Llamojha and Vanguardia Revolucionaria. See "Crónica de las luchas populares," *Tierra y liberación* 1, September 1978, 82. The prominent Peruvian magazine *Sur*—generally sympathetic to Vanguardia Revolucionaria—offered a very different perspective, praising Llamojha for the self-critical speech he made at the congress and criticizing Paredes's supporters for their continuing invective against the two other factions of the CCP. "Congreso Campesino en Quillabamba," 3.

50. "Congreso Campesino en Quillabamba," 3.

51. The National Agrarian Confederation was dissolved by Velasco's successor, Francisco Morales Bermúdez, in May 1978. "Informe especial V Congreso CCP," *Sur*

6, August 1978, 70. On the dissolution of the CNA, see "Congreso Nacional de la CNA," *Sur* 21, November 1979, 1.

52. "Representatividad," *Sur* 6, August 1978, 13.

53. After Paredes won a seat in the 1978 Constituent Assembly elections, joining a body that was to draft a new constitution for Peru and ease the country's scheduled return to democracy in 1980, he turned his energy and attention away from the CCP and toward his new political organization, the Frente Democrático Popular (Popular Democratic Front; FEDEP). By the early 1980s, Paredes's faction of the CCP had effectively ceased its operations. Interview with Dario Ventura, May 24, 2011.

CHAPTER 6: A WOUND THAT WON'T HEAL

1. On Peru's 1980–2000 internal war, see Berg, "Sendero Luminoso and the Peasantry of Andahuaylas," 165–196; Degregori, *Qué difícil es ser Díos*; La Serna, *Corner of the Living*; Palmer, *Shining Path of Peru*; Mitchell, *Peasants on the Edge*; Poole and Rénique, *Peru*; Rénique, "'People's War,' 'Dirty War,'" 309–337; Stern, *Shining and Other Paths*; Taylor, *Shining Path*.

2. Discussions of memory issues relating to the war appear in Degregori and Jelín, *Jamás tan cerca arremetió lo lejos*; del Pino and Yezer, *Las formas del recuerdo*; del Pino, "'En busca del gobierno'"; Drinot, "For Whom the Eye Cries," 15–32; Feldman, "Exhibiting Conflict," 487–518; Gavilán, *Memorias de un soldado desconocido*; González, *Unveiling Secrets of War in the Peruvian Andes*; Jiménez, *Chungui*; Milton, *Art from a Fractured Past*; Milton, "At the Edge of the Peruvian Truth Commission," 3–33; Ritter, "Complementary Discourses of Truth and Memory," 197–222; Theidon, *Intimate Enemies*; Yezer, "Anxious Citizenship."

3. For death toll numbers, see Rabe, *Killing Zone*, xxvii–xxviii. There is an enormous literature on the political violence that devastated Central America and the Southern Cone and a vibrant literature on memory issues linked to that violence. Key works include Gómez-Barris, *Where Memory Dwells*; Grandin, *Last Colonial Massacre*; Jelín, *State Repression and the Labors of Memory*; Stern, *Remembering Pinochet's Chile*; Todd, *Beyond Displacement*.

4. Herbert Rolando Llamojha Puklla statement to Supreme Court, September 10, 1981, fol. 935; summary of criminal trial against Máximo Hipolito Pizarro Ayala and others for the crime of armed attack against César Parodi Vassallo, case initiated July 25, 1980, fol. 536. Both documents in Archivo Regional de Ayacucho (ARA), Corte Superior de Justicia (CSJ), Cangallo Province criminal cases, dossier 188, file 28480. Very little has been written about this attack. Brief references to the assault appear in Pareja Pflucker, *Terrorismo y sindicalismo en Ayacucho (1980)*, and Gorriti, *Shining Path*, 61.

5. In an homage to La Torre, Abimael Guzmán wrote, "You initiated the popular war in Chuschi, and in its first campaign, you gave the highest action: Ayrabamba, on the 10th of July 1980. This proved, against all those who denied it, that we had initiated a Maoist guerrilla war and opened the path to encircling the cities from the countryside." Guzmán Reinoso, *De puño y letra*, 348.

6. Summary of criminal trial against Máximo Hipolito Pizarro Ayala and others for

the crime of armed attack against César Parodi Vassallo, case initiated July 25, 1980, ARA, CSJ, Cangallo Province criminal cases, dossier 188, file 28480, fols. 531, 540.

7. Summary of criminal trial against Máximo Hipolito Pizarro Ayala and others for the crime of armed attack against César Parodi Vassallo, case initiated July 25, 1980, ARA, CSJ, Cangallo Province criminal cases, dossier 188, file 28480, fols. 531, 534–535.

8. Mauro Antonio Castillo García statement to Supreme Court, December 1, 1980, fol. 446; Carlos Parodi Donayri statement to Supreme Court, August 29, 1980, fol. 546; summary of criminal trial against Máximo Hipolito Pizarro Ayala and others for the crime of armed attack against César Parodi Vassallo, case initiated July 25, 1980, fol. 532. All documents in ARA, CSJ, Cangallo Province criminal cases, dossier 188, file 28480.

9. Carlos Parodi Donayri statement to Supreme Court, August 29, 1980, fol. 547; Herbert Rolando Llamojha Puklla statement to Supreme Court, July 25, 1980, fol. 25; Herbert Rolando Llamojha Puklla statement to Supreme Court, September 10, 1981, fols. 934–935; summary of criminal trial against Máximo Hipolito Pizarro Ayala and others for the crime of armed attack against César Parodi Vassallo, case initiated July 25, 1980, fol. 535. All documents in ARA, CSJ, Cangallo Province criminal cases, dossier 188, file 28480.

10. Herbert Rolando Llamojha Puklla statement to Supreme Court, September 10, 1981, ARA, CSJ, Cangallo Province criminal cases, dossier 188, file 28480, fol. 932.

11. Interview with María Llamojha, November 9, 2011.

12. Concepción justice of the peace to Supreme Court, November 8, 1980, fol. 401; Herbert Rolando Llamojha Puklla statement to Supreme Court, September 10, 1981, fol. 935. Both documents in ARA, CSJ, Cangallo Province criminal cases, dossier 188, file 28480. The community council Herbert served on was an "administration and vigilance council." These bodies were created by the Revolutionary Government of the Armed Forces under General Juan Velasco.

13. Herbert R. Llamojha Puklla to presiding judge, March 25, 1981, ARA, CSJ, Cangallo Province criminal cases, dossier 188, file 28480, fol. 706.

14. Herbert R. Llamojha Puklla to presiding judge, May 12, 1981, fol. 49; Herbert Rolando Llamojha Puklla statement to Supreme Court, July 25, 1980, fol. 25. Both documents in ARA, CSJ, Cangallo Province criminal cases, dossier 188, file 28480. The Limeño is identified in Herbert's testimony only as "Víctor." Herbert testified that he had never previously met him.

15. Herbert R. Llamojha Puklla to presiding judge, May 12, 1981, fol. 49; Herbert Rolando Llamojha Puklla statement to Supreme Court, July 25, 1980, fol. 25; Sofia Sosa Ruíz statement to Supreme Court, December 5, 1980, fol. 560. All documents in ARA, CSJ, Cangallo Province criminal cases, dossier 188, file 28480. La Torre reserved some of the cash to dedicate to future struggles.

16. For more on Augusta La Torre, see Heilman, "Family Ties," 155–169; Kirk, *Monkey's Paw*, 89–94.

17. Herbert Rolando Llamojha Puklla statement to Supreme Court, July 25, 1980, fol. 25; Carlos Parodi Donayri statement to Supreme Court, August 29, 1980, fol. 547;

Sofia Sosa Ruíz statement to Supreme Court, December 5, 1980, fol. 561; Herbert Rolando Llamojha Puklla statement to Supreme Court, September 10, 1981, fols. 934–935; summary of criminal trial against Máximo Hipolito Pizarro Ayala and others for the crime of armed attack against César Parodi Vassallo, case initiated July 25, 1980, fol. 535. All documents in ARA, CSJ, Cangallo Province criminal cases, dossier 188, file 28480.

18. Herbert Rolando Llamojha Puklla statement to Supreme Court, July 25, 1980, fol. 25; summary of criminal trial against Máximo Hipolito Pizarro Ayala and others for the crime of armed attack against César Parodi Vassallo, case initiated July 25, 1980, fols. 531, 535–536. Both documents in ARA, CSJ, Cangallo Province criminal cases, dossier 188, file 28480. When César Parodi and the civil guards he had sought out finally arrived at the hacienda, Carlos Parodi and Flora Gutiérrez had been untied by sympathetic hacienda workers, and five other civil guards were already on scene.

19. Herbert Rolando Llamojha Puklla statement to Supreme Court, July 25, 1980, ARA, CSJ, Cangallo Province criminal cases, dossier 188, file 28480, fol. 25.

20. For initial reports, see police statement by Mauro Antonio Castillo García, December 1, 1980, fols. 426, 431; Flora Gutiérrez's accusation is referenced in Herbert R. Llamojha Puklla to presiding judge, December 4, 1980, fol. 420; César's accusation is provided in summary of criminal trial against Máximo Hipolito Pizarro Ayala and others for the crime of armed attack against César Parodi Vassallo, case initiated July 25, 1980, fol. 533. All documents in ARA, CSJ, Cangallo Province criminal cases, dossier 188, file 28480.

21. Herbert Rolando Llamojha Puklla statement to Supreme Court, September 10, 1981, fol. 935; summary of criminal trial against Máximo Hipolito Pizarro Ayala and others for the crime of armed attack against César Parodi Vassallo, case initiated July 25, 1980, fol, 536. Both documents in ARA, CSJ, Cangallo Province criminal cases, dossier 188, file 28480.

22. Herbert R. Llamojha Puklla to presiding judge, December 4, 1980, ARA, CSJ, Cangallo Province criminal cases, dossier 188, file 28480, fol. 420.

23. Herbert R. Llamojha Puklla to presiding judge, March 25, 1981, fol. 706; Herbert Rolando Llamojha Puklla statement to Supreme Court, September 10, 1981, fol. 935. Both documents in ARA, CSJ, Cangallo Province criminal cases, dossier 188, file 28480.

24. Herbert Rolando Llamojha Puklla statement to Supreme Court, September 10, 1981 ARA, CSJ, Cangallo Province criminal cases, dossier 188, file 28480, fol. 935.

25. Rufina Rosa Martínez Sulca to president of the Ayacucho Supreme Court of Justice, February 10, 1981, fol. 651; Félix Gómez Salvatierra statement to Supreme Court, September 10, 1981, fol. 931; Herbert Rolando Llamojha Puklla statement to Supreme Court, September 10, 1981, fol. 935; Marina Loayza Palomino statement to Supreme Court, September 21, 1981, fols. 953, 955. All documents in ARA, CSJ, Cangallo Province criminal cases, dossier 188, file 28480. To this day, Marina Loayza maintains her innocence and insists that she was not even in Ayrabamba on the day of the attack; interview with Marina Loayza, February 27, 2012. There is also a brief reference to this school-based conflict in Concepción campesinos to Ayacucho prefect, letter no. 182,

May 2, 1974, ARA, Subprefectura Cangallo (SC), Oficios remitidos a la superioridad 1974 dossier.

26. Marina Loayza Palomino statement to Supreme Court, September 21, 1981, ARA, CSJ, Cangallo Province criminal cases, dossier 188, file 28480, fol. 955. For a back history to these complaints against Víctor Llamojha, see Comuneros de la Comunidad Campesina de Concepción to presiding judge, July 3, 1977, ARA, CSJ, Cangallo Province criminal cases, dossier 149, file. 2977, fol. 21.

27. Víctor himself offered radically different sentiments in our own interview, denouncing local hacendados; criticizing the abusive district authorities Agüero, Castillo and Chávez; and praising his brother Manuel's activism. Without question, the context of the interview made it unlikely that Víctor would criticize his brother: Alicia and I were forthright in our initial description of the project, explaining that I was cowriting a life history with Manuel Llamojha, and Manuel's daughter María both arranged and participated in the interview. Interview with Víctor Llamojha, August 21, 2012. There has also been a partial reconciliation between the two brothers. As Llamojha described it, "Things are better now, they're okay. [Víctor] no longer speaks out against me. He no longer thinks ill of me. Before, he thought ill of me."

28. Civil guard Marcelino Muñoz Legua to presiding judge, November 30, 1980, fol. 1; Grimaldo Castillo Gutiérrez statement to Supreme Court, December 17, 1980, fol. 2. Both documents in ARA, CSJ, Cangallo Province criminal cases, dossier 187, file 13180. This file contains the court proceedings for both the downing of the telegraph poles and the bombing of Grimaldo Castillo's house.

29. Herbert Rolando Llamojha Puklla statement to Supreme Court, December 17, 1980, ARA, CSJ, Cangallo Province criminal cases, dossier 187, file 13180, fol. 23.

30. Dr. Germán Yanqui Takari to presiding judge, October 19, 1981, ARA, CSJ, Cangallo Province criminal cases, dossier 187, file 13180, fol. 81.

31. Civil guard Marcelino Muñoz Legua to presiding judge, November 30, 1980, ARA, CSJ, Cangallo Province criminal cases, dossier 187, file 13180, fol. 1.

32. Grimaldo Castillo Gutiérrez statement to Supreme Court, December 17, 1980, ARA, CSJ, Cangallo Province criminal cases, dossier 187, file 13180, fol. 2.

33. Grimaldo Castillo Gutiérrez statement to Supreme Court, December 17, 1980, ARA, CSJ, Cangallo Province criminal cases, dossier 187, file 13180, fol. 3.

34. Herbert Rolando Llamojha Puklla statement to Supreme Court, May 2, 1981, ARA, CSJ, Cangallo Province criminal cases, dossier 187, file 13180, fol. 61.

35. Supreme Court decision, June 18, 1981, ARA, CSJ, Cangallo Province criminal cases, dossier 187, file 13180, fol. 93; Supreme Court decision, November 4, 1981, ARA, CSJ, Cangallo Province criminal cases, dossier 188, file 28480, fol. 290.

36. Herbert Llamojha Puklla to presiding judge, September 26, 1980, ARA, CSJ, Cangallo Province criminal cases, dossier 188, file 28480, fol. 220.

37. Herbert Llamojha Puklla, Félix Gómez Salvatierra, Florentino Gómez Ochoa and Teodosia Gómez Ochoa to presiding judge, September 15, 1980, fol. 269; Herbert Llamojha Puklla, Félix Gómez Salvatierra, Florentino Gómez Ochoa and Teodosia Gómez Ochoa to presiding judge, September 17, 1980, fol. 328; Herbert Llamojha

Puklla to presiding judge, August 29, 1980, fol. 414; Herbert Llamojha Puklla to presiding judge, March 25, 1981, fol. 706. All documents in ARA, CSJ, Cangallo Province criminal cases, dossier 188, file 28480.

38. Herbert Llamojha Puklla, Félix Gómez Salvatierra, Florentino Gómez Ochoa, and Teodosia Gómez Ochoa to presiding judge, September 15, 1980, ARA, CSJ, Cangallo Province criminal cases, dossier 188, file 28480, fol. 269.

39. Herbert Llamojha Puklla, Félix Gómez Salvatierra, Florentino Gómez Ochoa and Teodosia Gómez Ochoa to presiding judge, September 17, 1980, ARA, CSJ, Cangallo Province criminal cases, dossier 188, file 28480, fol. 328.

40. Herbert Llamojha Puklla to presiding judge, December 4, 1980, fol. 420; Herbert Llamojha Puklla to presiding judge, March 27, 1981, fol. 701. Both documents in ARA, CSJ, Cangallo Province criminal cases, dossier 188, file 28480.

41. Herbert Rolando Llamojha Puklla and eleven others to president of Supreme Court, June 22, 1981, ARA, CSJ, Cangallo Province criminal cases, dossier 188, file 28480, fol. 863.

42. Herbert Roland Llamojha Puklla to president of the correctional tribunal, September 21, 1981, ARA, CSJ, Cangallo Province criminal cases, dossier 188, file 28480, fol. 944.

43. Santiago Salvatierra Puklla statement to Supreme Court, January 26, 1981, ARA, CSJ, Cangallo Province criminal cases, dossier 188, file 28480, fol. 506.

44. Santiago Salvatierra Puklla statement to Supreme Court, January 26, 1981, ARA, CSJ, Cangallo Province criminal cases, dossier 188, file 28480, fol. 507. Accusations and assumptions about Llamojha's supposed participation in the Ayrabamba assault endured. A 1983 story in the Peruvian newsmagazine *Oiga* offered a dramatic—but error-riddled—description of the events of July 10, 1980. See "En Airabamba comenzó la guerrilla," *Oiga* 119, April 4, 1983, 24–27.

45. Interview with María Llamojha, May 5, 2013.

46. Centro de Información para la Memoria Colectiva y los Derechos Humanos (CIMCDH), Testimony 200445; Comisión de la Verdad y Reconciliación (CVR), *Informe Final*, vol. 2, chap. 1, sec. 1.1, subsection 2. PCP-SL (Partido Comunista del Perú-Sendero Luminoso) 1980–82, 36. For the history of another detainee who escaped during the prison attack, see Mark Cox, *La verdad y la memoria*.

47. Llamojha, personal notebook for period October 22, 1989 to July 17, 2000, undated passage. Notebook in Llamojha's personal collection.

48. Interview with Hilda Llamojha, November 19, 2011.

49. Interview with Walter Llamojha, November 19, 2011.

50. Interview with María Llamojha, November 9, 2011.

51. "Edith Lagos dirigió ataque a Concepción," *La República* 1:117, April 5, 1982, 2. *La República* is available in the Biblioteca Nacional del Perú, in San Borja, Peru.

52. Grimaldo Castillo probably suffered the more brutal killing described above in *La República*.

53. Burt, *Political Violence and the Authoritarian State in Peru*, 103.

54. Kirk, *Monkey's Paw*, 189.

55. CIMCDH, interview with Magno Ortega, n.d. For the continuing divisions in the Peruvian left during the 1980s, see Feinstein, "How the Left Was Lost."

56. Interview with María Llamojha, November 9, 2011.

57. Interview with Walter Llamojha, November 19, 2011; Rénique, *La voluntad encarcelada*, 70. There was a simultaneous massacre at the Lurigancho prison, likewise in response to an uprising by Shining Path prisoners, where all 124 Shining Path inmates were killed. At the Santa Bárbara women's prison, two Shining Path prisoners were killed. Aguirre, "Punishment and Extermination," 194. See also CVR, *Informe Final*, vol. 7, chap. 2, sec. 2.67, "Las ejecuciones extrajudiciales en el penal de El Frontón y Lurigancho"; Feinstein, "Competing Visions of the 1986 Lima Prison Massacres," 1–40.

58. Llamojha, personal notebook for period October 22, 1989 to July 17, 2000, undated passage.

59. Interview with Hilda Llamojha, November 19, 2011.

60. Burt, *Political Violence and the Authoritarian State*; Conaghan, *Fujimori's Peru*; Degregori, *La década de la antipolítica*.

61. Llamojha, personal notebook for period October 22, 1989 to July 17, 2000, passage dated May 4, 2002.

62. Llamojha, personal notebook for period October 22, 1989 to July 17, 2000, undated passage.

63. Llamojha wrote this on a personal web page, previously available at http://www.fortunecity.com/victorian/hymn/30/historia.htm/ [accessed May 13, 2009]; unfortunately, the page is no longer available. "Cambio 90" literally means "Change 90." It was Fujimori's party when he ran in the 1990 presidential election.

64. Many residents of the Ayacucho community of Carhuanca, for example, returned to the community from Lima in 2000.

65. On the challenges of postwar reconciliation in Andean communities, see Theidon, *Intimate Enemies*.

AFTERWORD: "YOU HAVE TO STAND FIRM"

1. See Grandin and Joseph, *Century of Revolution*.

2. Grandin, "Living in Revolutionary Time," 10.

3. Grandin, *Last Colonial Massacre*, 11; Heilman, "Yellows against Reds."

4. Those presidents are Alejandro Toledo and Ollanta Humala.

5. This resurgence has been referred to as the "pink tide" and Latin America's "left turn." See Beasley-Murray, Cameron, and Hershberg, "Latin America's Left Turns," 319–330; Blanco and Grier, "Explaining the Rise of the Left in Latin America," 68–90.

6. Desmarais and Hernández, "Voices From Maputo," 22–26.

7. Grandin, *Last Colonial Massacre*, 198.

8. Degregori, "Harvesting Storms," 143–144.

9. Document from Llamojha's personal archive.

10. Llamojha's daughter María took responsibility for building a new home for her

parents, and the new residence is so lovely that Llamojha laughingly refers to it as a house suitable for a wealthy hacendado.

11. Personal communication with María Llamojha, May 6, 2012.

12. Salomon and Niño-Murcia discuss the importance of personal document and book collections in the Andean community of Tupicocha. See *The Lettered Mountain*, 3, 147.

13. Since suffering a massive stroke in 2014, Llamojha has no longer been able to write or teach.

14. Personal communication with María Llamojha, June 20, 2011.

15. Federación Universitaria Departamental Ayacuchana to minister of state, received August 5, 1959, Proyecto Especial de Titulación de Tierras Ayacucho (PETT), Concepción de Chakamarka dossier, official letter no. 86, fol. 986.

16. Llamojha Mitma, *Historia y tradición del Pueblo de Concepción*, unpublished manuscript in Llamojha's possession, 15.

17. Ricardo Caro and Valérie Robin, "El león de pampas," *La República*, September 5, 2010, http://larepublica.pe/05-09-2010/el-leon-de-pampas [accessed February 29, 2016].

18. Buck-Morss, *Dreamworld and Catastrophe*.

19. Llamojha, personal notebook for period January 1, 2011 to May 24, 2012, passage dated May 23, 2012. Notebook in Llamojha's personal collection.

20. Llamojha, personal notebook for period January 1, 2011 to May 24, 2012, passage dated May 24, 2012.

21. Interview with Hilda Llamojha, November 19, 2011.

22. Llamojha, personal notebook for period January 1, 2011 to May 24, 2012, passage dated January 3, 2012.

23. On witchcraft, see Vindal Ødegaard, *Mobility, Markets, and Indigenous Socialities*, 139–141.

24. Llamojha, personal notebook for period January 1, 2011 to May 24, 2012, passage dated May 23, 2012.

25. Llamojha, personal notebook beginning with undated essay titled "Manzanayoq" and ending with undated essay titled "Costumbres tradicionales [traditional customs]," passage dated July 18, 2004. Notebook in Llamojha's personal collection.

26. Llamojha, personal notebook for period January 1, 2011 to May 24, 2012, passage dated January 4, 2012.

27. Personal communication with María Llamojha, May 1, 2014.

BIBLIOGRAPHY

Aguirre, Carlos. *The Criminals of Lima and Their Worlds: The Prison Experience, 1850–1935.* Durham, NC: Duke University Press, 2005.

Aguirre, Carlos. "Punishment and Extermination: The Massacre of Political Prisoners in Lima, Peru, June 1986." *Bulletin of Latin American Research* 32 (March 2013): 193–216.

Albó, Xavier. "El retorno del Indio." *Revista Andina* 2 (December 1991): 299–345.

Angell, Alan. "Classroom Maoists: The Politics of Peruvian Schoolteachers under Military Government." *Bulletin of Latin American Research* 1:2 (1982): 1–20.

Angell, Alan. "The Left in Latin America since c. 1920." In *Cambridge History of Latin America,* vol. 6, *1930 to the Present,* pt. 2, *Politics and Society,* edited by Leslie Bethell, 163–232. Cambridge: Cambridge University Press, 1995.

Arce Espinoza, Elmer. *Perú 1969–1976: Movimientos Agrarios y Campesinos.* Lima: CEDEP, 2004.

Arias, Arturo, ed. *The Rigoberta Menchú Controversy.* Minneapolis: University of Minnesota Press, 2001.

Arroyo, Carlos. "La Experiencia Del Comité Central Pro-Derecho Indígena Tahuantinsuyo." *Estudios Interdisciplinarios de América Latina y El Caribe* 15:1 (June 2004): 1–24.

Banner, Lois. "Biography as History." *American Historical Review* 114:3 (June 2009): 579–586.

Bastinos, Antonio J. *Mosaico literario epistolar para ejercitarse los niños en la lectura de manuscritos: Colección de autógrafos de algunos hombres célebres contemporáneos.* 58th ed. Barcelona: Impr. Elzeviriana y Libr. Camí, 1941.

Beasley-Murray, Jon, Maxwell Cameron, and Eric Hershberg. "Latin America's Left Turns: An Introduction." *Third World Quarterly* 30:2 (March 2009): 319–330.

Becker, Marc. "In Search of Tinterillos." *Latin American Research Review* 47:1 (2012): 95–114.

Béjar, Héctor. *Perú 1965: Apuntes sobre una experiencia guerrillera.* Montevideo: Sandino, 1969.

Belaúnde Terry, Fernando. *Pueblo por pueblo.* Lima: Ediciones Tawantinsuyo, 1960.

Berg, Ronald. "Sendero Luminoso and the Peasantry of Andahuaylas." *Journal of Interamerican Studies and World Affairs* 28:4 (1986–87): 165–196.

Beverley, John. *Testimonio: On the Politics of Truth*. Minneapolis: University of Minnesota Press, 2004.

Blanco, Hugo. *Land or Death: The Peasant Struggle in Peru*. Translated by Naomi Allen. New York: Pathfinder Press, 1972.

Blanco, Luisa, and Robin Grier. "Explaining the Rise of the Left in Latin America." *Latin American Research Review* 48:1 (2013): 68–90.

Boesten, Jelke. "The State and Violence against Women in Peru: Intersecting Inequalities and Patriarchal Rule." *Social Politics: International Studies in Gender, State and Society* 19:3 (Fall 2012): 361–382.

Bourque, Susan Carolyn, and Kay B. Warren. *Women of the Andes: Patriarchy and Social Change in Two Peruvian Towns*. Ann Arbor: University of Michigan Press, 1981.

Brown, Michael, and Eduardo Fernández. *War of Shadows: The Struggle for Utopia in the Peruvian Amazon*. Berkeley: University of California Press, 1993.

Buck-Morss, Susan. *Dreamworld and Catastrophe: The Passing of Mass Utopia in East and West*. Cambridge, MA: MIT Press, 2000.

Burenius, Charlotte, and Zózimo Torres. *Testimonio de un fracaso Huando: Habla el sindicalista Zózimo Torres*. Lima: IEP, 2001.

Burns, Kathryn. *Colonial Habits: Convents and the Spiritual Economy of Cuzco, Peru*. Durham, NC: Duke University Press, 1999.

Burt, Jo-Marie. *Political Violence and the Authoritarian State in Peru: Silencing Civil Society*. New York: Palgrave Macmillan, 2007.

Caballero, José María. *Agricultura, reforma agraria y pobreza campesina*. Lima: IEP, 1980.

Campbell, Leon. "The Historiography of the Peruvian Guerrilla Movement." *Latin American Research Review* 8 (Spring 1973): 45–70.

Cant, Anna. "'Land for Those Who Work It': A Visual Analysis of Agrarian Reform Posters in Velasco's Peru." *Journal of Latin American Studies* 44:1 (February 2012): 1–37.

Castillo, Aracelio. *Reforma agraria por la vía campesina: Ccaccamarca, Pomacocha (Ayacucho)*. Lima: Universidad Nacional Mayor de San Marcos, 1974.

Cleaves, Peter S., and Martin J. Scurrah. *Agriculture, Bureaucracy, and Military Government in Peru*. Ithaca, NY: Cornell University Press, 1980.

Comisión de la Verdad y Reconciliación. *Informe Final: Perú, 1980–2000*. Lima: Universidad Nacional de San Marcos, 2004.

Comité Interamericano de Desarrollo Agrícola (CIDA). *Tenencia de la Tierra y Desarrollo Socio-Económico del Sector Agrícola Perú*. Washington, DC: Union Panamericana, 1966.

Conaghan, Catherine. *Fujimori's Peru: Deception in the Public Sphere*. Pittsburgh: University of Pittsburgh Press, 2005.

Confederación Campesina del Perú. *Estatutos y declaración de principios de la Confederación Campesina del Perú*. Lima, 1963.

Confederación Campesina del Perú. *IV Congreso Nacional Campesino. Torreblanca, Huaral. 5, 6, 7 de Mayo 1974. Informe Central.* N.p., n.d.

Confederación Campesina del Perú. "Justiniano Minaya Sosa." *Conclusiones y resoluciones del V Congreso Nacional de la Confederación Campesina del Perú "Justiniano Minaya Sosa."* N.p., 1978.

Confederación Campesina del Perú. *Cuarto Congreso Nacional, 1973, Eccash-Ancash, Conclusiones y Resoluciones.* Lima: Ediciones Voz Campesina, 1978.

Contreras, Carlos. *El aprendizaje del capitalismo: Estudios de historia económica y social del Perú republicano.* Lima: IEP, 2004.

Cox, Mark. *La verdad y la memoria: Controversias en la imagen de Hildebrando Pérez Huarancca.* Lima: Pasacalle, 2012.

Davies, Thomas. *Indian Integration in Peru: A Half-century of Experience, 1900–1948.* Lincoln: University of Nebraska Press, 1974.

Degregori, Carlos Iván. "Harvesting Storms: Peasant *Rondas* and the Defeat of Sendero Luminoso in Ayacucho." In *Shining and Other Paths: War and Society in Peru, 1980–1995,* edited by Steve J. Stern, 128–157. Durham, NC: Duke University Press, 1998.

Degregori, Carlos Iván. *La década de la antipolítica: Auge y huida de Alberto Fujimori y Vladimiro Montesinos.* Lima: IEP, 2000.

Degregori, Carlos Iván. *Qué difícil es ser Dios: El Partido Comunista del Perú-Sendero Luminoso y el conflicto armado interno en el Perú: 1980–1999.* Lima: IEP, 2010.

Degregori, Carlos Iván, and Elizabeth Jelín, eds. *Jamás tan cerca arremetió lo lejos: memoria y violencia política en el Perú.* Lima: IEP, 2003.

de la Cadena, Marisol. *Indigenous Mestizos: The Politics of Race and Culture in Cuzco, 1919–1991.* Durham, NC: Duke University Press, 2000.

del Pino, Ponciano. "'En busca del gobierno': Comunidad, política, y la producción de la memoria y los silencios en Ayacucho, Perú, siglo XX." PhD diss., University of Wisconsin–Madison, 2008.

del Pino, Ponciano, and Caroline Yezer, eds. *Las formas del recuerdo: Etnografías de la violencia política en el Perú.* Lima: IEP, 2013.

de Oliviera, Orlandina, and Bryan Roberts. "Urban Growth and Urban Social Structure in Latin America, 1930–1990." In *The Cambridge History of Latin America,* vol. 6, *1930s to the Present,* pt. 1, *Economy and Society,* edited by Leslie Bethell, 251–324. Cambridge: Cambridge University Press, 1995.

Desmarais, Annette Aurélie, and Luis Hernández. "Voices from Maputo: La Vía Campesina's Fifth International Conference." NACLA *Report on the Americas* 42:3 (May/June 2009): 22–26.

Diez Hurtado, Alejandro. *Comunes y haciendas: Procesos de comunalización en la Sierra de Piura (siglos XVIII al XX).* Piura, Peru: CBC, 1998.

Drinot, Paulo. "For Whom the Eye Cries: Memory, Monumentality, and the Ontologies of Violence in Peru." *Journal of Latin American Cultural Studies* 18:1 (March 2009): 15–32.

Drinot, Paulo. Introduction to *Che's Travels: The Making of a Revolutionary in 1950s*

Latin America, edited by Paulo Drinot, 1–20. Durham, NC: Duke University Press, 2010.

Drinot, Paulo. *The Allure of Labor: Workers, Race, and the Making of the Peruvian State*. Durham, NC: Duke University Press, 2011.

Drinot, Paulo. "Creole Anti-communism: Labor, the Peruvian Communist Party, and APRA, 1930–1934." *Hispanic American Historical Review* 92:4 (November 2012): 703–736.

Drysdale, Robert S., and Robert G. Myers. "Continuity and Change: Peruvian Education." In *The Peruvian Experiment: Continuity and Change under Military Rule*, edited by Abraham F. Lowenthal, 254–301. Princeton, NJ: Princeton University Press, 1975.

Feierman, Steven. *Peasant Intellectuals: Anthropology and History in Tanzania*. Madison: University of Wisconsin Press, 1990.

Feinstein, Tamara. "How the Left Was Lost: Remembering Izquierda Unida and the Legacies of Political Violence in Peru." PhD diss., University of Wisconsin–Madison, 2013.

Feinstein, Tamara. "Competing Visions of the 1986 Lima Prison Massacres: Memory and the Politics of War in Peru." *A Contracorriente* 11:3 (Spring 2014): 1–40.

Feldman, Joseph. "Exhibiting Conflict: History and Politics at the Museo de la Memoria de ANFASEP in Ayacucho, Peru." *Anthropological Quarterly* 85:2 (Spring 2012): 487–518.

Fioravanti, Eduardo. *Latifundio y sindicalismo agrario en el Perú. El caso de los valles de La Convención y Lares (1958–1964)*. Lima: IEP, 1976.

Flores Galindo, Alberto. "Apuntes sobre las ocupaciones de tierras y el sindicalismo agrario, 1945–1964." *Allpanchis* 11 (1978): 175–184.

Flores Galindo, Alberto. *Buscando un Inca: Identidad y utopía en los Andes*. 4th ed. Lima: Editorial Horizonte, 1994.

Forgacs, David, ed. *An Antonio Gramsci Reader: Selected Writings 1916–1935*. New York: Schocken Books, 1988.

García, María Elena. *Making Indigenous Citizens: Identities, Education, and Multicultural Development in Peru*. Stanford, CA: Stanford University Press, 2005.

García, María Elena. "Introduction: Indigenous Encounters in Contemporary Peru." *Latin American and Caribbean Ethnic Studies* 3:3 (2008): 217–226.

García, María Elena, and José Antonio Lucero. "Un País Sin Indígenas? Rethinking Indigenous Politics in Peru." In *The Struggle for Indigenous Rights in Latin America*, edited by Nancy Grey Postero and León Zamosc, 158–188. Portland, OR: Sussex Academic Press, 2004.

García, María Elena, and José Antonio Lucero. "Exceptional Others: Politicians, Rottweilers, and Alterity in the 2006 Peruvian Elections." *Latin American and Caribbean Ethnic Studies* 3:3 (2008): 253–270.

García, María Elena, and José Antonio Lucero. "Authenticating Indians and Movements: Interrogating Indigenous Authenticity, Social Movements, and Fieldwork in Contemporary Peru." In *Histories of Race and Racism: The Andes and Mesoamerica from Colonial Times to the Present*, edited by Laura Gotkowitz, 278–298. Durham, NC: Duke University Press, 2011.

García Bryce, Iñigo. "A Revolution Remembered, a Revolution Forgotten: The 1932 Aprista Insurrection in Trujillo, Peru." *A Contracorriente* 7:3 (2010): 277–322.

Gavilán, Lurgio. *Memorias de un soldado desconocido: Autobiografía y antropología de la violencia*. Lima: IEP, 2012.

Gelles, Paul H. "Andean Culture, Indigenous Identity and the State in Peru." In *The Politics of Ethnicity: Indigenous Peoples in Latin American States*, edited by David Maybury-Lewis, 239–266. Cambridge, MA: Harvard University Press, 2002.

Glave, Luis Miguel, and Jaime Urrutia. "Radicalismo político en élites regionales: Ayacucho, 1930–1956." *Debate Agrario* 31 (August 2000): 1–37.

Gómez-Barris, Macarena. *Where Memory Dwells: Culture and State Violence in Chile*. Berkeley: University of California Press, 2009.

González, Olga. *Unveiling Secrets of War in the Peruvian Andes*. Chicago: University of Chicago Press, 2011.

González-Cueva, Eduardo. "Conscription and Violence in Peru." *Latin American Perspectives* 27:3 (May 2000): 88–102.

González Prada, Manuel. *Páginas libres; Horas de lucha*. Caracas: Biblioteca Ayacucho, 1985.

Gorriti, Gustavo. *The Shining Path: A History of the Millenarian War in Peru*. Translated by Robin Kirk. Chapel Hill: University of North Carolina Press, 1999.

Gott, Richard. *Rural Guerrillas in Latin America*. Harmondsworth, England: Penguin Books, 1973.

Gould, Jeffrey. "Solidarity under Siege: The Latin American Left, 1968." *American Historical Review* 114:2 (April 2009): 348–375.

Grandin, Greg. *The Last Colonial Massacre: Latin America in the Cold War*. Chicago: University of Chicago Press, 2004.

Grandin, Greg. "Living in Revolutionary Time: Coming to Terms with the Violence of Latin America's Long Cold War." In *A Century of Revolution: Insurgent and Counterinsurgent Violence during Latin America's Long Cold War*, edited by Greg Grandin and Gilbert M. Joseph, 1–42. Durham, NC: Duke University Press, 2010.

Grandin, Greg, and Gilbert M. Joseph, eds. *A Century of Revolution: Insurgent and Counterinsurgent Violence during Latin America's Long Cold War*. Durham, NC: Duke University Press, 2010.

Greenblatt, Stephen. *Renaissance Self-Fashioning: From More to Shakespeare*. Chicago: University of Chicago Press, 1980.

Greene, Shane. "Getting Over the Andes: The Geo-eco-politics of Indigenous Movements in Peru's Twenty-first-century Inca Empire." *Journal of Latin American Studies* 38:2 (May 2006): 327–354.

Greene, Shane. *Customizing Indigeneity: Paths to a Visionary Politics in Peru*. Stanford, CA: Stanford University Press, 2009.

Guzmán Reinoso, Abimael. *De puño y letra*. Los Olivos, Peru: Manoalzada, 2009.

Halbwachs, Maurice. *On Collective Memory*. Edited and translated by Lewis A. Coser. Chicago: University of Chicago Press, 1992.

Handelman, Howard. *Struggle in the Andes: Peasant Political Mobilization in Peru*. Austin: University of Texas Press, 1975.

Harris, Olivia. "Complementarity and Conflict: An Andean View of Women and Men." In *Sex and Age as Principles of Social Differentiation*, edited by Jean Sybil La Fontaine, 21–40. New York: Academic Press, 1978.

Harvey, Penelope. "Domestic Violence in the Peruvian Andes." In *Sex and Violence: Issues in Representations and Experience*, edited by Penelope Harvey and Peter Gow, 66–90. New York: Routledge, 1994.

Hazen, Dan C. "The Awakening of Puno: Government Policy and the Indian Problem in Southern Peru, 1900–1955." PhD diss., Yale University, 1974.

Heilman, Jaymie Patricia. "We Will No Longer Be Servile: 'Aprismo' in 1930s Ayacucho." *Journal of Latin American Studies* 38:3 (August 2006): 491–518.

Heilman, Jaymie Patricia. *Before the Shining Path: Politics in Rural Ayacucho, 1895–1980*. Stanford, CA: Stanford University Press, 2010.

Heilman, Jaymie Patricia. "Family Ties: The Political Genealogy of Shining Path's Comrade Norah." *Bulletin of Latin American Research* 29:2 (2010): 155–169.

Heilman, Jaymie Patricia. "To Fight Soviet Agents in the Fatherland: Anti-communism in Ayacucho's APRA, 1945–1948." *A Contracorriente* 9:3 (Spring 2012): 94–120.

Heilman, Jaymie Patricia. "Yellows against Reds: Campesino Anti-communism in 1960s Ayacucho, Peru." *Latin American Research Review* 50:2 (2015): 154–175.

Hinojosa, Iván. "On Poor Relations and the Nouveau Riche: Shining Path and the Radical Peruvian Left." In *Shining and Other Paths: War and Society in Peru, 1980–1995*, edited by Steve J. Stern, 60–83. Durham, NC: Duke University Press, 1998.

Hobsbawm, E. J. "Peasant Land Occupations." *Past and Present* 62 (February 1974): 120–152.

Horton, Douglas E. *Haciendas and Cooperatives: A Study of Estate Organization, Land Reform and New Reform Enterprises in Peru*. Dissertation series no. 67. Ithaca, NY: Cornell University Latin American Studies Program, 1976.

Isbell, Billie Jean. *To Defend Ourselves: Ecology and Ritual in an Andean Village*. 2nd ed. Prospect Heights, IL: Waveland, 1985.

Jacobsen, Nils. *Mirages of Transition: The Peruvian Altiplano, 1780–1930*. Berkeley: University of California Press, 1993.

James, Daniel. *Doña María's Story: Life History, Memory, and Political Identity*. Durham, NC: Duke University Press, 2000.

Jelín, Elizabeth. *State Repression and the Labors of Memory*. Translated by Judy Rein and Marcial Godoy-Anatiria. Minneapolis: University of Minnesota Press, 2003.

Jiménez, Edilberto. *Chungui: Violencia y Trazos de Memoria*. Lima: IEP, 2005.

Joseph, Gilbert M. "What We Now Know and Should Know: Bringing Latin America

More Meaningfully into Cold War Studies." In *In from the Cold: Latin America's New Encounter with the Cold War*, edited by Gilbert M. Joseph and Daniela Spenser, 3–46. Durham, NC: Duke University Press, 2007.

Joseph, Gilbert M., and Daniela Spenser, eds. *In from the Cold: Latin America's New Encounter with the Cold War*. Durham, NC: Duke University Press, 2007.

Kapsoli Escudero, Wilfredo. *Ayllus del sol: Anarquismo y utopía andina*. Lima: TAREA, 1984.

Kessler-Harris, Alice. "Why Biography?" *American Historical Review* 114:3 (June 2009): 625–630.

Kirk, Robin. *The Monkey's Paw: New Chronicles from Peru*. Amherst: University of Massachusetts Press, 1997.

Klaiber, Jeffrey L. *Religion and Revolution in Peru, 1824–1976*. Notre Dame: University of Notre Dame Press, 1977.

Klaiber, Jeffrey L. *The Catholic Church in Peru, 1821–1985: A Social History*. Washington, DC: Catholic University of America Press, 1992.

Klarén, Peter F. *Modernization, Dislocation, and Aprismo: Origins of the Peruvian Aprista Party, 1870–1932*. Austin: University of Texas Press, 1973.

Klarén, Peter F. *Peru: Society and Nationhood in the Andes*. New York: Oxford University Press, 2000.

Koc-Menard, Silvia Nathalie. "Social Mediation and Social Analysis: The Discourse of Marginality in a Theater of War." PhD diss., University of Michigan, 2011.

Kuczynski, Pedro-Pablo. *Peruvian Democracy under Economic Stress: An Account of the Belaúnde Administration*. Princeton, NJ: Princeton University Press, 1977.

Larico Yujra, Mariano, and José Luis Ayala. *Yo fui canillita de José Carlos Mariátegui: (Auto)biografía de Mariano Larico Yujra*. Lima: Kollao, 1990.

La Serna, Miguel. *The Corner of the Living: Ayacucho on the Eve of the Shining Path Insurgency*. Chapel Hill: University of North Carolina Press, 2012.

Leibner, Gerardo. "Radicalism and Integration: The Tahuantinsuyo Committee Experience and the 'Indigenismo' of Leguía Reconsidered." *Journal of Iberian and Latin American Studies* 9:2 (December 2003): 1–23.

Linde, Charlotte. *Life Stories: The Creation of Coherence*. New York: Oxford University Press, 1993.

Llamojha Mitma, Manuel. "Las luchas campesinas y la Confederación Campesina del Perú." *Campesino* 5 (1972): 43–67.

Lowenthal, Abraham F., ed. *The Peruvian Experiment: Continuity and Change under Military Rule*. Princeton, NJ: Princeton University Press, 1975.

Lund Skar, Sarah. *Lives Together, Worlds Apart: Quechua Colonization in Jungle and City*. New York: Oxford University Press, 1994.

Lüthi, Lorenz M. *The Sino-Soviet Split: Cold War in the Communist World*. Princeton, NJ: Princeton University Press, 2008.

Lynch, Nicolás. *Los jóvenes rojos de San Marcos: El radicalismo universitario de los años setenta*. Lima: El Zorro de Abajo, 1990.

Mallon, Florencia. *The Defense of Community in Peru's Central Highlands: Peasant*

Struggle and Capitalist Transition, 1860–1940. Princeton, NJ: Princeton University Press, 1983.

Mallon, Florencia. *Peasant and Nation: The Making of Postcolonial Mexico and Peru*. Berkeley: University of California Press, 1995.

Mallon, Florencia. "Chronicle of a Path Foretold? Velasco's Revolution, Vanguardia Revolucionaria, and 'Shining Omens' in the Indigenous Communities of Andahuaylas." In *Shining and Other Paths: War and Society in Peru, 1980–1995*, edited by Steve J. Stern, 84–117. Durham, NC: Duke University Press, 1998.

Mallon, Florencia. "*Barbudos,* Warriors, and *Rotos*: The MIR, Masculinity, and Power in the Chilean Agrarian Reform, 1965–1974." In *Changing Men and Masculinities in Latin America*, edited by Matthew C. Gutmann, 179–215. Durham, NC: Duke University Press, 2003.

Mallon, Florencia. *Courage Tastes of Blood: The Mapuche Community of Nicolás Ailío and the Chilean State, 1906–2001*. Durham, NC: Duke University Press, 2005.

Mallon, Florencia. "Introduction: Decolonizing Knowledge, Language and Narrative." In *Decolonizing Native Histories: Collaboration, Knowledge and Language in the Americas*, edited by Florencia Mallon, 1–19. Durham, NC: Duke University Press, 2012.

Manrique, Nelson. *Yawar Mayu: Sociedades terratenientes serranas, 1879–1910*. Lima: DESCO, 1988.

Mantilla, Luis Felipe. *Libro de lectura*. New York: Ivison, Blakeman, Taylor and Co., 1876.

Masterson, Daniel M. *Militarism and Politics: Peru from Sánchez Cerro to Sendero Luminoso*. New York: Greenwood Press, 1991.

Matos Mar, José. *Desborde popular y crisis del Estado. El nuevo rostro del Perú en la década de 1980*. Lima: IEP, 1984.

Matos Mar, José, and José Manuel Mejía. *La reforma agraria en el Perú*. Lima: IEP, 1980.

Mayer, Enrique. *Ugly Stories of the Peruvian Agrarian Reform*. Durham, NC: Duke University Press, 2009.

McClintock, Cynthia. *Peasant Cooperatives and Political Change in Peru*. Princeton, NJ: Princeton University Press, 1981.

Méndez, Cecilia. "Tradiciones liberales en los Andes, o la ciudadanía por las armas: Campesinos y militares en la formación del Estado peruano." In *La mirada esquiva: Reflexiones históricas sobre la interacción del Estado y la ciudadanía en los Andes (Bolivia, Ecuador, Perú), Siglo XIX*, edited by Marta Irurozqui Victoriano, 125–153. Madrid: Consejo Superior de Investigaciones Científicas, 2005.

Mercado, Rogger. *Las guerrillas del Perú*. Lima: Fondo de Cultura Popular, 1967.

Milton, Cynthia. "At the Edge of the Peruvian Truth Commission: Alternative Paths to Recounting the Past." *Radical History Review* 98 (May 2007): 3–33.

Milton, Cynthia, ed. *Art from a Fractured Past: Memory and Truth-telling in Post–Shining Path Peru*. Durham, NC: Duke University Press, 2014.

Ministerio de Guerra. *Las guerrillas en el Perú y su represión*. Lima: Editorial Ministerio de Guerra, 1966.

Mitchell, William P. *Peasants on the Edge: Crop, Cult and Crisis in the Andes*. Austin: University of Texas Press, 1991.

Montoya, Rodrigo, ed. *La Sais Cahuide y sus contradicciones*. Lima: Universidad Nacional de San Marcos, 1974.

Montoya, Rodrigo. *Lucha por la tierra: Reformas agrarias y capitalismo en el Perú del siglo xx*. Lima: Mosca Azul, 1989.

Muñoz, Erasmo, José Matos Mar, and Jorge Carbajal. *Erasmo Muñoz, yanacón del Valle de Chancay: Biografía*. Lima: IEP, 1974.

Myerhoff, Barbara. "Life History among the Elderly: Performance, Visibility and Remembering." In *A Crack in the Mirror: Reflexive Perspectives in Anthropology*, edited by Jay Ruby, 99–120. Philadelphia: University of Pennsylvania Press, 1982.

Nasaw, David. "Historians and Biography: Introduction." *American Historical Review* 114:3 (June 2009): 573–578.

Neira, Hugo. *Los Andes: Tierra o muerte*. Lima: Editorial Zyx, 1968.

Nora, Pierre. *Realms of Memory: Rethinking the French Past*. Translated by Arthur Goldhammer. New York: Columbia University Press, 1996.

Nugent, David. *Modernity at the Edge of Empire: State, Individual and Nation in the Northern Peruvian Andes, 1885–1935*. Stanford, CA: Stanford University Press, 1997.

Oficina Nacional de Estadística y Censos. *Censos Nacionales de Población, Vivienda y Agropecuario 1961*. Vol. 5. *Departamento de Ayacucho*. Lima: Oficina Nacional de Estadistica y Censos, 1969.

Orlove, Benjamin. "Putting Race in Its Place: Order in Colonial and Postcolonial Peruvian Geography." *Social Research* 60:2 (1993): 301–336.

Orlove, Benjamin. "Down to Earth: Race and Substance in the Andes." *Bulletin of Latin American Research* 17:2 (May 1998): 207–222.

Palmer, David Scott, ed. *The Shining Path of Peru*. 2nd ed. New York: St. Martin's Press, 1994.

Pareja Pflucker, Piedad. *Terrorismo y sindicalismo en Ayacucho (1980)*. Lima, 1981.

Peloso, Vincent C. *Peasants on Plantations: Subaltern Strategies of Labor and Resistance in the Pisco Valley, Peru*. Durham, NC: Duke University Press, 1999.

Pévez, Juan H., and María Teresa Oré. *Memorias de un viejo luchador campesino: Juan H. Pévez*. Lima: Tarea, 1983.

Poole, Deborah. "Performance, Domination, and Identity in the *Tierras Bravas* of Chumbivilcas (Cusco)." In *Unruly Order: Violence, Power and Cultural Identity in the High Provinces of Southern Peru*, edited by Deborah Poole, 97–131. Boulder, CO: Westview Press, 1994.

Poole, Deborah, and Gerardo Rénique. *Peru: Time of Fear*. London: Latin America Bureau, 1992.

Portelli, Alessandro. *The Death of Luigi Trastulli and Other Stories: Form and Meaning in Oral History*. Albany: State University of New York Press, 1991.

Portocarrero, Gonzalo, and Patricia Oliart. *El Perú desde la escuela*. Lima: Instituto de Apoyo Agrario, 1989.

Pratt, Mary Louise. *Imperial Eyes: Travel Writing and Transculturation*. New York: Routledge, 1993.

Quintanilla, Lino. *Testimonio de Andahuaylas*. Lima: Círculo de Cultura e Investigación José María Arguedas, 1974.

Quintanilla, Lino. *Andahuaylas: La lucha por la tierra (Testimonio de un militante)*. Lima: Mosca Azul Editores, 1981.

Quiroz, Alfonso W. *Corrupt Circles: A History of Unbound Graft in Peru*. Baltimore: Johns Hopkins University Press, 2008.

Rabe, Stephen G. *The Killing Zone: The United States Wages Cold War in Latin America*. New York: Oxford University Press, 2012.

Radcliffe, Sarah. "'People Have to Rise Up—Like the Great Women Fighters': The State and Peasant Women in Peru." In *Viva: Women and Popular Protest in Latin America*, edited by Sarah A. Radcliffe and Sallie Westwood, 197–218. New York: Routledge, 1993.

Ranque, Axel. "Les origines et les divisions des partis maoistes peruviens dans les annees 1960." MA thesis, University of Paris, 1992.

Rappaport, Joanne. *Intercultural Utopias: Public Intellectuals, Cultural Experimentation, and Ethnic Pluralism in Colombia*. Durham, NC: Duke University Press, 2005.

Rappaport, Joanne, and Abelardo Ramos. "Collaboration and Historical Writing: Challenges for the Indigenous-Academic Dialogue." In *Decolonizing Native Histories: Collaboration, Knowledge and Language in the Americas*, edited by Florencia Mallon, 122–143. Durham, NC: Duke University Press, 2012.

Rasnake, Roger. *Domination and Cultural Resistance: Authority and Power among an Andean People*. Durham, NC: Duke University Press, 1988.

Reforma Agraria Peruana: Documentos. Lima: Editorial Thesis, 1963.

Remy, María Isabel. "The Indigenous Population and the Construction of Democracy in Peru." In *Indigenous Peoples and Democracy in Latin America*, edited by Donna Lee Van Cott, 107–130. New York: St. Martin's Press, 1994.

Rénique, Gerardo. "'People's War,' 'Dirty War': Cold War Legacy and the End of History in Postwar Peru." In *A Century of Revolution: Insurgent and Counterinsurgent Violence during Latin America's Long Cold War*, edited by Greg Grandin and Gilbert M. Joseph, 309–337. Durham, NC: Duke University Press, 2010.

Rénique, José Luis. *La voluntad encarcelada: Las "luminosas trincheras de combate" de Sendero Luminoso del Perú*. Lima: IEP, 2003.

Rénique, José Luis. *La batalla por Puno: Conflicto agrario y nación en los Andes peruanos, 1866–1995*. Lima: IEP, 2004.

Reuque Paillalef, Rosa Isolde. *When a Flower Is Reborn: The Life and Times of a Mapuche Feminist*. Edited and translated by Florencia Mallon. Durham, NC: Duke University Press, 2002.

Ritter, Jonathan. "Complementary Discourses of Truth and Memory: The Peruvian Truth Commission and Canción Social Ayacuchana." In *Music, Politics, and*

Violence, edited by Susan Fast and Kip Pegley, 197–222. Middletown, CT: Wesleyan University Press, 2012.

Rothwell, Matthew. *Transpacific Revolutionaries: The Chinese Revolution in Latin America*. New York: Routledge, 2012.

Rubio Giesecke, Daniela. "Las guerrillas peruanas de 1965: Entre los movimientos campesinos y la teoría foquista." *Histórica* 32:2 (2008): 121–165.

Rus, Jan, and Diane L. Rus. "The Taller Tzotzil of Chiapas, Mexico: A Native Language Publishing Project, 1985–2002." In *Decolonizing Native Histories: Collaboration, Knowledge and Language in the Americas*, edited by Florencia Mallon, 144–174. Durham, NC: Duke University Press, 2012.

Salomon, Frank. "Unethnic Ethnohistory: On Peruvian Peasant Historiography and Ideas of Autochthony." *Ethnohistory* 49:3 (Summer 2002): 475–506.

Salomon, Frank, and Mercedes Niño-Murcia. *The Lettered Mountain: A Peruvian Village's Way with Writing*. Durham, NC: Duke University Press, 2011.

Scheper-Hughes, Nancy. *Death without Weeping: The Violence of Everyday Life in Brazil*. Berkeley: University of California Press, 1993.

Seligmann, Linda J. *Between Reform and Revolution: Political Struggles in the Peruvian Andes, 1969–1991*. Stanford, CA: Stanford University Press, 1995.

Silverblatt, Irene. *Moon, Sun and Witches: Gender Ideologies and Class in Inca and Colonial Peru*. Princeton, NJ: Princeton University Press, 1987.

SINAMOS [Sistema Nacional de Apoyo a la Movilización Social]. *Vanguardia Revolucionaria*. Lima: Cenpla, 1975.

Sorensen, Diana. *A Turbulent Decade Remembered: Scenes from the Latin American Sixties*. Stanford, CA: Stanford University Press, 2007.

Starn, Orin. "Missing the Revolution: Anthropologists and the War in Peru." *Cultural Anthropology* 6:1 (February 1991): 63–91.

Starn, Orin. "Rethinking the Politics of Anthropology: The Case of the Andes." *Current Anthropology* 35:1 (February 1994): 13–38.

Starn, Orin. *Nightwatch: The Politics of Protest in the Andes*. Durham, NC: Duke University Press, 1999.

Stein, Steve. *Populism in Peru: The Emergence of the Masses and the Politics of Social Control*. Madison: University of Wisconsin Press, 1980.

Stern, Steve J., ed. *Shining and Other Paths: War and Society in Peru*. Durham, NC: Duke University Press, 1998.

Stern, Steve J. *Remembering Pinochet's Chile: On the Eve of London, 1998*. Durham, NC: Duke University Press, 2004.

Sulmont, David. "Race, Ethnicity and Politics in Three Peruvian Localities: An Analysis of the 2005 CRISE Perceptions Survey in Peru." *Latin American and Caribbean Ethnic Studies* 6:1 (March 2011): 47–78.

Sulmont, Denis. *El movimiento obrero peruano, 1890–1980*. Lima: Tarea, 1980.

Taylor, Lewis. *Bandits and Politics in Peru: Landlord and Peasant Violence in Hualgayoc, 1900–1930*. Cambridge: Centre of Latin American Studies, University of Cambridge, 1987.

Taylor, Lewis. "The Origins of Apra in Cajamarca, 1928–1935." *Bulletin of Latin American Research* 19 (2000): 437–459.

Taylor, Lewis. *Shining Path: Guerrilla War in Peru's Northern Highlands, 1980–1997.* Liverpool: Liverpool University Press, 2006.

Theidon, Kimberly. *Intimate Enemies: Violence and Reconciliation in Peru.* Philadelphia: University of Pennsylvania Press, 2013.

Todd, Molly. *Beyond Displacement: Campesinos, Refugees, and Collective Action in the Salvadoran Civil War.* Madison: University of Wisconsin Press, 2010.

Tula, María Teresa. *Hear My Testimony: María Teresa Tula, Human Rights Activist of El Salvador.* Edited and translated by Lynn Stephen. Cambridge: South End Press, 1994.

Valderrama, Mariano. "Movimiento campesino y la reforma agraria en el Perú." *Nueva Sociedad* 35 (1978): 103–113.

Valderrama, Ricardo, and Carmen Escalante. *Gregorio Condori Mamani, autobiografía.* Cusco: Centro de Estudios Rurales Andinos "Bartolomé de las Casas," 1977.

Vargas Llosa, Mario. *La ciudad y los perros.* Barcelona: Editorial Seix Barral, 1962.

Villanueva, Víctor. *Un año bajo el sable.* Lima: Empresa Grafica, 1963.

Vindal Ødegaard, Cecilie. *Mobility, Markets, and Indigenous Socialities: Contemporary Migration in the Peruvian Andes.* Burlington, VT: Ashgate, 2010.

Warren, Kay B. *Indigenous Movements and Their Critics: Pan-Maya Activism in Guatemala.* Princeton, NJ: Princeton University Press, 1998.

Wilson, Fiona. "Transcending Race? Schoolteachers and Political Militancy in Andean Peru, 1970–2000." *Journal of Latin American Studies* 39:4 (November 2007): 719–746.

Yezer, Caroline. "Anxious Citizenship: Insecurity, Apocalypse and War Memories in Peru's Andes." PhD diss., Duke University, 2007.

Zolov, Eric. "Expanding Our Conceptual Horizons: The Shift from an Old to a New Left in Latin America." *A Contracorriente* 5:2 (Winter 2008): 47–73.

INDEX

Note: Italicized page numbers point to figures and maps.

administration and vigilance councils, 210n12

abandon: personal, 47, 68, 83, 90–91, 131, 142, 144; political, 22

agrarian reform, by 1962–1963 military government, 100; by 1968–1980 military government, 132–34, 143; by Fernando Belaúnde Terry, 100, 114; CCP's calls for 108–9, 114, 132,142, 203n31; Latin America, 4, 132; leftist opposition to 132–34; peasant need for land, 4; Llamojha's views on 1, 4, 6, 110, 129

Agüero, Raúl, 60, 68–69, 71, 106, 144, 157, 162, 212n27. *See also* authorities, abusive

Alarcón Mitma, Alejandro, 90–91

Albania, 115, 140

Alcedo, Otoniel, 102

alcohol, 54–55, 72, 88, 96, 111

Alfaro, Abel, 72, 76–77, 80, 91–96

Amazon, 4, 113, 125, 191n28

Andahuaylas, 55, 68, 116, 143, 198n6

anticolonial sentiment, 10, 12, 43, 101, 103, 149, 182

anticommunism, 42, 58, 176

anti-Indianism, 1, 3–4, 19, 66, 71, 177

APRA (Alianza Popular de la Revolucíon Americana): agrarian reform and, 100; anticommunism, 58; and class identity,

191n28, in El Frontón, 34; and land struggles, 34–35; Llamojha's sympathies for 20, 33–35, 197n35; rise of, 6; tensions with military, 33, 100, 201n2

Apurímac, 4, 116, 144, 198n6. *See also* Andahuaylas; Rurunmarca

archives: Llamojha's personal, 9, 14, 51, 179–80, 205n56; state and notarial, 13, 45, 57, 69, 83, 105

authoritarianism, 66, 176

authorities, abusive: appointments of, 39, 69; in Ayacucho, 7, 39, 69; in Concepción, 38–39, 60, 69, 71, 106, 131, 144, 157, 162, 167–68; in Peru, 195n39; Shining Path and 7–8, 167–68; status of, 7, 71. *See also specific authorities*

auto-ethnography, 193n48

Ayacucho: administrative divisions, ix, 23; authorities, 49–50, 62, 65, 81, 85, 91, 96, 101–4, 106, 205n57; bishopric, 56; bureau of Indian affairs, 67, 69, 95; campesino congress, 148; Communist Party in, 59; court, 74, 128, 162, 166; hacendados in, 50, 196n9; history of, 180, 182; hospitals, 186–87; indigenous population, 4, 12, 20; internal war and, 164, 172, 179; land struggles, 1, 4, 99, 102, 142, 201n8; literacy rates, 9; postwar return to, 173, 214n64; poverty, 1, 4; Shining Path and, 147, 153–54

Ayala, Moisés, 51, 54, 58–61

Ayrabamba: abuses of peasants, 26–27, 72, 91, 157, 161; border conflict with Concepción, 38, 91, 126–28, 162, 182; Concepción authorities and, 67–68, 72, 159; economic connections with peasants, 70, 84, 88, 96; false accusations by owners, 73–76, 82; Herbert Llamojha and, 155, 157–61, 165–66; Shining Path attack on, 8, 155, 157–58, 162, 166, 209n5, 211n25, 213n44; title, 127–28, 205n57. *See also* Parodi, Carlos; Parodi, César; Vassallo de Parodi, Elodia

Bandera Roja. See Partido Comunista del Perú-Bandera Roja
Bandera Roja (newspaper), 124, 142, 203n28
Béjar, Héctor, 11, 205n6
Belaúnde Terry, Fernando: agrarian reform, 100, 114; counterinsurgency in 1960s, 100; counterinsurgency in 1980s, 178; election of, 100; meeting Llamojha, 113–14, 204n38
biography, 14, 192n38
Blanco, Hugo, 11, 109, 136
books: historical, 179–80; legal, 72; of Mao Zedong, 121; Marxist, 138; of oligarchs, 35, 49; religious, 31, 56–57; schoolbooks, 24–25; seizure by courts, 9, 57; seizure during internal war, 9, 179; written by Llamojha, 182. *See also* co-authorship; Mantilla, Luis Felipe; *Mosaico*
bourgeoisie, 142, 146
bureau of Indian affairs, 27, 51, 57, 59, 67, 95, 202n16, 202n20

Cambio, 90, 172, 214n63. *See also* Alberto Fujimori
Cangallo Provincial Peasant Federation. *See* Federación Campesina Provincial de Cangallo
Cangallo: administrative division of, ix; authorities, 38, 62, 73, 91, 93, 95–96, 102–3; Belaúnde Terry in, 114; courts in,

51–52; police in, 82; prison in, 61–62, 155, 161, 166; rural conflicts in, 101–3
capitalism, 134, 137–38, 149, 184
Cárdenas, Alonso, 46–47
Cárdenas, Antonio, 46–47
Cárdenas, Benigno, 45–46
Cárdenas, Carlos, 47, 52–55, 58–59, 61–63, 197n35
Cárdenas, Ernesto, 47, 51–55, 59, 61–63, 197n35
Caro Cárdenas, Ricardo, 184, 187
Carrasco Gutiérrez, Alicia, 16–17, 79, 88, 165, 184, 193n45, 204n47, 212n27
Castillo Gutiérrez, Grimaldo: as abusive authority, 39, 60, 68–9, 71, 106, 144, 157, 162–63, 212n27; assassination of, 39, 167–68, 213n52; Ayrabamba and, 158–9; bombing of home, 160; father of, 198n6; Shining Path and, 158, 160, 167–68
Catholic Church, 22, 28, 30–31, 56–57. *See also* priests
Ccaccamarca. *See* Jhajhamarka
CCP. *See* Confederación Campesina del Perú
Chacari, 126, 140, 157
Chávez, Joaquín, 60, 68–69, 71, 106, 144, 157, 162, 212n27. *See also* authorities, abusive
Chávez Oré, Pelayo, 115
China: funding of foreign activists, 139–40, 206n17; Llamojha's sympathies for, 138–39; Llamojha's trip to, 2, 99, 114, 117, 119–21, 124–25, 204n41, 204n48; Paredes and, 139–40; Partido Comunista del Perú-Bandera Roja and 107–8, 139; Peruvian travels to, 115; representatives in Cuba, 116; representatives in Soviet Union, 117, 119. *See also* Maoism; Mao Zedong; Sino-Soviet split
Christianity, 92, 104, 202n14
civil guards: accusations by, 54, 58, 102, 104; hacendados and, 60; and internal war, 155, 158, 160–62, 166, 211n18;

land invasions and, 109; searches for Llamojha, 144, 147; solidarity with Llamojha, 55, 111–13. *See also* police co-authorship, 13–17, 43

Cold War, 6–7, 42, 58, 99–100, 111, 124, 129, 184, 196n3

colonialism, 14, 45, 55, 101, 103, 149, 182, 191. *See also* anti-colonial sentiment

Colonial Penal Agrícola del Sepa, 113

Columbus, Christopher, 12, 101

comedor popular, 170

Comisión de la Verdad y Reconciliación, 13, 16, 178, 193n46, 204n49

Comité Pro-Comunidad Indígenas de Concepción Chacamarca, 36–38, 95, 108, 127, 182. *See also* migrant clubs

Comité Pro-Derecho Indígena Tawantinsuyo, 27, 190–91n27

communism: accusations of, 7, 58, 61, 103–4, 106, 129; Llamojha's sympathies for, 117, 138. *See also* anticommunism; Cold War; Soviet Union

Communist Party. *See* Partido Comunista del Perú

Comrade Norah. *See* Augusta La Torre

Concepción, *21*; abusive authorities, 38–39, 60, 67, 69, 71, 106, 144, 159, 163; conflict with Abel Alfaro, 76–77, 80–83; conflict with Ayrabamba, 26–27, 34, 72–75, 127–28, 162; conflicts with haciendas, 39, 42, 66, 72, 91–94, 160; counter-insurgency in, 154–55, 165, 167, 178–79; history, 9, 14, 182; Llamojha's birth in, 20; Llamojha's burial in, 188; migrants from, 29, 36–37, 95, 108, 164; police post, 111, 173, 180; postwar return to, 173, 180; recognition as indigenous community, 36–37; reorganization as district, ix, 79, 184; schools, 21, 159; Shining Path and, 158, 160, 162; support for Llamojha, 70–71, 95–97, 142, 184; title, 127–28; village council, 67–71, 95–96, 157, 183

Confederación Campesina del Perú (CCP): agrarian reform proposals of,

108–9, 114, 132, 142, 203n31; Bandera Roja and, 138; Belaúnde's agrarian reform and, 114; and Concepción, 96–97; congresses, 107–8, 110, 137, 141, 148, 150, 203n32, 206n18, 207n26, 208n49; and Decree Law 19400, 134–35; early years of, 49, 101, 107, 190–91n27; fracture of, 2, 7, 131–32, 136, 140–42, 150, 208n49; Llamojha's election as secretary general, 1–2, 97, 99–100, 107–8, 203n29; Llamojha's faction of, 8, 141–42, 148, 150–51, 207n26; Llamojha's work as secretary general, 109–11, 114, 124, 129, 136, 139; Paredes and, 107–9, 117, 140–42, 147, 150–51, 203n29, 206n18, 208n49, 209n53; and Pomacocha, 101; present day, 11, 187–88; repression under Odría, 49, 107; Shining Path and 8, 147–48; statist collaboration and, 136; strength of, 126–27, 140–41, 203n29, 205n56; unification attempts, 150; Vanguardia Revolucionaria and, 140–45, 150–51, 207n26; Velasco agrarian reform and, 133–34, 142–43

Confederación Nacional Agraria (CNA), 134, 150, 208n51

congress: agrarian reform and, 114; deputies, 84, 205n57; elections, 99, 105–6; Fujimori and, 172

constituent assembly, 209n53

Convento de San Francisco, 29–30

Convento de Santa Clara, 45–46, 101–2

cooperatives, agrarian, 121, 132, 134, 143

corruption, 83, 172–73

counterfeit money, 66, 93–94, 200n45

counterinsurgency. *See* internal war, 1980–2000

courts. *See* justice system

Cuba: agrarian reform in, 6; Llamojha's travels to, 2, 99, 114–17, 119, 121–22; Peruvians' travels to, 115; revolution, 99–100, 106, 138. *See also* Guevara, Ernesto "Che"

Cuba, Celia, 78

Cuzco: agrarian reform in, 105; campesino congresses in, 150, 208n49; guerrilla struggles in, 123–24; Hugo Blanco and, 136; indigenous population, 4; land struggles in, 65, 109–10, 136, 139, 201n8; support for Llamojha in, 108, 141–42, 148, 150. *See also* La Convención; Quillabamba

CVR. *See* Comisión de la Verdad

decolonization of knowledge, 10
Degregori, Carlos Iván, 13, 208n43
de-Indianization, 191n29, 194n12
de la Cadena, Marisol, 191n29, 194n12
De la Puente, Luis, 11, 122
demoralization, 141, 188
dirty war, 8, 154, 176
disappearance, 2, 8, 154, 162, 165–67, 173, 176, 179. *See also* Llamojha, Herbert
documents: abuses surrounding, 25, 46, 72–73, 92–93, 95, 163, 173; archives and, 45, 54, 57, 80, 83, 127, 162; delivery of, 49, 62, 66, 78, 84–85; forgery, 57, 94; Herbert Llamojha and, 157, 161–62; identity, 32, 112, 123, 145, 164–65; and Llamojha's employment, 66, 146; Llamojha's personal archive, 14, 51, 179–80; Llamojha's political roles and, 67, 82–83; orthography in, 43; power of, 49, 51, 103, 106, 128; preparation of, 10, 12, 48–49, 51–53, 60, 62, 72, 82–85, 109; stamps for, 49, 50, 51, 186; testimonial biography and, 15. *See also* tinterillos

Eccash, 139, 141, 207n25
Echegaray, Juan, 72, 96
editing process, 15, 17, 192n39, 193n46
education, 20–22, 30–31, 71, 156, 176. *See also* literacy; schools
Ejército de Liberación Nacional (ELN, National Liberation Army), 123
El Frontón prison, 34–35, 46, 113, 154, 171
elections, 11, 13, 100, 105, 131, 177, 184, 204n38, 209n53, 214n63

El Sepa. *See* Colonial Penal Agrícola del Sepa
envarados, 70, 182
Expreso, 104, 202n20

Federación Campesina Provincial de Cangallo, 102–4, 142
Fernández, Leoncio, 47–48, 52
feudalism, 108, 109, 137–38, 149, 161, 173
forgery, 57, 65, 94–96, 164–65
France, 122, 186
franchise. *See* voting
Frente de Liberación Nacional (FLN), 105–6
Fujimori, Alberto, 172–73, 214n63

Gadea, Hilda, 116
gamonales, 45, 95, 105, 111, 133, 161, 166. *See also specific individuals*
García, Alan, 170–71
gender, 79, 118, 176, 198n18. *See also* fatherhood; masculinity; women
generation, 14, 183–84
genocide, 12, 171, 182
Gorriti, Gustavo, 8
Gramsci, Antonio, 9, 189n14
Greenblatt, Stephen, 193n8
Guamán Poma de Ayala School, 148
guerrilla struggles, 2, 99–100, 123–24, 209n5
Guevara, Ernesto "Che," 2, 116
Gutiérrez, Demetrio, 70, 96
Gutiérrez, Flora, 155, 158, 211n18
Guzmán, Abimael: arrest of, 172; and CCP, 147–48; encounters with Llamojha, 147–48, 168; and land invasions, 207n33; and La Torre, 155, 209n5; notoriety of, 11; and Paredes, 140, 147; and teachers, 147–148

hacendados: and agrarian reform, 114, 133–34, 143; Concepción's struggle against in 1920s and 1930s, 26–28, 34; Concepción's struggle against in 1940s, 34, 36, 38–39, 42; Concepción's struggle against in 1950s, 65, 72–73, 76–77, 91–97; Concepción's struggle against in 1960s, 127–28; and courts, 48, 127, 161; in Cuzco, 109; denunciations of Llamojha by, 56–61, 73, 76, 80–81, 84, 92–96, 102, 168; and district authorities, 67–68, 158–59, 162; gamonales and, 45, 133, 161; Jhajhamarka's struggle against, 41, 46–49, 51–52, 54–55, 58, 62–63; in Latin America, 6, 41; and national authorities, 95; paternalism of, 72; in Peru, 27, 108–10, 112; racism of, 71; and regional authorities, 50–51, 54, 68, 93, 96, 196n9; and schools, 21–22. *See also specific hacendados*

haciendas. *See* hacendados

Haya de la Torre, Víctor Raúl, 34–35

hierbaje, 26, 28, 73

Hobsbawm, Eric, 41

hospitals, 125–26, 185–87

Huancavelica, 4, 110

Ica, 78, 127–28, 205n57

identity: Andean, 190n24; campesino, 11–13, 190n26, 189–90n27, 194n12; documents, 32, 57, 94, 112, 115, 164–65; indigenous, 11–13, 69, 121–22, 189n5, 190n24, 190–91n27, 194n12; mestizo, 191n29. *See also* self-fashioning

illiteracy, 9, 25, 31, 52, 61, 70, 93, 106, 194n12

indigeneity, 11–12, 121, 178, 194n12. *See also* identity; Quechua

indigenous communities: abusive authorities in, 195n39; educational opportunities in, 9, 19; envarados in, 70; and haciendas, 4, 6, 65; and hierbaje, 26; labelling, 12, 191n28, 197–98n40; priests in, 28, 195n39; recognition of, 36–37, 85; solidarity in, 45; village councils, 67–68

indigenous population, 4, 13, 19, 27, 189n5, 190–91n27

indios leídos (literate Indians), 51, 93

Inka, 9, 11–13, 43, 149, 182

internal refugees, 2, 8, 154, 170, 173, 176

internal war, 1980–2000: civil guards and, 155, 158, 160–62, 166, 211n18; internal refugees and, 2, 8, 154, 170, 173, 176, 182; Llamojha's archives and, 2–3, 7–8, 154, 170, 173, 178, 182; military and, 153, 161–64, 170–71, 178–79, 182; Shining Path and, 2–3, 7–8, 209n5

international travels: Latin American activists and, 99, 114; Llamojha to China, 99, 114, 119–23, *120*; Llamojha to Cuba, 99, 114–17, 121–22; Llamojha to France, 122; Llamojha's imprisonment following, 122–26; Llamojha to Soviet Union, 99, 114, 117–19; outlawed to communist-bloc countries, 115–16, 124, 204n45; Peruvian activists and, 114–15

interview dynamics: apocryphal stories and, 17; context and, 212n27; gender and 79; goals and, 17–18, 81, 192n33, 193n51; ideological sympathies and, 137–38; memory and, 16, 183, 187; nostalgia and, 181; power disparities and, 17; research assistant and, 16, 193n44; trauma and, 16, 165

Izarra, Alberto, 101, 110, 213n61

jail. *See* prison

Jhajhamarka: accusations of communism and, 58–61; denunciations of abuse in, 51, 54; history, 43–47; orthography, 43; recognition as community, 63; repression, 56–57, 62; sharecropping, 53–54; start of Llamojha's work with, 41, 47; strike, 62–63; unionization, 48–50, 52

Jesus Christ, 20, 28, 58, 104, 182

justice: Herbert Llamojha's calls for, 161; Llamojha's efforts for, 1–2, 4, 19–20, 41, 58, 66, 102, 131, 137, 176–78, 182–83, 188; Llamojha's interview statements about, 36, 50, 180; Llamojha's written calls for, 13, 38, 52, 91–92, 103, 114; *Sierra*'s calls for, 81

142–45; as CCP secretary general, 1–2, 97, 99–100, 107–11, 114, 124, 129, 136, 139, 203n29; clash between reputation and appearance, 102, 111–13; and Concepción, 34, 42, 65–67, 71–73, 78, 91–93, 95–97, 126–28, 178–79; hardships associated with, 73–75, 80–81, 88; as head of CCP faction, 8, 141–42, 148, 150–51, 207n26; and Jhajhamarka, 41, 47–49, 51–52, 54–56, 58–63; and marginalization, 149, 151; and migrant club, 36–39; and Pomacocha, 101–2; racialized assumptions about, 10, 31, 33, 123; and writing, 2, 9, 14, 33, 52, 62, 65, 91–92. *See also* documents; international travels; prison

Llamojha Mitma, Manuel, childhood: aspirations, 19, 25, 27–33; birth, 20; friendships, 25–26; hacienda abuses during, 26–28; migration to Lima, 29, *30*; rural labor in, 22, 25; studies, 22, 24–25, 31, 49, 176; violence in, 22, 28

Llamojha Mitma, Manuel, as elderly man: activist work, 178–79, 183; concern over younger generations, 183–84; death, 188; death of wife, 185, 187; determination, 175, 177, 188; health, 186–88; intellectual work, *174*, 175, 180–82; legacies of internal war, 173, 179; Llamojha's children and, 179–80, 184, *185*, 186; loneliness, 185–86; memory loss, 3, 11, 16, 175, 181, 183, 185–88; mortality, 15–16, 181, 186; nostalgia, 181, 183; recognition of, 184, *185*, 188

Llamojha Mitma, Manuel, employment: agricultural labor, 28, 66, 84; construction, 168, *169*; difficulty finding, 29, 170; milk delivery, 29; office work, 84, *85*, 199n27; in oligarchs' homes, 35; poverty, 2, 18, 29, 84, 88; railway station, 66; security guard, 170; teacher's cooperative, 145–47, 151, 156, 163; unpaid activist work, 2, 66, 86, 88, 111

Llamojha Mitma, Manuel, false accusations against: by abusive authorities,

162–63; of APRA membership, 33–34, 171; of being a communist, 6, 41, 58–61, 99, 102, 106, 138; of betraying peasants, 147, 150; of break with Concepción campesinos, 142; of collaboration with military government, 140, 143; of counterfeiting money, 66, 93–94; of forgery, 65, 92–93, 95–96; of impersonating priests, 56–57, 61; of inciting land invasions, 94, 102; of inciting violence, 54, 76–77; of manipulating peasants, 54, 65, 92–93, 96, 199, 213n44; of membership in Shining Path, 2, 8, 146–47, 153–54, 162–63; of participation in Ayrabamba attack, 162; of terrorism, 153, 162–63, 168, 173; by Víctor Llamojha, 163

Llamojha Mitma, Manuel, as intellectual: historical writing, 9, 12, 43, 110, 149, 182, 190n17; internet writing, 172–73, 214n63; notebooks, 12, 25, 166, 171–72, 182, 186–87; organic intellectual, 9; poetry, 9, 181; radio program, 180; reading, 9, 35, 56, 138, 180, 186; speeches, 10, 12, 79, 117, 122, 146, 149; teaching, 9–10, 25–26, 137–38, 180–81; and typewriter, 47–49, 51, 55, 62, 65, 74, 85, 92. *See also* archives; books; documents; literacy

Llamojha Mitma, Manuel, political affiliations and views: APRA, 20, 34–35, 197n35; communism, 106; Frente de Liberación Nacional (FLN), 105–106; indigenism, 149, 151; Maoism, 117; Marxism, 138; Partido Comunista del Perú, 7, 41, 58–60, 102, 106; Partido Comunista del Perú-Bandera Roja, 125, 138–40, 151; Partido Comunista del Perú-Sendero Luminoso, 2, 8, 147–48, 151; party membership, 106, 138–39; Patria Roja, 125; "philosophy of the peasantry," 137; socialism, 138; Soviet political line, 117, 136; Trotskyism, 136–37; Vanguardia Revolucionaria, 141–45, 151, 207n26

Llamojha Mitma, Natividad, 90

Llamojha Mitma, Víctor, 90, 158–59, 163, 212n27

Llamojha Puklla, Delia, *135*, 185
Llamojha Puklla, Herbert: activism,
   156–57, 210n12; attack on Ayrabamba, 8,
   157–58, 161, 166, 210n14; childhood, 77,
   155–56, *156*, *167*; disappearance, 8, 154,
   162, 165–67, 176, 179; imprisonment, 155,
   158–62
Llamojha Puklla, Hilda, 66, 88, 91, *135*, 154,
   166, 172, *185*, 185–87
Llamojha Puklla, María, 10, *135*, 156, 164,
   166, 170, 173, 179–80, *185*, 185–86, 212n27
Llamojha Puklla, Walter, 66, 88, 90–91,
   154, 164, 166, 170–72, *185*, 187
Loayza Palomino, Marina, 159, 166, 211n25
Luna Vargas, Andrés, 140–41, 187–88,
   207n26
Lurigancho prison, 171, 214n57

Mallon, Florencia, 15, 189n1, 193n42, 196n2
Mantilla, Luis Felipe, 24
Maoism, 117, 136–37, 139–40, 206n12,
   209n5
Mao Zedong, 121
map making, 37, 85–86, *87*
marriage, 28, 42, 56, 94. *See also* Esther
   Honorata Puklla
Martinelli, Alfonso, 72, 94–95, 196n9,
   200n48
Marxism, 9, 103, 137–38, 184, 189n14
masculinity, 2. *See also* fatherhood
Medina, Luis, 61, *62*
memory: failing, 16, 28, 187; historical,
   17, 110; literature on, 193n48; nostalgia,
   11, 129, 181; traumatic, 173. *See also* oral
   history
migrant clubs, 36, 47. *See also* Comité Pro-
   Comunidad Indígena de Concepción
   Chacamarca
migration, to Lima, 6, 29, 36, 42, 47, 66–67,
   77, 176
military: 1927 indigenous mobilization
   and, 190–91n27; 1965 guerrilla struggle and, 100; Cold War and, 42, 100;
   conscription, 32; internal war and, 153,
   162–64, 170–71, 178–79, 182; land inva-

sions and, 79, 100; Llamojha's desire to
   join, 19, 31–32; Llamojha's detention in
   barracks, 113, 123–26; Llamojha's experience in, 1, 32–34; seizure of Llamojha's
   archive, 9, 14, 51, 179, 205n56; tensions
   with APRA, 33, 201n2
military dictatorships, Latin American,
   8, 154
military government, 1948–1956: CCP and,
   49, 107; repression of left by, 49, 58, 66.
   See also Odría, Manuel
military government, 1962–1963: agrarian
   reform, 100; coup, 100; Cuzco and, 100,
   109; mass arrests of leftists, 99, 111–13
military government, 1968–1980: administration and vigilance councils, 210n12;
   agrarian reform, 132–34, 143; coup by,
   132, Decree Law 19400, 136; leftists and,
   132–33, 142–43, 207n33; Llamojha's
   views on, 133–34, 136; second phase,
   132; SINAMOS, 140, 142–43, 206n18;
   teachers' cooperative and, 208n36. *See
   also* Velasco Alvarado, Juan; Morales
   Bermúdez, Francisco
MIR. *See* Movimiento de la Izquierda
   Revolucionaria
Miraflores, 32, 35, 125
Mitma Vásquez, Paulina, 20, 24, 26, 29, 42,
   73, 88, 90–91
Montesinos, Vladimiro, 172
morale, 62, 141
Morales Bermúdez, Francisco, 208n51
morality, 70, 75, 94–95, 199n25
Mosaico, 24, 49, 194n11
Moscow, 115, 117–19, 124. *See also* Soviet
   Union
Movement of the Revolutionary Left.
   See Movimiento de la Izquierda
   Revolucionaria
Movimiento de la Izquierda
   Revolucionaria (MIR), 122–24
murder: accusations of attempted, 38, 80;
   attempts against Llamojha, 132, 140–41;
   of Benigno Cárdenas, 42, 46; of Castillo,
   167–68, 213n52

music, 21–22, 28, 56–57, 78, 110, *129*, 184
Myerhoff, Barbara, 16

newspapers, 81, 96, 104, 119, 124, 142, 184, 190n17, 202n12. *See also specific newspapers*
North Korea, 115
Nuñez Lafore, Ramón, 136

Odría, Manuel, 49, 58, 107
oligarchy, 35, 103, 183
oral history, 17, 193n47
organic intellectuals, 9, 189n14
orthography, 10, 43, 57

pacha vela, 73
Paredes, Saturnino: Albanian turn, 139; CCP and, 107–9, 203n29; China and, 139–40; Frente Democrático Popular, 203n26, 209n53; land invasions and, 207n33; meeting Llamojha, 107–8; PCP-Bandera Roja and, 107–8, 117; Shining Path and, 140, 147; split of CCP, 141–42, 150–51, 208n49; split with Llamojha, 139–40, 142, 147, 150, 206n18; Vanguardia Revolucionaria and, 140, 142
Parodi Donayri, Carlos, 155, 157–58, 211n18
Parodi, César, 72, 75–76, 128, 155, 158, 166, 211n18
Partido Comunista del Perú, 6, 41, 58–60, 105
Partido Comunista del Perú-Bandera Roja, 108, 117, 125, 138–39, 203n28. *See also* Paredes, Saturnino
Partido Comunista del Perú-Sendero Luminoso (Shining Path): attack on Huamanga jail, 8, 154, 165; Ayrabamba attack and, 8, 154–58; criticisms of Llamojha, 149, 151; founding of, 140; Herbert Llamojha accused of membership in, 160; Llamojha's attitudes toward, 149, 168; Llamojha falsely accused of belonging to, 2, 8, 146–47, 153, 162; participation in CCP, 148–49; prison massa-

cres, 171, 214n57; Saturnino Paredes and, 147; teachers and, 147; violence of, 7–8, 39, 138, 147, 153, 167–68, 170, 175. *See also* Guzmán, Abimael; La Torre, Augusta
Partido Comunista del Perú-Unidad, 108, 203n28
Patria Roja, 125
Patrice Lumumba University, 115
Pereyra, Nelson, 11, 146–47
personero legal: abuses by, 38; CCP and, 96–97, 103; Llamojha's work as, 70–72, 91, 94–96; and village councils, 67, 69
Peru, 5; activists, 11; Catholic Church, 31; constitution, 53, 91; economy, 154, 170, 172; health care, 126; history, 43, 45; injustices in, 31, 177; political system, ix, 10, 21–22, 28, 36, 50, 52, 92, 176; indigenous population, 4, 13, 19, 27, 189n5, 190–91n27; land struggles, 41, 48–49, 63, 65, 103; Llamojha's desire to transform, 31, 159; Maoism in, 117; racism and classism, 10, 19
Piura, 110, 139, 142, 148, 206n16
police: abuses, 76–77, 81, 90, 176, 180; denunciations of Llamojha, 51, 57–58, 95, 106, 173; and hacendados, 26, 54, 76, 80, 92, 94, 110; Hugo Blanco and, 137; and internal war, 159, 163–65, 170–72, 182; Llamojha's detention by, 61, 74–75, 81–83, 171–172; Llamojha's evasions of, 6, 10, 66, 75, 77–78, 81, 90, 153, 163–64; sympathetic, 55, 82, 111. *See also* civil guards
Pomacocha, 83, 101–2, 104, 110, 126, 139, 142
Pontificia Universidad Católica del Perú, 207n35
Portelli, Alessandro, 17, 193n47
Pratt, Mary Louise, 193n48
prefects, ix. *See also* Ayacucho: authorities
priests: Anselmo Llamojha and, 22, 28; Liberation Theology and, 202n14; Llamojha accused of impersonating, 56–58, 61; Llamojha's desire to become, 19, 28–31, 34; Llamojha's encounters with, 29–30; status, 28, 31, 195n39

teachers' cooperative, 145–47, 151, 156, 163, 208n36

terrorism, 138, 147, 153–54, 160, 163, 172–73

testimonial biography, 1, 13–15

testimonio, 14–15

tinterillos, 93, 199n25

torture, 2, 99, 113, 128, 154, 161, 174

travel. *See* international travels

trickster, 81

Trotskyists, 109, 136–37, 142, 205n6

truth commission. *See* Comisión de la Verdad

unions: Chinese, 204n48; of Jhajhamarka campesinos, 48–49, 52–54, 60; of La Convención campesinos, 65; rural, 42, 84, 100, 103, 106, 111, 115, 148, 151; Shining Path and, 148–49, 151; of teachers, 145; of students, 146

United States, 7, 16, 115

Universidad Nacional San Cristóbal de Huamanga (UNSCH), 140, 147–48, 181, 185

university students: arrests of, 111; collaboration with Llamojha, 101, 146, 148, 181; Lino Quintanilla and, 207n35; Llamojha's speeches to, 9, 146, 181; in Moscow, 115; Quechua and, 122; visits to Llamojha, 10, 125–26, 180–81

Universidad Nacional de San Marcos, 101, 125, 181, 205n55

Vanguardia Revolucionaria, 144; CCP faction of, 140–41, 150–51, 187, 207n26; conflict with Llamojha, 142–43; formation, 207n34; land seizures by, 143; opposition to Paredes, 140, 208n49. *See also* Quintanilla, Lino; Letts Colmenares, Ricardo; Luna Vargas, Andrés

varayocs. *See* envarados

Vassallo de Parodi, Elodia, 27, 38, 72–73, 75–76, 79, 127–28

Velasco Alvarado, Juan, 132–34, 140, 142–43, 191n28, 197–98n40, 206n18, 207n33, 208n36, 210n12. *See also* military government, 1968–1980

Vilcashuamán, ix, 43, 72, 85–86, 102, 187

village councils, 36, 65, 67, 79, 183. *See also* personero

Vischongo, ix, 57, 73, 126, 144

voting: for district authorities, 38–39, 68; right to vote, 9, 25, 38, 67, 176; for village councils, 36, 67–71, 95–96

Voz campesina, 205n56

witchcraft, 16, 186–87

women, 28, 51, 72, 76–79, 101, 118, 170, 176, 178, 198n18, 214n57. *See also specific women*

working class, 55, 103, 106, 108, 117, 131, 171

yanaconas (sharecroppers), 53–54

Zea, Juan, 38, 102. *See also* authorities, abusive